ENCOUNTERING FAITH IN THE CLASSROOM

ENCOUNTERING FAITH IN THE CLASSROOM

Turning Difficult Discussions into Constructive Engagement

Edited by

Miriam Rosalyn Diamond

Foreword by Art Chickering

STERLING, VIRGINIA

The *Wingspread Declaration on Religion and Public Life: Engaging Higher Education* is reproduced by kind permission of the Society for Values in Higher Education. Copyright © 2005 by the Society for Values in Higher Education.

Published by Stylus Publishing, LLC
22883 Quicksilver Drive
Sterling, Virginia 20166–2102

Library of Congress Cataloging-in-Publication-Data
Encountering faith in the classroom : turning difficult discussions into constructive engagement / edited by Miriam Rosalyn Diamond.—1st ed.
    p. cm.
    Includes index.
    ISBN 978-1-57922-236-9 (cloth : alk. paper)—
    ISBN 978-1-57922-237-6 (pbk. : alk. paper)
1. Religion in the public schools—United States. 2. Universities and colleges—United States—Religion. I. Diamond, Miriam Rosalyn.
LC111.E52   2008
379.2'8—dc22   2007026528

13-digit ISBN: 978-1-57922-236-9 (cloth)
13-digit ISBN: 978-1-57922-237-6 (paper)

Printed in the United States of America

All first editions printed on acid free paper that meets the American National Standards Institute Z39-48 Standard.

Bulk Purchases

Quantity discounts are available for use in workshops and for staff development.
Call 1-800-232-0223

First Edition, 2008

10 9 8 7 6 5 4 3 2 1

This book is lovingly dedicated to the blessed memory of my father,
Michael Diamond (1918–2007),
who expressed deep faith through his vocation as an educator.

"Who is wise? One who learns from all people."

—Sayings of the Fathers

CONTENTS

ACKNOWLEDGMENTS

Many people made this book possible. First, I thank John von Knorring, president and publisher of Stylus Publishing, who approached me with the initial concept of this book and gave me the opportunity to take on this important project. I appreciate the sage advice of Lois Calian Trautvetter, whose words of wisdom guided me through many steps of putting together this work. I esteem all of the contributors for their enthusiasm and insights, as well as willingness to engage in dialogue about their ideas. I am honored that Arthur Chickering provided his reflections in the foreword. And I thank Jeffrey Solotoroff for his feedback on drafts of this material.

I am grateful to participants in Northeastern University's faculty book group on Spiritual Aspects of Teaching and Learning for sparking my interest in this area of inquiry in the first place. I appreciate the encouragement of Gregory Light to join Northwestern's Religion and Science Working Group (RSWG), where I gained further understanding of faculty concerns regarding conflicts between course material and student religious convictions. I am thankful to members of the RSWG for welcoming me into their meetings, allowing me to contribute to discussions and hear about their experiences.

I thank Marvin Kaiser and the Society for Values in Higher Education for granting permission to reprint the Wingspread Declaration on Religion and Public Life.

Finally, I cherish the support and encouragement my parents provided as I worked on this project.

Many thanks to all of you.

FOREWORD

I feel lucky and honored to have been invited to write the foreword for this timely and excellent book. I appreciate having an early chance to encounter this important work. As a lifelong teacher concerned about improving higher education's effectiveness with diverse learners, I value learning from others who address the complex and gritty challenges in our classrooms with students. I have spent forty years arguing that higher education needs to be more intentional and explicit about attending to major dimensions of student development so, not surprisingly, I am heartened to meet a collection of experienced and thoughtful authors who address this critically important area.

Since the 1960s, at least, there has been an ongoing body of research and writing concerning student quests for purpose and meaning, for developing authenticity, identity, and integrity. But until the terrorist attacks of 9/11 and the ongoing conflicts and tensions in the Middle East, the religious and spiritual dimensions of these developmental concerns received only scant attention. Now issues of religious and spiritual diversity—in addition to race and gender—have leapt to our screens. Our general understanding of this arena has been enriched by the University of California at Los Angeles Higher Education Research Center's national surveys and follow-up studies of students, by their faculty survey, and by their focus group studies. There is an emerging literature concerning single institution responses and varied programmatic interventions. But to respond effectively to these challenges, from our students and from the larger political and social context, we must address them where the rubber meets the road—in our courses and classes.

I am not aware of another book that has put together a collection of penetrating and thoughtful writing from experienced teachers that tackles these bedrock complexities. Chapter 1, Faith and Reason: Higher Education's Opportunities and Challenges, puts these complexities in our current cultural context. Two other chapters help us understand how these issues are experienced by African Americans, fundamentalists, and evangelicals. We get basic information concerning legal protections and prohibitions as they

apply to classroom teaching and faculty roles. We learn from concrete examples of varied courses and pedagogical strategies across the curriculum, in law
and education, and for graduate study in student affairs. The special poten-
tials of carefully constructed service-learning opportunities are thoughtfully
articulated. We are brought to a deeper understanding of complexities concerning faculty roles and responsibilities. We are introduced to a wide range
of pertinent literature and research findings. There is lively use of metaphor
and analogy, and the writers are authentically present and candid about the
dilemmas they have faced and their attempts to respond. It is clear that each
contributor has a deep and personal investment in doing the very best he or
she can to meet these difficult challenges.

I especially appreciated the sensitivity to how important many of these
issues are to students. Roger Baker, for example, in "Teaching Secular Bible
Reading to Religiously Committed Students," says, "I have affection for students who struggle and I don't want to be a professional iconoclast who
breaks their often fragile images, images that still want the refiner's fire of
study and experience. Although good scholarship requires that those who
study willingly ask any question about any text, being a teacher requires that
the teacher only break an image that can be replaced with something better,
and I am often in no position to replace what I could easily tear down."

In "Philosophy and Religious Disagreements in the College Classroom,"
Dona Warren says, "Ideally, students are brought to appreciate points of
agreement, as well as points of disagreement, between themselves and individuals who hold beliefs they don't share. Students who object to particular
philosophical positions can be assured that their *agreement* is not the issue;
their *charitable comprehension* is." (Italics in the original.) The authors also
recognize the need for personal authenticity. For example, David Hall ("The
Role of Religion and Spirituality in the Law School Classroom") says, "Our
search for an educational model that teaches to the whole student also hinges
on our ability as legal educators to model the type of spiritual behavior and
values this perspective offers to the world. The cry 'Physician, heal thyself'
will be transformed to 'Educator, teach thyself,' unless we live the spirituality
that we offer to others." Those are critical perspectives for all of us.

In the closing chapter Nash and Baskette make another critical point.
"We have found that, at times, it is necessary to separate out the *cognitive*
from the *emotional* dimensions of religio-spiritual conversation in the
classroom. . . . We try to recognize, and validate, the powerful emotional

content of our students' religio-spiritual convictions. To this end, we encourage our students to express the intensity of their beliefs freely, but always in a mutually respectful and sensitive manner. One way we try to maintain a balance between the cognitive and emotional in our seminar is to rule out of order favoring one or another perspective. Rational and emotional approaches to subject matter have equal worth as learning styles in our seminar." (Italics in the original.) I believe that making this clear distinction, together with respecting and validating both the cognitive and emotional dimensions of varied views, is a critical ingredient. But note that they are talking about "learning styles." They are NOT talking about the evidentiary basis for a particular conviction.

This book can be read selectively. I trucked right on through from beginning to end, but you don't need to do that. The major sections provide useful conceptual organizers. But each chapter is a discrete individual expression. They do not require prior understandings from preceding pages. I do think it is important to read the Diamond and Copre "Faith in Learning: An Overview" first to get the general orientation for the book. And then read Thomas and Bahr, "Faith and Reason: Higher Education's Opportunities and Challenges" with the accompanying Wingspread Declaration. That chapter puts the subsequent, more specifically focused, chapters in our larger political and cultural condition. Then you could go Diamond's "Afterword." Here she provides some very helpful perspectives emerging from the contributions of the varied contributors. With this material in mind you can pick and choose in the order that suits your fancy. Having said this, I encourage every reader to read all the chapters. I learned from every one. Taken together they enriched my understanding of some important conceptual distinctions and gave me some concrete, practical, and useful ideas for my own teaching.

My thanks go to Miriam Diamond and her contributors for sharing this useful and important work.

Art Chickering
Special Assistant to the President
Goddard College
Plainfield, Vermont

Introduction

FAITH IN LEARNING

An Overview

Miriam Rosalyn Diamond and Christina Copre

In social company avoid, if possible, all discussion with whom you may not agree, especially of politics and religion.

—Alexander Murdock Gow (1873, p. 202)

It was an excellent course, don't get me wrong, but we all cleverly avoided really talking about God. Didn't we?

—Feedback from an undergraduate taking the course, The Bible as Literature, cited in Susan Handelman's 1999 "We Cleverly Avoided Talking About God: Personal and Pedgogical Reflections on Academia and Spirituality" (p. 103)

Religion in the secular classroom is a hot topic on today's campuses, one that is becoming increasingly consequential. As an instructor, my first encounter with religion in the classroom was self-initiated. It was 1998, and I was teaching a seminar on the Psychology of Adult Development to first-year undergraduates at a private, nonsectarian university. Due to time limitations, I had to decide which topic to include in the curriculum—gender issues, moral development, or faith and spirituality. I opted to let the students make the choice. To my surprise, the response was overwhelmingly enthusiastic; the students wanted an opportunity to explore the role of religion in adulthood. I had a moment of panic. "What did you get yourself into, Miriam? How can you teach such an emotionally laden topic? How will you manage the conflicts and tensions that may arise?"

I elected to facilitate discussion by dividing the class into small groups, maximizing the religious diversity represented in each section. I provided a questionnaire to foster discussions on the faiths in which they were raised or with which they identified. Items included: "What basic questions and concerns are religions set to answer? What does your religion say about why we are here? What religious questions do you think would be of greater concern to people at certain ages or going through particular life events?" As a group, students looked at Fowler's stages of faith development (1995) and explored several examples.

Although most of the students seemed reluctant and even embarrassed to strongly state agreement with a formal religious belief, they were eager to listen to and compare faiths of origin with each other. In fact, they seemed hungry to do so. I got the sense they did not have many opportunities on campus to have this kind of interfaith discourse in a safe setting. At the end of the term, students ranked this session as the most valuable of the entire class.

Since then, I have included this session in subsequent renditions of the course and received the same positive response. I noticed that, as time went on, more students articulated strong ties to a particular faith.

Years later, a group of faculty convened a committee to discuss ways of working with students who expressed religious beliefs that contradicted the subject matter. As a member of the Center for Teaching Excellence, the group asked if I would be willing to participate and facilitate discussions about student learning amid controversy. This was an intriguing opportunity, and I accepted the offer. Together we considered means of supporting critical thinking, the role of emotions in learning, and the effect of increased parental attention on students' educational experiences. Involvement with this team sparked my interest and led me to explore the issues further.

Do institutions of higher education have a responsibility to address—or avoid—matters of faith? What happens when students raise the topic, even if faculty try to keep it out of the equation? In situations where we choose to do so, how do we broach discussions related to belief in the academic classroom? Developmentally speaking, what do students need and want around this issue? What do we do about conflicts among students and their religiously rooted worldviews? And how do we respond to contradictions between religious and academic ideologies?

In the early years of American higher education, this was not a controversial matter. In fact, the first American universities were founded as institutes to foster religious thought and practice in conjunction with providing students' academic training. British education provided the model for American universities as institutions for training clergy, the elite of those being educated. Harvard University, the nation's oldest, was founded in 1636 originally to "advance Learning and perpetuate it to Posterity; dreading to leave an illiterate Ministry to the Churches" (President and Fellows of Harvard University, 2005b, para. 4). Some members of the Puritan tradition, including Increase Mather, the sixth president of Harvard, and his son, Cotton Mather, saw Harvard as too religiously liberal. These Puritans' desire for an educational institution more grounded in religion led to their support of Yale University, then known as the Collegiate School (Yale University, 2006). As late as the mid-19th century, private institutions with sectarian ties were commonly being established, such as Northwestern University, founded in 1851 with the oversight of the Methodist Episcopal Church (Northwestern University, 2002). "By the time of the Civil War there had been founded 182 permanent colleges, and out of these 175 were under the control of the various religious denominations" (Kohlbrenner, 1961, p. 46).

The early American universities eventually began to incorporate an increasingly diversified offering of courses in the 18th and early 19th centuries. While religion and divinity colleges were still at the forefront of academics, their curricula were expanded to reflect a more well-rounded institution. In 1708, John Leverett, Harvard's first elected lay president, encouraged placing greater curricular emphasis on the sciences (President and Fellows of Harvard University, 2005a). Yale presented the first modern science course in the country when Benjamin Silliman Sr. began teaching chemistry in 1802. These actions paved the way for the introduction of the bachelor of science degree at Harvard in 1851. Professors in these fields generally saw no contradiction between their fields of study and religion, and they often felt that science supported their beliefs (Rudolph, 1962). However, these developments set the stage for an ideological transformation in colleges.

Changes in higher education became more striking at the end of the 19th century. As advances in science and technology became more apparent in daily life, colleges increasingly emphasized objective, empirical approaches to study. This led to a decoupling of religion from the study of both sciences and humanities (Kliever, 2001), and educational institutions expected less student religious participation (such as required attendance at services and prayers at the start of classes) in and around their studies (Stamm, 2006).

This era also meant changes for public university systems. Although the earliest state institutions maintained religious influences, new demands in the years following the Civil War spurred growth in this sector of higher education and led to different missions. Notably, these institutions increasingly provided training for the professions at the undergraduate level (Jenks & Riesman, 1968; Rudolph, 1962).

As the turn of the 20th century approached, additional forces further separated many institutions from their religious ties. As higher education increasingly became a training ground for professions, a wider—and more diverse—student population began participating. The notion of colleges educating primarily the elite often gave way to German-style university systems, with multiple majors, professional schools, and graduate degrees. Fiscal factors also influenced the secularization of higher education: pursuant to the legal separation of church and state, public financing was no longer available to sectarian institutions (Kohlbrenner, 1961). Private monies such as the Carnegie Pension Fund made financial support available to colleges that were expressly not religiously affiliated or that had renounced previous denominational oversight (Kohlbrenner, 1961; Marsden, 1994). As a result, through the early 20th century, many universities distanced themselves from their founding theological missions and roots, while others struggled regarding the role of religion in their mission or gradually loosened ties. Still others were founded purely on nonsectarian bases (Marsden, 1994).

Two major events in the mid-20th century challenged the traditional private institution that was founded on religion. World War II sparked changes in society at large, and specifically in academia. "During the postwar era . . . forces drove American higher education to unprecedented levels of growth and achievement: the rising tide of economic prosperity, the baby boom, and the revolution in federal science policy" (Graham & Diamond, 1997, p. 11). In addition, the Cold War led to initiatives that expanded American emphasis on scientific and technological accomplishments.

Social and political unrest in the country at large and on college campuses in particular contributed the other major influence during this era. The civil rights movement became more prominent, controversy grew over the war in Vietnam, and other social and political conditions were questioned. University roles and responsibilities in social action were deemed less effective and relevant than in previous generations. Although they remained active through community ministries, private universities were unable to simultaneously sustain their social efforts, their intellectual objectives, and their often-sectarian roots (Sloan, 1994).

By the 1970s, religion had found its way back in the American university but in a different form. The "passage of the landmark Immigration Act in 1965 opened America as never before to non-European immigration and the beginning of a new chapter in American racial, ethnic and religious pluralism" (Stamm, 2007, para. 24). In addition, admissions quotas that had limited cultural and ethnic minority group access to many institutions were abandoned (Synnott, 1979). These developments, along with the civil rights movement, ushered in a wave of diversity—religious as well as ethnic and cultural diversity—on American campuses. Furthermore, this era heralded greater interest in finding personal meaning in life, and religions—including Eastern faiths—were identified as a means to individual spiritual fulfillment. Students often expressed their religious faiths in more individualized and egalitarian forms than had been practiced traditionally (Stamm, 2007).

In the beginning of the 21st century, faith and religion experienced a resurgence of interest in society at large as well as in academia. The tragedy of September 11, 2001, ignited conversations about communicating and building relationships in the global community, pointing toward religious understanding as key to this process. This incident also led many Americans on a search for means of dealing with calamity on personal, national, and global levels (Stamm, 2007). The result has been more college course offerings generating discourse about various religions and religion in general. Greater student interest in Middle Eastern studies and Islam, for instance, has led to greater demand for and attendance in courses addressing religion (Prothero, 2007). (For examples, see Hicks, 2002; Krache, 2006.) In turn, faculty grappled with responding to these calls for exploring such topics.

The controversy regarding the role of religion in college studies is far from being resolved. In 2006, a Task Force at Harvard University's College of Arts and Sciences proposed amending core undergraduate requirements to include courses on "Reason and Faith." After considerable debate over the reference to religion, the recommendation was broadened and resubmitted to address subjects related to "Culture and Belief" (Miller, 2007). Authors of the proposal maintain that the study of religion still falls under this category and is important because:

Religion has historically been, and continues to be, a force shaping identity and behavior throughout the world. Harvard is a secular institution, but religion is an important part of our students' lives. When they get to college, students often struggle to sort out the relationship between their own beliefs and practices and those of fellow students, and the relationship of religious belief to the resolutely secular world of the academy. It is also important for students to have the opportunity to learn something about the impact that religious belief and practice has on the world, as well as on themselves. (Report on the Task Force, 2007, pp. 11–12)

What concerns do today's faculty have about teaching subjects that students may find controversial and may contradict their religious beliefs? In the fall of 2006, I held a series of meetings with professors who were actively dealing with these issues. They articulated the following challenges:

- overcoming student resistance to—and fear of—hearing ideas that contradict their understanding of how the universe functions;
- dealing with emotions that arise when students are taught something that runs counter to what they believe;
- fostering an environment where students can struggle with different concepts and explanations for the same phenomena;
- addressing learner misconceptions of what the scientific method is and how that differs from religious understanding; and
- increasing student trust in the sciences, while at the same time respecting religious beliefs.

Those who had been teaching for a while noted recent changes in student responses to discussions about reproduction, evolution, origins of the universe, and anthropology. They identified the time of this change to be around the start of the 21st century. According to one faculty member, today's students find it more "intellectually acceptable" than did previous cohorts to speak out against these topics in class on the grounds of religious ideology.

The purpose of this book is to explore what happens—and what can happen—in today's college classroom when course content meets or collides with students' religious beliefs. Those episodes can be intentional, as when David Hall or Robert Nash and Sue Baskette encourage students to explore their beliefs and the role these worldviews play in their vocations. In other cases, student responses to class material may occur unexpectedly, as Mano Singham relays in his experience teaching introductory physics. In still other instances, evoking reactions on the basis of personal faith may be par for the course, as Roger Baker describes in his classes on the Bible as literature.

How can learning take place in an environment where students may feel threatened, angry, or misunderstood, or that their convictions are being discredited? This book aims to serve as a resource for those in higher education, providing ways of conceptualizing, engaging, and responding to student beliefs. Included are models for raising topics related to religion and suggestions for responding to students who contend that course material contradicts their worldviews.

This book is divided into four sections. In the first, Nancy Thomas and Ann Marie Bahr provide an overview of the Wingspread initiative and rationale for including faith in higher education. In the second section, Lois Trautvetter, Judy Rogers, and Patrick Love reveal findings about student and faculty perspectives on addressing religion in college classes.

The third portion of the book provides tools for conceptualizing and addressing student religious convictions in the teaching-learning experience. Peggy Catron discusses fundamentalism and affective development, while Tamara Rosier offers ways of managing issues of cognitive dissonance. Mark Giles, Odelet Nance, and Noelle Witherspoon offer insights regarding diversity, belief, and the learning process, particularly with regard to African American students' experiences. And Barbara Lee delineates legal perspectives on broaching controversial issues in the college classroom.

The final section focuses on how faculty in a variety of disciplines and institutions respond to and work with student religious convictions in their classes. Kent Koth considers educational outcomes of student service-learning placements in religious facilities. Dona Warren presents ways of fostering productive disagreement in her religion and philosophy classes, and Mano Singham describes his experiences as a physicist teaching a course on science and religion. Roger Baker explores approaches to teaching the Bible as literature in a religiously affiliated institution. David Hall elucidates why and how he encourages students to examine their religious ideologies in law school classes, while Robert Nash and Sue Baskette do the same in education courses.

Religion is often a highly personal, emotionally laden topic. It also provides an opportunity to further understanding—about oneself, one's peers, the world, and human nature. The contributors hope this book will serve as an inspiration and guide to faculty navigating the controversial, sensitive— yet illuminating—lessons that can be learned when religion takes a seat in the classroom.

References

Fowler, J. W. (1995). *Stages of faith: The psychology of human development and the quest for meaning*. San Francisco: Harper.

Gow, A. M. (1873). *Good morals and gentle manners: For schools and families*. Cincinnati, New York: Van Antwerp, Bragg.

Graham, H. D., & Diamond, N. (1997). *The rise of American research universities: Elites and challengers in the postwar era*. Baltimore, MD: Johns Hopkins University Press.

Handelman, S. (1999). We cleverly avoided talking about God: Personal and pedagogical reflections on academia and spirituality. *A Journal of Research and Thought in Jewish Education 1999–2000, 1,* 101–120.

Hicks, S. (2002). *Duke students flood 9/11-related courses*. Retrieved March 5, 2007, from http://www.dukenews.duke.edu/mmedia/features/911site/sept11_courses .html

Kliever, L. D. (2001, May–June). Review of *The sacred and the secular university*. Retrieved October 25, 2007, from http://www.aaup.org/AAUP/pubsres/academe/ 2001/MJ/BR/Klie.htm

Jenks, C., & Riesman, D. (1968). *The academic revolution*. Garden City, NY: Doubleday.

Kohlbrenner, B. J. (1961). Religion and higher education: An historical perspective. *History of Higher Education Quarterly, 1*(2), 45–56.

Krache, D. (2006, September 8). *9/11 changes focus for class of '07*. Retrieved March 5, 2007, from http://www.cnn.com/2006/US/09/01/911.students/index.html

Marsden, G. M. (1994). *The soul of the American university: From Protestant establishment to established nonbelief*. New York: Oxford University Press.

Miller, L. (2007). Beliefwatch: Harvard's fuss over faith. *Newsweek*. Retrieved March 14, 2007, from http://www.msnbc.msn.com/id/16610014/site/newsweek/

Northwestern University. (2002). *Historic moments: Planning a university to serve the Northwest Territory*. Retrieved December 4, 2006, from http://www.northwest ern.edu/features/historic_moments/10_21_00_founders.html

President and Fellows of Harvard College. (2005a). *New schools and new houses*. Retrieved December 4, 2006, from http://www.news.harvard.edu/guide/intro/ hist2.html

President and Fellows of Harvard College. (2005b). *The early history of Harvard University*. Retrieved December 4, 2006, from http://www.news.harvard.edu/guide/intro/index.html

Prothero, S. (2007, March 16). Worshiping in ignorance. *The Chronicle of Higher Education, 53*(28), B6. Retrieved March 29, 2007, from http://chronicle.com/weekly/v53/i28/28b00601.htm

Report on the Task Force on General Education. (2007). Harvard University Faculty of Arts and Sciences. pp. 11–12. Retrieved March 14, 2007, from http://www.fas.harvard.edu/curriculum-review/general_education.pdf

Rudolph, F. (1962). *The American college and university: A history*. New York: Alfred A. Knopf.

Sloan, Douglas. (1994). *Faith and knowledge: Mainline Protestantism and American higher education*. Louisville, KY: Westminster/John Knox Press.

Stamm, Liesa. (2006). The influence of religion and spirituality in shaping American higher education. In Arthur W. Chickering, Jon C. Dalton, & Liesa Stamm (Eds.), *Encouraging authenticity and spirituality in higher education*. San Francisco: Jossey-Bass.

Stamm, Liesa. (2007). Can we bring spirituality back to campus? Higher education's re-engagement with values and spirituality. *Journal of College and Character, 2*. Retrieved February 28, 2007, from http://www.collegevalues.org/articles.cfm?a = 1&id = 1075

Synnott, Marcia. (1979). The admission and assimilation of minority students at Harvard, Yale and Princeton, 1900–1911. *History of Education Quarterly, 19*(3), 285–304.

Yale University. (2006). *Illustrated timeline of Yale's history*. Retrieved December 4, 2006, from http://www.yale.edu/timeline/1701/index.html

PART ONE

SOCIETY, LEARNING, AND RELIGION

I

FAITH AND REASON

Higher Education's Opportunities and Challenges

Nancy L. Thomas and Ann Marie B. Bahr

In July 2005, educators representing various disciplines, institutions, and roles in higher education, met for two and a half days at the Wingspread Conference Center in Racine, Wisconsin. We came to discuss changes in the landscape of religion and public life and to define higher education's role in response to these changes. We shared concerns over how little Americans seem to know about their own religion, much less the religions of others, the uncertain role of reason and inquiry in society and in student learning, and whether to respond to interest a majority of students evince in including a spiritual dimension to their learning. We worked out of concern over the divisiveness of public discourse when matters of culture, morality, or religion are at stake. Our deliberations slowed over seemingly intractable problems, but in the end we agreed to develop a statement on the critical issues facing higher education with regard to religion and public life and a framework for further exploration. The resulting recommendations were captured in a 2006 *Wingspread Declaration on Religion and Public Life: Engaging Higher Education* (see the appendix to this chapter).

This chapter begins with an assessment of the role of higher education in maintaining democratic institutions and practices in American society. We argue that it is higher education's responsibility to engage in study, dialogue, critique, and action on issues emerging from the changing role of

The authors would like to thank Gregory R. Peterson for providing comments on an earlier version of the manuscript.

religion in American public life, and we present a framework for doing so. We then examine specific challenges facing the academy as it addresses religion, faith, and spirituality in student learning.

Higher Education as American Democracy's Critical Partner

The work at Wingspread was grounded in the belief that higher education is essential to American democracy. Although definitions of democracy vary, we can probably agree that a strong and effective democracy has these characteristics: (a) an educated and informed citizenry, (b) inclusive social and political systems open to all voices, (c) the active engagement of citizens in civic life and public policy making, and (d) policy decisions that are subject to revisions resulting from citizen questioning and dissent. A democratic society guards certain principles, particularly freedom, justice, and equal opportunity. We have yet to realize this ideal, but as a nation we continue to implement reforms, albeit with difficulty and slowly, to increase equity and access to educational, social, and political systems. Levels of citizen engagement and responsiveness of public policy makers fluctuate, and commentators on American public life continue to express concern that both are lackluster.

As educators of the next generation of informed citizens, colleges and universities are essential partners in American democracy. However, higher education also plays a critical role in shaping inclusive social and political systems. Since World War II, colleges and universities have worked to increase equity in American society by providing access to education to women, people of color, immigrants, people with disabilities, the poor, and other historically underrepresented groups. Education is widely viewed as the best antidote to economic and social injustice. Discussions in and beyond the classroom enable students to practice the arts of democratic dialogue, informed deliberation, and decision making. Although these images may be more ideal than realized, the point is that the hard work of strengthening democracy rests partly with the academy.

Even in the most harmonious times, democratic dialogue, informed reasoning, and collaborative decision making are difficult. Issues of power and privilege can trump inclusiveness. Individuals harbor deeply felt views based on experience, learning, culture, and other influences that can cause a process of engagement to break down or never to begin at all. In recent years Americans seem more polarized than ever, separated across cultural divides, distrustful of political systems and politicians, and disengaged from each other socially. Public Agenda has reported that Americans demonstrate a weakening in their ethic of tolerance and less willingness to compromise with others of different beliefs or values (Public Agenda, 2005).

The Changing Role of Religion in Public Life

Nearly 90% of Americans have long said they believe in God or a higher authority (Harris Poll, 2003), but for the past 50 years or more, religion has been marginalized in the public sphere. This is changing; religion is a growing cultural force in American public life (Pew Forum, 2005). In the 2004 presidential election, religious affiliation aligned with national voting patterns (Pew Forum, 2005). At the same time, the religious landscape has continued to diversify because of revised immigration quotas. According to the American Religious Identity Survey (ARIS), the following categories grew by more than 100% between 1990 and 2000: nonreligious/secular, Islam, Buddhism, Hinduism, Native American religion, Baha'i, new age, Sikhism, and deism (Kosmin, Mayer, & Keysar, 2001). Concerned with perceived declines in morality and increases in excessive individualism, many Americans are drawn to the more conservative forms of their religious beliefs and practices.[1] At the same time, the number of Americans who claim they are spiritual but have no religious preference has doubled,[2] proving the dictum that in turbulent times people tend toward both extremes.

These changes—increasing religious diversity, fewer people practicing moderate religions, growth in both conservative congregations and personal spiritual exploration, increased political activism by religious groups, and a commingling of public policy decisions and religious practices—have led many to worry that Americans are becoming increasingly intolerant. The public square has devolved into a hostile place where people are divided into camps and remain unwilling to engage each other, much less explore their shared values and seek common solutions.

The Changing Role of Religion on Campus

Few campuses can claim that religion is irrelevant. Witness students who demand exemptions based on their sincerely held religious beliefs; accusations of indoctrination and discrimination by students against faculty for behavior the students view as "liberal" or biased toward a secular view; parents and legislators challenging assignments or academic programming that offend their religious views; student blogs on the out-of-class speech of their professors; religiously affiliated high schools suing universities to force them to accept credit for courses that use textbooks that place "God's word above science"; and concerns over the distinction between "sincerely held religious beliefs" and sham excuses. These are matters of academic freedom, of who can teach, what should be taught, who should be taught, how university property is used, and who decides.

Students today are undeniably interested in exploring meaning and purpose in their lives. They are seeking a venue in which they can express their religious ideas and grow spiritually, and they expect colleges and universities to help them attain these goals (Higher Education Research Institute [HERI], 2004).

These concerns, which prompted the Wingspread gathering, generated discussion that led to the creation of the *Declaration*, a document that identifies three areas of concern:

- Both the religious and the nonreligious need to know more about themselves and each other. The group agreed to call on higher education to address widespread religious illiteracy in this nation.
- Both the religious and the nonreligious need to be open to inquiry, critique, and exploration of the foundations of their views. Knowing how important it is to have a fair and equitable framework for discussions involving opposing worldviews, we asked higher education to affirm academic freedom and to promulgate standards of rational inquiry that are both open to religion and academically rigorous.
- Colleges and universities must be intentional about whether and how they respond to student interest in meaning and purpose.

Finally, the Wingspread participants challenged colleges and universities to model the arts of democracy—inclusive dialogue, informed deliberation, and collaborative action—in examining the issues outlined in the Declaration.

Religious Literacy

Each section of the *Wingspread Declaration on Religion and Public Life* opens with questions for consideration by institutions, administrators, and faculty. In this section, we posed these questions:

- What do graduates need to know about religion in a diverse democracy and global society?
- How well are we educating students for a religiously pluralistic democracy?

Following the questions are recommendations to provoke discussion, not to mandate action. We recommended developing programs to address:

- The historical and contemporary role of religion across the disciplines and in the professions
- The relevance of religion to public life
- Teaching about religion at the elementary and secondary school levels
- Faculty development

Two significant points: At Wingspread, the participants agreed that these tasks cannot be relegated to religious studies programs alone. And the *Declaration* clearly was written to convey the message that, rather than teach religion (meaning, teach how to practice a religion), colleges and universities should teach *about* religions.

Defining Religious Literacy

What is "religious literacy"? To answer this question, universities need to determine what students need to know, value, and be able to do regarding religion by the time they graduate. Some institutions, both religious and secular, oppose guidelines or standards on teaching and learning about religion in higher education, believing that religion is a private matter that individuals should pursue outside the classroom. The Wingspread participants disagreed. Religion is a significant force nationally and globally, they agreed, and colleges and universities should grapple with how and when to teach it.

Several works concerned with religious literacy have appeared in recent decades. Charles C. Haynes (1987) raised the issue of defining religious literacy as early as 1987. In 1998, the Association for Supervision and Curriculum Development (ASCD) published *Taking Religion Seriously Across the Curriculum* (Nord & Haynes, 1998), in which the authors argue for including religion in the K–12 curriculum. California, Massachusetts, and Texas include religion in their state standards for history-social science and English.[3] Two new works on religious literacy were published in 2007: Stephen Prothero's *Religious Literacy: What Every American Needs to Know—And Doesn't*, in which the author traces the roots of religious illiteracy and argues for the importance of reversing that trend, and Diane L. Moore's *Overcoming Religious Illiteracy: A Cultural Studies Approach to the Study of Religion in Secondary Schools*, which argues that religious literacy is a critical component of liberal education in a multicultural and multireligious democracy. Despite these efforts, standards for religious literacy remain largely undefined.

If the task of teaching religious literacy belongs throughout the curriculum, then who is responsible for designing curricula for this purpose? There are some highly visible national efforts to involve legislative bodies in these decisions, and that seems ill advised. This responsibility should not be relegated to campus ministry either, even if it is an interfaith ministry, as the purpose of campus ministry is to tend to the personal religious beliefs of students. Nor does it belong in an office of campus diversity, unless that office is part of the academic structure of the institution and is responsible for designing courses and programs that adhere to rigorous disciplinary standards. Ultimately, each institution will have to decide who designs the curriculum and where it is housed in the academic program.

Access

The *Declaration* also encourages development of means of access to academically sound religion content for both faculty and students. This might be easier to accomplish if programs in religious studies were as ubiquitous as programs in English or history, but they are not. According to the American Academy of Religion's *Religion & Theology Programs Census* (2001), approximately 50% of all higher education institutions meet one or more of the following criteria: (a) offer a major in religion, (b) offer a minor in religion, or (c) offer courses in religious studies that are required for graduation. Only 25% of these are public institutions, suggesting that only one-eighth of public institutions offer religion programs. At the same time, almost 75% of all college and university students are enrolled in public institutions of higher education (Carnegie Foundation for the Advancement of Teaching, 2004). In short, to the extent that programs teaching religious literacy exist at all, they are clustered in private colleges rather than in institutions that reach the greatest number of students.

Perhaps more of a problem is that less than half (46%) of the programs in the American Academy of Religions' census offer courses that address religions other than Christianity. "Religious literacy" means knowledge and understanding of multiple religions, not just the historically dominant religion in the United States.

Religion Across the Curriculum

Since the *Declaration*'s publication, faculty members nationally have communicated their reluctance to add religion to their courses and programs. Because integrated programs of this nature were not part of these faculty members' disciplinary training, they feel they lack the skills and knowledge to do it well. We acknowledge that religion is complex and difficult to teach. Ideally, the nonexpert who wishes to incorporate material on religion should learn something about multiple religions; critical theory; a variety of humanities and social science approaches to religion; the personal, social, and political ramifications of religious beliefs and practices; standards of academic freedom; and techniques for managing discussions about controversial or volatile topics. Nonexperts may begin by consulting publications by the First Amendment Center;[4] the webpage of the Religion and Public Education Resource Center (established 1995) at California State University, Chico; and *Religion and the Founding of the American Republic* (Library of Congress (1995); *The Islamic World to 1600* (Applied History Research Group, 1998–2001); and *Divining America: Religion and the National Culture, Religion and the Founding of the American Republic* (National Humanities Center, 2005).

Standards of Intellectual Inquiry, Reason, and Academic Freedom

This section in the *Declaration* leads with these questions:

- How do academics preserve standards of intellectual inquiry, public reason, and academic freedom when faced with religiously grounded assertions?
- How can the classroom be open to religious insights without promoting or denigrating specific religious beliefs?

- What are the ground rules for civic discourse on matters of religion and public life? How do we encourage civility, candor, and diversity of perspectives through our educational programs?

We followed these questions with these recommendations:

- Establish standards for academic inquiry and reason that reflect the principles of rational discourse.
- Foster a spirit of tolerance for both religious and secular perspectives.
- Apply principles of academic freedom in ways that welcome religious views when germane to the subject and protect the right of faculty to subject those views to reasonable challenge and critique.
- Resist ideological interference, especially when it threatens intellectual integrity and academic freedom.
- Support public scholarship.
- Develop and teach models of public discourse and deliberation that work with even the most divisive and difficult issues.

Academic freedom is both a professional standard and a legal concept. As a professional standard, it dates back to the early 20th century and international debates on how to create learning environments that foster free and open research, teaching, and learning. The results of these debates were codified in the *1940 Statement of Principles on Academic Freedom and Tenure*, published by the American Association of University Professors, and that statement—or variations of it—can be found in university handbooks and faculty contracts nationally. Academic freedom is also a legal standard, articulated in *Sweezy v. New Hampshire* (1957) as the *university's* right to maintain a learning environment that is most conducive to speculation, experiment, and creation. *Sweezy* identified the "four essential freedoms" of a university: to determine who may teach, what may be taught, how it shall be taught, and who may be admitted to study. It is commonly accepted that a university's academic mission is most likely achieved through "a robust exchange of ideas" (*Keyishian v. Board of Regents*, 1967) and the unfettered exploration of controversial or unpopular questions.

What happens, then, when a student refuses to study a particular text, citing his or her right to the free exercise of religion? How should a university respond to the faculty member who teaches the Apocalypse as part of a history class? What should a professor do if a student refuses to engage another student in class, claiming religious reasons? May a professor at a public university teach intelligent design in a biology class?

Academic freedom entitles the faculty, as agents of the institution, to set standards, design courses and programs, establish learning outcomes at the programmatic and institutional level, evaluate student learning, and otherwise create and maintain an appropriate setting for learning. There are some limits: faculty cannot coerce or exploit students, and they cannot discriminate on the basis of race, gender, religion, and other protected categories. They have to be competent—a scientist cannot teach that the earth revolves around the sun. A geography professor cannot deny the existence of Israel. And they should stay on point and address issues that are germane to the subject. They must also evaluate students fairly. Professors can ask controversial or unpopular questions and can use provocative teaching methods, but they cannot indoctrinate. Students are not protected from being offended; they are, however, entitled not to be humiliated or harassed.

These standards are easier to recite than to apply. Distinctions between critique and challenge or indoctrination and discrimination on the basis of religion may tread a fine line. There will be times when standards and religious views conflict, or when it is appropriate for a faculty member to challenge a faith-based perspective as unreasonable. The trick is to do so in ways that do not denigrate the student, religion in general, or the religion with which the student is affiliated.

Faculty members at Wingspread expressed concern over the boldness of students and their demand for special treatment in the name of their religious beliefs. They or their colleagues sometimes felt bewildered or even threatened by claims that, as a whole, they indoctrinate students toward a liberal perspective or are intolerant of religious worldviews. At the same time, students, particularly religious conservatives, feel intimidated by what they view as a dominant liberal culture on most campuses.

In addition to the *Wingspread Declaration*, several other statements can serve as discussion materials and foundations for study, critique, dialogue, and policy development at the institutional level. Some are controversial, but one message of the *Wingspread Declaration* is that colleges and universities should never be averse to conflict. These sources include:

- *1940 Statement of Principles on Academic Freedom and Tenure* (with interpretive comments; American Association of University Professors [AAUP], 1940)

- *Academic Bill of Rights* (proposed legislation by conservative activist David Horowitz; Students for Academic Freedom, 2006)
- *Statement on Academic Rights and Responsibilities* (American Council on Education et al., 2005)
- Statement on Academic Freedom and Educational Responsibility (Association of American Colleges and Universities [AACU], 2006)
- *Joint Statement on Rights and Freedoms of Students* (American Academy of Religion [AAR], 1967)
- *AAR Statement on Academic Freedom and the Teaching of Religion* (AAR, 2006)

The Wingspread participants discussed whether broader standards of rational inquiry would ease tensions between religious and secular worldviews. The *Declaration* urges the academy to consider broadening standards of rationality by incorporating principles of rational inquiry that are not tied to earlier worldview commitments but that seek the kind of genuine understanding that is both open to possibility and opposed to dogma and intellectual gullibility. Although some would counter that principles of rational inquiry cannot be separated from worldviews, the Wingspread participants thought it should be possible to find ways to engage in rigorous rational inquiry that do not require a particular worldview. Those interested in this debate may wish to consult recent work wrestling with the relationship of religion and science, for example, J. Wentzel van Huyssteen's *The Shaping of Rationality: Toward Interdisciplinarity in Theology and Science* (1999) and Mikael Stenmark's *How to Relate Religion and Science: A Multidimensional Model* (2004).

Students Seeking Purpose and Spiritual Meaning

The *Declaration* poses these questions regarding spirituality:

- What is the responsibility of colleges and universities to respond to growing spiritual concerns among students?
- To the extent that a college or university enables students' search for purpose or spiritual quest, how does it simultaneously adhere to standards of intellectual inquiry and academic excellence?
- If an institution's mission includes a commitment to educating students for personal and social responsibility, is a spiritual framework an appropriate template for student development?

The group recommended that:

- Colleges and universities should be intentional about whether they will address students' search for meaning and purpose.
- Programs designed to address students' search for meaning and purpose, whether academic or co-curricular, should complement and enrich course content.
- Research is necessary to determine whether attention to spiritual development influences student learning.

The Wingspread group split over whether matters of purpose, meaning, and/or spirituality are relevant to discipline-based learning. Providing students with opportunities for worship, dialogue, counseling, or mentoring linked to their personal exploration was fine beyond the classroom, many felt, but this dimension of student development lacks intellectual rigor and is not a valid part of serious disciplinary study. Others disagreed.

The historical background of our disagreement lies in higher education's progressive incorporation of Enlightenment ideals of rationality over the past several centuries. Spirituality, which deals with practices that cannot be tested by scientific methods, fails to conform to Enlightenment norms.

Traditionally, religious studies programs in secular institutions have been guarded about including spirituality. Typically, a religious studies professor in such an institution describes the beliefs and practices of various religions. The professor can demonstrate the significance of religion for individuals, cultures, and societies, and teach students to empathize with religious traditions other than their own. All of this can be done without crossing the line separating teaching *about* religion and facilitating spiritual development, particularly if "spirituality" is a veiled term for a particular religion or perspective. Consider, for example, that for decades religious studies professors have asked their students to suspend both belief and disbelief to understand and empathize with a variety of religious and antireligious perspectives. Professors themselves are trained to check their personal beliefs at the classroom door.

These pedagogical methods have proven fruitful and effective. They silence angry debates, make space for rational discussion of religion, and advance intercultural learning and respect for difference. On the other hand, serious questions have been raised regarding their underlying pedagogical assumptions.

According to the model, professors should dispense information, but they should not attempt to engender any personal changes in religious belief or disbelief. When these methods are used in religious studies classrooms, various distinctions are made to facilitate student understanding of the nature of the religious studies classroom vis-à-vis the life of faith. Some advise students that understanding something is one thing, believing it is another. In other words, one can understand something and demonstrate that comprehension on a test, yet not believe it to be true (Burns, 2006, p. 7).

Such explanations can be effective in reducing the cognitive dissonance that a devout but naïve believer typically experiences when first encountering the academic study of religion. As Charlene Burns points out, they grant a kind of permission to "learn without changing beliefs" (2006, p. 7). The problem is not that these techniques fail to shelter students from intellectual interference in their faith lives or that they fail to respect the line between teaching about religion and teaching religion. The problem is this: Perhaps it is necessary to generate cognitive dissonance if one wants students to learn. Is it really possible to "learn without changing?"

Consider, for example, a science class on earth systems of which climate change is a significant curricular piece. This course could be taught without any suggestions regarding personal responsibility, but most hope that students leave the course more conscious of how their own choices affect the environment. The desired outcome is that students become more knowledgeable *and* conscientious. The hope is that they have been personally affected—that their education has been transformational.

Is it right to assume that education in certain disciplines (e.g., environmental science) will be transformational, but education in religion cannot be so because it will be viewed as indoctrination? Are we exempting the study of religion from its responsibility to contribute, as other disciplines do, to education of the whole person?

For those who wish to explore the arguments for including spirituality within disciplinary and professional study, we suggest the following resources:

- *Education as Transformation: Religious Pluralism, Spirituality, and a New Vision for Higher Education in America* (Kazanjian & Laurence, 2000)

- *Encouraging Authenticity and Spirituality in Higher Education* (Chickering, Dalton, & Stamm, 2005)
- "In the New Millennium: The Role of Spirituality and the Cultural Imagination in Dealing with Diversity and Equity in the Higher Education Classroom" (Tisdell, 2007)

Either pedagogical method—facilitating students' search for purpose and meaning or avoiding such issues in the classroom—can be effective. These are questions of institutional mission and individual style, not a call for either mandating or excluding spirituality. What *is* called for is a high level of intentionality at an institutional level and dialogue between professor and students about how spiritual dimensions to learning will be managed and why.

Conclusion

Americans seem to be engaged in a new debate about the appropriate role of religion in public life. These discussions include concerns over long-held assumptions regarding separation of church and state, the role of religion in public policy making, how religious pluralism affects our ability as citizens to work together to solve pressing social and moral problems, and the role of objectivity and reason and whether religious and ideological frameworks belong in schools, politics, and the public square.

We view higher education as "our nation's think tank," and in that capacity, it must engage matters of religion and public life proactively. Matters of religion and spirituality provide colleges and universities with myriad opportunities for study, dialogue, interdisciplinary learning, and scholarship. The academy can begin by designing new programs that promote religious literacy. It can review the history and diversity of competing theories regarding what counts as rationality and genuine knowledge. It can affirm standards of intellectual inquiry, reason, and academic freedom and simultaneously examine the anxieties and assumptions about how religious beliefs and practices might affect teaching and learning. It can tackle hostility and divisiveness exhibited in the public sphere by promoting respectful and candid interfaith dialogue, particularly in the classroom. It can address assumptions that the academy should be "values neutral," when religious beliefs are involved yet not necessarily when "safer" values, such as protecting the environment, are involved. Institutions need to settle the question of whether they will guide students in purpose, meaning, and spirituality. To the extent that the spiritual dimension of student development matters, institutions need to find ways to be open to religious insights without alienating others or advancing a specific religious practice.

This list is formidable and calls for faculty dialogue, study, and experimentation. Yet the emergent role of religion in public life presents colleges and universities with exciting opportunities, particularly to tackle the profound intellectual and educational questions facing this generation of educators. Higher education has been handed an opportunity to model exemplary practices in democratic discourse and social action, and in so doing, to demonstrate its worth to society in ways that go beyond facilitating economic and personal gain for individuals. Here is an opportunity, should institutions decide to accept it, to ponder anew fundamental questions about the mission of higher education: What do our graduates need to know, value, and be able to do to live in a diverse democracy and a complex world? Do our academic programs provide students with opportunities to experience things they have never experienced before and to explore new intellectual questions? Do we do enough to challenge them to analyze, think critically, engage in difficult dialogues, and solve thorny social and moral problems? Are we, as individual faculty members and academic leaders, prepared to teach in these ways?

Religion presents opportunities for colleges and universities to consider from a new perspective how effective and integrative their programs and activities are. Finally, academics have new opportunities to reach out to the public on matters of concern to many of them: ethics and values, lifestyle choices, democratic institutions and processes, and the unique historical and demographic landscape of contemporary America.

References

American Academy of Religion. (1967). *Joint statement on rights and freedoms of students*. Retrieved March 25, 2007, from www.aaup.org

American Academy of Religion. (2001). *Religion & theology programs census: The study of religion counts*. Retrieved April 1, 2007, from http://www.aarweb.org/department/RSNAARCensus.pdf

American Academy of Religion. (2006). *AAR statement on academic freedom and the teaching of religion*. Retrieved March 25, 2007, from http://www.aarweb.org/about/board/resolutions/academicfreedom.asp

American Association of University Professors (AAUP). (1940). *1940 statement of principles on academic freedom and tenure*. Retrieved March 25, 2007, from www.aaup.org

American Council on Education et al. (2005). *Statement on academic rights and responsibilities*. Retrieved March 25, 2007, from http://www.acenet.edu

Applied History Research Group. (1998–2001). *The Islamic world to 1600*. Retrieved May 7, 2007, from http://www.ucalgary.ca/applied_history/tutor/islam/

Association of American Colleges and Universities (AACU). (2006). Academic freedom and educational responsibility. *Liberal Education, 92*(2), 6–13.

Burns, C. P. E. (2006). Cognitive dissonance theory and the induced-compliance paradigm: Concerns for teaching religious studies. *Teaching Theology and Religion, 9, 7.*

Carnegie Foundation for the Advancement of Teaching. (2004). *Classifications: Enrollment profile tables.* Retrieved March 25, 2007, from http://www.carnegiefoundation.org/classifications/index.asp?key = 802

Chickering, A. W., Dalton, J. C., & Stamm, L. (2005). *Encouraging authenticity and spirituality in higher education.* New York: Wiley.

First Amendment Center. (2002). *A teacher's guide to religion in the public schools.* Retrieved March 25, 2007, from http://www.firstamendmentcenter.org/

First Amendment Center and the Pew Forum on Religion & Public Life. (2003). *Teaching about religion in public schools.* Retrieved March 25, 2007, from http://www.firstamendmentcenter.org/

Glenmary Research Center. (2002). *Religious congregations & membership: 2000.* Retrieved April 1, 2007, from http://www.glenmary.org/grc/RCMS_2000/release.htm

Harris Poll #11. (2003). *The religious and other beliefs of Americans 2003.* Retrieved March 28, 2007, from http://www.harrisinteractive.com

Haynes, C. C. (1987). Religious literacy in the social studies. *Social Education, 51*(7), 488–490.

Higher Education Research Institute, University of California Los Angeles (HERI). (2004). *Spirituality in higher education: A national study of college students' search for meaning and purpose.* Retrieved March 25, 2007, from http://spirituality.ucla.edu

Kazanjian, V. H., Jr., & Laurence, P. L. (Eds.). (2000). *Education as transformation: Religious pluralism, spirituality, and a new vision for higher education in America.* New York: Peter Lang.

Keyishian v. Board of Regents, 385 U.S. 589 (1967).

Kosmin, B. A., Mayer, A., & Keysar, A. (2001) *American religious identification survey.* Retrieved March 25, 2007, from http://www.egonmayer.com/emayer _aris.pdf

Library of Congress. (1998). *Religion and the founding of the American republic.* Retrieved March 28, 2007, from http://www.loc.gov/exhibits/religion

Moore, D. L. (2007). *Overcoming religious illiteracy: A cultural studies approach to the study of religion in secondary schools.* New York: Palgrave Macmillan.

National Humanities Center. (2005). *Divining America: Religion and the national culture.* Retrieved March 28, 2007, from http://www.nhc.rtp.nc.us/tserve/ divam.htm

Nord, W. A., & Haynes, C. C. (1998). *Taking religion seriously across the curriculum.* Alexandria, VA: Association for Supervision and Curriculum Development. Retrieved March 25, 2007, from http://www.freedomforum.org

Pew Forum on Religion & Public Life. (2005). *A faith-based partisan divide.* Retrieved March 28, 2007, from http://pewresearch.org/assets/files/trends2005 -religion.pdf

Prothero, S. (2007). *Religious literacy: What every American needs to know—and doesn't.* San Francisco: Harper.

Public Agenda. (2005). *Religion and public life, 2000–2004.* Retrieved March 25, 2007, from http://www.publicagenda.org/research/research_reports_details.cfm? list = 1

Religion and Public Education Resource Center, California State University, Chico. (1995). Retrieved March 31, 2007, from http://www.csuchico.edu/rs/rperc/ index.html.

Robinson, B. A./Ontario Consultants on Religious Tolerance. (1995–2006). *New age spirituality.* Retrieved March 31, 2007, from http://www.religioustolerance.org/ newage.htm

Stenmark, M. (2004). *How to relate religion and science: A multidimensional model.* Grand Rapids, MI: Eerdmans.

Students for Academic Freedom. (2006). *Academic bill of rights.* Retrieved March 25, 2007 from http://www.studentsforacademicfreedom.org.

Sweezy v. Hew Hampshire, 354 U.S. 234 (1957).

Tisdell, E. J. (2007). In the new millennium: The role of spirituality and the cultural imagination in dealing with diversity and equity in the higher education classroom. *Teachers College Record, 109*(3), 531–560.

van Huyssteen, J. W. (1999). *The shaping of rationality: Toward interdisciplinarity in theology and science.* Grand Rapids, MI: Eerdmans.

Endnotes

1. The Glenmary Research Center (2002) reported that, between 1990 and 2000, the Presbyterian Church U.S.A. experienced an 11.6% decline in membership,

the United Methodist Church lost 6.7%, the Episcopal Church was down 5.3%, the United Churches of Christ declined 14.8%, and the American Baptist Churches declined 5.7%. All of these denominations are considered "mainstream." During the same decade, conservative churches gained membership: the Presbyterian Church in America experienced a membership increase of 42.4%; the Evangelical Free Church, 57.2%; the Assemblies of God, 18.5%; and the Church of God, 40.2%.

2. Personal spiritual exploration is difficult to survey, but the Ontario Consultants on Religious Tolerance claim that one subset of spiritual practices, New Age spirituality, is practiced to some degree by 20% of the North American population (B. A. Robinson/Ontario Consultants on Religious Tolerance, 1995–2006).

3. California State Board of Education. (2006, February 1). History-social science academic content standards for kindergarten through grade twelve. Retrieved March 31, 2007, from *http://www.cde.ca.gov/be/st/ss/hstmain.asp*

California State Board of Education. (2006, October). English-language arts academic content standards for kindergarten through grade twelve. Retrieved March 31, 2007, from *http://www.cde.ca.gov/be/st/ss/engmain.asp*

Massachusetts Department of Education, Dr. David P. Driscoll, Commissioner of Education. (2003, August). Massachusetts history and social science curriculum framework. Retrieved March 31, 2007, from *http://www.doe.mass.edu/frameworks/hss/final.pdf*

Massachusetts Department of Education, Dr. David P. Driscoll, Commissioner of Education. (2001, June). Massachusetts English language arts curriculum framework. Retrieved March 31, 2007, from *http://www.doe.mass.edu/frameworks/ela/0601.pdf*

Massachusetts Department of Education, Dr. David P. Driscoll, Commissioner of Education. (2004, May). Supplement to the Massachusetts English language arts curriculum framework. Retrieved March 31, 2007, from *http://www.doe.mass.edu/frameworks/ela/0504sup.pdf*

Texas Education Code, §28.002. (1998, September 1). Chapter 113. Texas essential knowledge and skills for social studies, Subchapter C. High School. Retrieved March 31, 2007, from *http://www.tea.state.tx.us/rules/tac/chapter113/ch113c.html*

Texas Education Code, §28.002. (1998, September 1). Chapter 110. Texas essential knowledge and skills for English language arts and reading, Subchapter C. High School. Retrieved March 31, 2007, from *http://www.tea.state.tx.us/rules/tac/chapter110/ch110c.html*

4. Some of these materials are aimed at public secondary school teachers. We included the First Amendment Center because both public schools and public colleges and universities face common considerations regarding separation of church and state and religious inclusiveness.

Wingspread Declaration on Religion and Public Life: Engaging Higher Education*

In July 2005, scholars from public and private colleges and universities—representing diverse disciplines, geographic regions, and faith perspectives—came together at the historic Wingspread Conference Center in Racine, Wisconsin. The purpose of this gathering, entitled "Religion and Public Life: Engaging Higher Education," was to discuss the growing awareness of and concern about the intersection between religion and public life, and to define the role higher education must play in response to those concerns. In animated and sometimes difficult conversations, conference participants narrowed and defined the areas of focus. At the end of the gathering, participants agreed that the points of concern raised at the Wingspread conference called for study, dialogue, critique, and action. The academy had to examine how it teaches about religion; how it welcomes students' diverse religious views and spiritual interests; and how it factors religion into its educational programs and initiatives to strengthen deliberative democracy, all the while preserving standards of intellectual inquiry, public reason, and academic freedom.

This document is a result of a collaborative effort by the conference participants while at Wingspread and through remote consultation in the months that followed. Each section begins with critical questions that scholars might ask themselves and their institutions. Following the questions are specific observations and suggestions intended to foster conversation rather than to serve as final or definitive answers to the questions.

Overview

Religion has always played a significant role in shaping American society. The nation's religious heritage, including its pluralism, remains deeply intertwined with American culture and identity. In recent decades, however, public prominence of religious views has grown even as the nation's religious

*Compiled on behalf of participants in a Wingspread Conference by the Society for Values in Higher Education.

diversity has increased. In this context, maintaining a pluralistic democracy demands a corresponding advance in our citizens' capacity to understand religious differences as well as in the ability and willingness to engage across differences of belief for the sake of the common good.

We are disturbed by surveys that reveal a citizenry inexperienced in engaging others on issues of religious and moral differences and moral debate. It is also worrisome that studies suggest Americans are increasingly less tolerant of others' religious views and less likely to compromise when their religious views are at stake. That all of this is happening at a time when an increasingly large segment of the American public is studying in higher education institutions raises the issue of the academy's appropriate response to these developments.

We assume that colleges and universities serve as our nation's collective think tank and, arguably, its conscience. Changes in the landscape of religion in American public life provide the academy with myriad opportunities for fulfilling that role—for study, dialogue, critique, and action. However, religion all too often is confined to religious studies programs and campus ministries and accepted without critical inquiry. In this statement, we challenge colleges and universities to reexamine how religion is studied and taught. All students, regardless of their beliefs and values, need to understand how religions work. They need to know the constructive and critical appraisals of religion's historic and contemporary significance and, in particular, its impact on public life. We call for a renewed commitment to intellectual inquiry standards, reason, and academic freedom and urge the academy to examine religion in those contexts. Further, we urge colleges and universities to be intentional about how they facilitate students' search for public purpose, self-understanding, and spirituality. We conclude with a call for further attention to the arts of a democratic citizenry. Despite different beliefs and perspectives, students—and their teachers—should be able to engage in a civic or classroom dialogue both thoughtfully and respectfully.

How might this vision be realized? There is no uniform approach, and each university will pursue its own programs and initiatives. We are particularly sensitive to the diverse missions among colleges and universities —religious institutions, nonreligious private institutions, and public institutions. This statement addresses the common goal of colleges and universities: to prepare students to understand and participate in public life.

We encourage colleges and universities to consider the following framework, questions, and recommendations:

Religious Literacy

We recognize and value the contributions of religious studies scholars and programs at universities, but they cannot be expected to bear sole responsibility for advancing religious literacy. We challenge colleges and universities to examine their courses and curricula to put into practice new ways to educate students about religion's dimensions and influence. Students need to understand the historical relationship between religion and the disciplines—sciences, humanities, arts, and social sciences—and the professions as well as the contemporary relevance of religion to the disciplines, the professions, and public life. Students should understand the need to adhere rigorously to disciplinary procedures for constructing hypotheses and disciplinary standards for evaluating theories and truth claims.

Higher education must direct more attention to teacher education with respect to these concerns. American elementary and secondary schools frequently avoid the study of religion partly because it is viewed as too controversial, because of the scarcity of adequately prepared teachers, texts, and tested curricula, and due to confusion or concern regarding First Amendment freedoms. Teacher training is key to addressing these shortcomings.

Religion has resurfaced in American public life and global society as a source of conflict, violence, and corruption and, conversely, as a source of personal strength, civic engagement, creative solutions, and social change. Colleges and universities need to provide students with multiple interdisciplinary opportunities to engage in dialogue and grapple with these glaring contrasts and to understand their personal and social implications.

Colleges and universities must support faculty development so that faculty will learn how to manage both discussion and critique in ways that do not advocate for or denigrate religious views. Teaching about religion requires understanding of and respect for agnostics, atheists, and secularists, as well as for a broad range of religious perspectives. It would be naïve to assume that most faculty are already fully prepared to negotiate the philosophical complexities of debates concerning the rationality of belief or skepticism, to cope with religious diversity, to teach the value of religious pluralism, or to negotiate First Amendment principles.

- What do graduates need to know about religion in a diverse democracy and global society?
- How well are we educating students for a religiously pluralistic democracy?

Standards of Intellectual Inquiry, Reason, and Academic Freedom

- How do academics preserve standards of intellectual inquiry, public reason, and academic freedom when faced with religiously grounded assertions?
- How can the classroom be open to religious insights without promoting or denigrating specific religious beliefs?
- What are the ground rules for civic discourse on matters of religion and public life?
- How do we encourage civility, candor, and diversity of perspectives through our educational programs?

Nearly all colleges and universities aspire to prepare students to be informed, responsible, and engaged citizens in their communities, in American society, and in a complex, global world. As valuable as religious studies scholars and programs are, they alone cannot accomplish the objectives of this Declaration. We urge the academy to consider as a framework for discussion the 1963 U.S. Supreme Court ruling, *Abington Township v. Schempp*, in which the court said:

> It might well be said that one's education is not complete without a study of comparative religion or the history of religion and its relationship to the advancement of civilization. It certainly may be said that the Bible is worthy of study for its literary and historic qualities. Nothing we have said here indicates that such study of the Bible or of religion, when presented objectively as part of a secular program of education, may not be effected consistently with the First Amendment. (*Abington Township v. Schempp*, 374 U.S. 203, 225 [1963])

The academy must preserve and enlarge its understanding of public reason by setting standards for inquiry and discourse. These standards of public reason should reflect the principles of rational discourse that lie at the basis of all academic inquiry. It is important to distinguish the ideals of rational inquiry—which are common features of many of the world's great religious traditions as well as Western philosophy and science—from both religious and secularist worldviews. Debate among worldviews is a valid, though often contentious, part of intellectual life. One of the university's most valuable contributions to democratic society lies in modeling how rational inquiry can contribute to these difficult and important kinds of public argument.

Higher education must foster a spirit of tolerance and actively champion an attitude of mutual respect and affirmation of the value of pluralism in a democracy without implicitly or explicitly privileging secularist worldviews or particular religious perspectives in the search for truth. Academics must explore ways to work with, rather than exclude, religious communities, and all parties must abide by the rules of rational, academic inquiry.

The principles of academic freedom should be applied in ways that preserve the right to subject religious assertions to critique, challenge, and appropriate standards of argumentation, proof, and evidence and that welcome religious perspectives and secularist worldviews when they are relevant to the search for truth.

Higher education must preserve the essential principles of intellectual integrity and academic freedom in the face of pressures of ideological interference, whether religious or secular, from across the political spectrum. It is particularly important to preserve the minority voice. Religious minorities have the same right to the public square as religious majorities; committed nonbelievers and passionate believers are equally entitled to academic freedom.

Colleges and universities must support public scholarship and encourage public discourse and other exchanges among faculty and students and in partnership with surrounding communities. Both scholarship and programs should address the pressing ethical and social issues in American democracy and do so in ways that result in heightened public awareness, civility, and civic engagement.

Colleges and universities must support faculty development opportunities that help faculty engage in democratic dialogue that is both probative and inclusive.

Higher education must develop and practice models of deliberative democracy that strengthen communities and society in general. The academy must also mediate conversations between those motivated by the desire for greater freedom of religious expression in the public square and those who believe that a more secular public square offers the best hope for religious freedom and interreligious peace. Colleges and universities must be models for American democracy.

Students Seeking Purpose and Spiritual Meaning

- What is the responsibility of colleges and universities to respond to growing spiritual concerns among students?
- To the extent that a college or university enables students' search for purpose or spiritual quest, how does it simultaneously hold these students to standards of intellectual inquiry and academic excellence?
- If an institution's mission includes a commitment to educating students for personal and social responsibility, is a spiritual framework an appropriate template for student development?

In April 2005, the Higher Education Research Institute (HERI) of the University of California, Los Angeles (UCLA) issued a report on the spiritual life of college students. The study revealed that three of every four college and university students say they are "searching for meaning/purpose in life" and that they regularly discuss the meaning of life with friends. Students want to use their time in college partly to find meaning and purpose in their personal lives and their academic studies.

We recognize the tensions within academia the study of spirituality raises. Many academics argue that secular colleges and public universities have no business facilitating students' spiritual formation; these institutions' responsibility is to provide an educational environment in which students are able to acquire knowledge, skills, and a sense of personal and social responsibility through disciplined questioning and intellectual challenges. Others respond, however, that this more limited view promotes a form of secularism that ignores the role of faculty as mentors. Students learn in the context of their personal values, beliefs, and experiences. Teaching and learning that ignores this dimension of student learning and development lacks authenticity or, worse, effectiveness. This mentor-teacher model applies to secular colleges and public universities as well, provided the approach does not include religious formation.

We call for each college and university to examine its mission and curricula, to engage in campus-wide dialogues, and to be intentional about whether and how it helps students explore their sense of purpose and the public relevance of their academic studies.

Programs designed to address students' search for purpose and self-understanding, whether such programs are academic or nonacademic, should complement and enrich a student's educational experience.

Colleges and universities must work together or with existing consortia, associations, and other structures for multi-institutional collaboration to create new courses and programs.

Researchers must study and assess how attention to spiritual development in students influences student learning.

Conclusion

The study of religion and its public relevance is a crucial dimension to liberal education. All students should engage that study in ways that affirm intellectual inquiry, reason, and academic freedom. The study of religion and public life should never compromise rational discourse on campus nor should it subvert knowledge attained through disciplinary inquiry. Challenges to disciplinary or professional knowledge and practice should be raised through reasoned debate and academically accepted methods that enrich student learning.

Colleges and universities must make a genuine commitment to deliberative democracy by making a commitment to principles of inclusiveness and respect as foundations for dissent, dialogue, and action. Without these ground rules for democratic discourse, the relationship between those motivated by religious beliefs and those motivated by other values will be defined by who is in the majority or in power, a rule that applies both in public life and on campus. This impasse is increasingly unacceptable to both the academy and the nation. It is the academy's responsibility to model a more positive, productive, and educationally sound form of engagement.

The Wingspread conference, "Religion and Public Life: Engaging Higher Education," was sponsored by the Society for Values in Higher Education (SVHE) and the Johnson Foundation. Wingspread is an educational conference center in Racine, Wisconsin, designed by Frank Lloyd Wright and managed by the Johnson Foundation (www.johnsonfdn.org). The

Society for Values in Higher Education (www.svhe.org) is a community of scholars who care about the ethical issues—particularly integrity, diversity, social justice, and civic responsibility—facing higher education and the wider society.

Participants in the Wingspread conference, Religion and Public Life: Engaging Higher Education, were:

Ann Marie B. Bahr, Professor
Department of Philosophy and Religion, South Dakota State University
Brookings, South Dakota

Christopher Beem, Program Officer
Democracy, Community, and Family, The Johnson Foundation
Racine, Wisconsin

Joel Carpenter, Provost
Calvin College
Grand Rapids, Michigan

Douglas F. Challenger, Professor of Sociology
Franklin Pierce College
Rindge, New Hampshire

Tony C. Chambers, Associate Vice Provost and Assistant Professor
Theory and Policy Studies, University of Toronto
Ontario, Canada

Arthur Chickering, Office of the President
Goddard College
Plainfield, Vermont

Marion Danis**, Head
Section on Ethics and Health Policy, National Institute of Health
Bethesda, Maryland

Allen Dunn, Editor
Soundings, Society for Values in Higher Education
Professor
Department of English, University of Tennessee
Knoxville, Tennessee

Karyn Halmstad, Student
Mount Mary College
Milwaukee, Wisconsin

David A. Hoekema, Professor of Philosophy
Former President, Society for Values in Higher Education, Calvin College
Grand Rapids, Michigan

Marvin A. Kaiser, Executive Director
Society for Values in Higher Education
Dean, College of Liberal Arts and Science, Portland State University
Portland, Oregon

Edward T. Linenthal, Professor of History
University of Indiana

Editor, *Journal of American History*
Bloomington, Indiana

Stephen L. Macedo, Professor of Politics
University Center for Human Values, Princeton University
Princeton, New Jersey

Richard B. Miller, Professor
Department of Religious Studies
Director, The Poynter Center for the Study of Ethics and American
    Institutions
Indiana University
Bloomington Indiana

R. Eugene Rice, Senior Scholar
Association of American Colleges & Universities
Washington, D.C.

Carol Geary Schneider, President
Association of American Colleges & Universities
Washington, D.C.

Mark Silk, Director and Associate Professor
Leonard E. Greenberg Center for the Study of Religion in Public Life
Trinity College
Hartford, Connecticut

Robert A. Spivey, President
Society for Values in Higher Education
Tallahassee, Florida

William M. Sullivan, Senior Scholar
The Carnegie Foundation for the Advancement of Teaching
Stanford, California

Convener/Facilitator*
Nancy L. Thomas, Director
Democracy Project, Society for Values in Higher Education
Portland, Oregon

Acknowledgments
* Abington Township v. Schempp, 374 U.S. 203, 225 (1963)

**The opinions expressed here are those of the authors and are not a reflection of the National Institute of Health or the Department of Health and Human Services.

Direct questions or comments to society@pdx.edu.

PART TWO

STUDENT AND FACULTY PERSPECTIVES

2

UNDERGRADUATE PERSPECTIVES ABOUT RELIGION IN HIGHER EDUCATION

Lois Calian Trautvetter

Undergraduate students are expressing more interest in questions of values, faith, and religion as well as frustration with how rarely those ideas are explored in the classroom. Many students are unsure what they believe, are interested in grappling with such questions as the meaning of life, and are looking for ways to incorporate these questions into their college experience. In a recent Higher Education Research Institute (HERI, 2005) spirituality survey, more than half of the respondents reported they believed it is essential that colleges encourage their personal expression of spirituality. In addition, students want to associate with faculty who are willing to assist them in their search for meaning and purpose.

Another HERI (2006) national survey on faculty spirituality revealed that more than half of the faculty respondents believe it is important to enhance students' self-understanding and to develop moral character and values; however, most are uncomfortable addressing religious/spiritual issues in class and anticipate that students may feel this way, as well. Faculty are being encouraged to reassess their responsibility to contribute to the faith, spiritual, religious, moral, and character development of the students they teach (e.g., Braskamp, Trautvetter, & Ward, 2006; Chickering, Dalton, & Stamm, 2006).

A desired image of a faculty member is emerging, with a portrayal consisting of fellow learners in the communal search for truth, good company, fellow travelers, encouragers of dialogue rather than one-way communicators of truth, and the "guide on the side" (e.g., Baxter Magolda & King, 2004; Palmer, 1998; Parks, 2000). Faculty need not leave their "person hat at the door" of the classroom if education is to be transformative (Tisdell, 2003, p. 254). If faculty are to help students explore their purpose and meaning in life as part of the educational process and guide them with "life's big questions" as Parks (2000, p. 166) suggests, "faculty likely will need to re-think their roles" (Lageman, 2003, p. 11).

In an academic culture where students do explore their individuality, it seems the student's own personal quest of making meaning of life may be missing. Even though many institutions, both private and public, have people working with students of a particular religious affiliation, many do not address the overall spiritual development of their students. Buley-Meissner, Thompson, and Tan (2000) argue that "students with spiritual interests suppress their spiritual life or split their spiritual life apart from their formal education" (p. 15). This results in many college students experiencing a period of displacement, confusion, and discomfort as they develop (Love, 2002). The concept of educating the "whole student" is returning with a more modern appreciation for diverse beliefs and backgrounds, including different faith and religious perspectives. Holistic student development stresses connections among and between the cognitive, interpersonal, and intrapersonal dimensions of development (e.g., Braskamp et al., 2006).

The objectives of this chapter are (a) to understand undergraduates' search for meaning today; (b) to explore some undergraduate perspectives about religion, faith, and spirituality; and (c) to acknowledge the contributions faculty can make and strategies they can use in and out of the classroom to develop personal values, meaning making, and faith development of students, along with intellectual learning outcomes. This chapter uses empirical evidence from surveys and focus group interviews of undergraduate students gathered from a private, nonsectarian, elite university in the Midwest to shed light on undergraduate perspectives on religion, as well as data from case studies of 10 church-related campuses committed to holistic student development to learn more about the role of faculty in guiding students.

College Students Search for Meaning, Faith, and Religion

We are reminded that today's college students are often portrayed as compassionate and caring individuals, immersed in service and community activities (e.g., HERI, 2005; Howe & Strauss, 2003). They are also becoming increasingly interested in religion and spirituality for meaning, comfort, and certitude (e.g., Astin, 2004; HERI, 2005). In the HERI spirituality survey at 236 institutions, 100,000 first-year undergraduate students responded they are interested in spirituality (80%), searching for meaning in life (76%), using their beliefs for guidance (69%), discussing life philosophies with friends (74%), attending religious services (81%), believing in God (79%), and praying (69%) (HERI, 2005). In fact, many of these students reported they expected their colleges, including faculty members, to provide opportunities for them to develop and continue their search for meaning and purpose.

Spiritual and religious development often has not been included as a component of a holistic approach to students. More recently, the terms faith, spirituality, religious commitment, character, and vocation are now common terms in the literature on college student development (e.g., Astin, 2004; Chickering et al., 2006; Fowler, 1981; Love, 2002; Parks, 2000), as well as society, in general; yet, they tend to be avoided on college campuses for fear of overstepping boundaries or offending students. These terms can serve as conversation starters or stoppers, because they are very often emotional and sometimes explosive. These terms are also often institution-dependent, with different terms having very different meanings and interpretations at different colleges. For example, *being spiritual* at an evangelical college is often integrated with the religious views of the campus, whereas at a secular campus, the term *spiritual* is used as a more generic term separate from any religious connotations.

Faith usually refers to an intentional effort to make meaning of one's life or to obtain a higher stage of moral reasoning. For example, Fowler (1981) describes faith as "the ways we go about making and maintaining meaning in life" (p. xii). Faith has "both affective and cognitive dimensions . . . [it] is the ground of ethics and the moral life. Faith is intimately linked with a sense of vocation—an awareness of living one's life aligned with a larger frame of purpose and significance" (Parks, 2000, p. 26). Furthermore, faith is conveyed as the "interior" of one's life (Astin, 2004).

Dalton, Eberhardt, Bracken, and Echols (2006) argue that *spirituality* is a more general term that includes religion. They state that "spirituality" often includes "all forms of reflection and introspection in which the primary goal is to explore one's relationship to the transcendent in order to deepen and enrich practice as well as non-religious or secular beliefs and practices in which the inward search for meaning and purpose, authenticity, and wholeness is the guiding purpose" (p. 5). Palmer (1990) defines spirituality as "turning inward to oneself," but in such a way as to experience "an encounter with otherness" (p. 5). Spirituality is also referred to as not merely an emotional quest, as it touches the core of our being and existence—to help to know oneself (Astin, 2004), to claim an authentic identity, cohesiveness, integration, and wholeness (Tisdell, 2003), and to be socially and morally responsible (Dalton, Russell, & Kline, 2004). It is finding one's purpose in life through inner reflection and introspection and taking action that may lead to vocation. This inward journey or quest that college students take is an attempt to answer the "big" questions of life (Parks, 2000).

Usually, developing an authentic spiritual identity involves moving away from or deeply questioning one's childhood religious tradition and the authorities to which one has been exposed, in favor of a critical-reflective process. This kind of development typically occurs among college students (Fowler, 1981; Parks, 2000; Tisdell, 2003) and can have a religious faith orientation or not. Dalton and colleagues (2006) have categorized college student spiritual seekers into two groups, religious and secular. The secular seekers are identified as being mindfulness seekers, those who focus their inner search on ways to heighten self-awareness and understanding, and wellness seekers, those engaged in spiritual activities to achieve a more holistic, healthy, and integrated way of life.

Some college students' (e.g., religious seekers') development is within the context of religious faith orientation or *religious commitment*, in the sense that faith and the practice of faith are intractably connected. The terms religion and religious commitment are associated with a set of beliefs about supernatural power(s) and one's relationship to a transcendent source or being that often has a set of doctrinal standards and involves public expression, worship, and sacraments and implies community with shared beliefs, commitments, convictions, and celebrating and mourning the lives of others (Marty, 2000). Dalton and colleagues (2006) also believe that college students who are religious seekers can be multireligious in nature as they seek to deepen their religious spirituality and faith through interfaith and multireligious exploration, dialogue, and practice.

There are interrelationships among faith, religious commitment, spirituality, and intellectual dimensions; all are involved in a student's journey of meaning making. But colleges vary in how interrelated they are and can be. Helping to define these terms on a campus or in a class provides the right start in developing undergraduates' convictions and articulating their views of the world and their place in it.

Undergraduates' Perspectives About Their Religious Lives at College

Data were collected in 2006 from both first-year and upperclass (sophomores, juniors, and seniors, equally distributed) through surveys and follow-up focus group interviews to learn more about religious life on campus at a private, nonsectarian elite university ("Midwest University"). Students were asked separately to describe the campus culture; their experience of how questions of meaning, morality, and religion manifest themselves in the classroom and beyond; their interactions with faculty and others; and the campus community and beyond.

The survey was distributed to a randomized sample of first-year ($N = $ 244, 30% response) and upperclass students ($N = 663$, 20% response). It is important to note that the response rate for a survey of this nature may have had a high representation of religious students participating. Although, the respondents were representative of the student population by school affiliation, ethnicity, and religion, there were slightly more female respondents (59%). The respondents gave themselves religious labels such as: Christian (40%), Jewish (16%), agnostic (12%), atheist (11%), Hindu (4%), Muslim (3%), spiritual (2%), Eastern Orthodox (1%), Buddhist (1%), Bahai'i (1%), Sikh (1%), seeker/inquirer (1%), and none (7%). At a quick glance, the respondents showed similar results to the above national survey: interested in spirituality (86%), searching for meaning in life (76%), using their beliefs for guidance (63%), discussing life philosophies with friends (75%), attending religious services (53%), believing in God (79%), and praying (65%). They also reported feeling unsettled about spiritual or religious matters (89%) and feeling disillusioned with their religious upbringing (55%).

It is interesting to note that only 22% of the first-year and 77% percent of the upperclass students reported knowing their religion very well or somewhat. The first-year and upperclass students also reported that spiritual growth and practice of religious beliefs are very or somewhat important to them—68% and 70%, respectively. Regarding their level of religious participation, 44% of the upperclass students reported the same level, 35% increased participation, and 21% decreased participation. Only 40% reported they were very or somewhat satisfied with opportunities for religious/spiritual reflection on campus. One student respondent said: "I've really been looking for a source of information [in matters of truth] I feel I can trust, someone genuinely interested in my spiritual development, not just converting me to their religion."

Both sets of students, first-year and upperclass, reported they felt very comfortable in interactions with people of different religions—77% and 80%, respectively. In fact, 80% of all students reported having an interest in different religious traditions. Many students reported being positively affected by "living and interacting with people of different religions" from their own. As one student stated, "Being from a very homogeneous Mormon community, I never had exposure to other faiths. Since coming to [Midwest University], I have been glad to see that people of varying faiths can still practice as much as they please while being tolerant and respectful of other faiths." On the other hand, one student expressed his concerns: "I have no problem with the various religious activities on campus and think they should continue. However, I do not choose to participate . . . and sometimes feel a little overwhelmed by the religious presence on campus. Just because I'm not religious, [that] doesn't make me bad."

Both sets of students showed a strong degree of comfort discussing their personal beliefs with close friends, family, acquaintances, in classes, and strangers, as shown in Table 2.1.

TABLE 2.1
Percentage of Students Who Are Comfortable Discussing Personal Beliefs

	First-year students	*Upperclass students*
With close friends	97	97
With family	87	88
With acquaintances	79	86
In classes	63	71
With strangers	54	59

It is interesting to note that students generally reported reasonable comfort with talking about their personal beliefs in class. More important, the upperclass students reported on those who have contributed most to their spiritual growth or religious identity: friends (30%), student organization(s) (16%), a class (14%), religious services on campus (12%), professor (6%), religious advisor (6%), campus minister or rabbi (6%), and coach, student life, or residential life administrator (1%). It is not surprising that friends and student organizations rank the highest because peers are very important to college student development (e.g., Chickering & Reisser, 1993); however, it is worth noting that classes also ranked high for contributing the most to students' spiritual growth/religious identity. Class is an important time for many students to be stimulated and share these new ideas.

Furthermore, some upperclass students also reported that professors could talk about their personal religious beliefs and discuss religious beliefs other than their own, as shown in Table 2.2.

One student stated:

> While I'm not a religious person, I enjoy hearing speakers and discussing the philosophical and sociological roles of religion and faith . . . there have been courses . . . along the lines of discussion of philosophical works by the likes of Hume and Kant, as well as the role of religion in modern, technology-dominated life. These activities, I feel, are only available when you're in a college environment and are very enriching.

TABLE 2.2
Percentage of Students Who Considered It Appropriate for Their Professors to Discuss Personal Religious Beliefs and Religious Beliefs Other Than Their Own

	Personal religious beliefs	*Other religious beliefs*
Any class	19	38
Only certain classes	69	82
Office hours	51	55
Research opportunity	46	54
Advising	42	48
Co-curricular activities on campus	56	65
Co-curricular activities off campus	65	69
Residence hall program	53	63

Furthermore, an engineering student said, "I think that in discussing certain topics . . . you might not agree with that perspective, approach, or theory, but in understanding the other theories and why they're not feasible, it helps with your comprehension of your own personal theories." However, expression of personal religious beliefs in class generally is limited to times "when such expressions relate to the topic on which the professor is lecturing or leading a discussion." Otherwise the lecture becomes "less effective as a teaching tool and/or certain unprepared students may feel marginalized or under attack."

Upperclass students also reported how frequently they experienced different kinds of feedback from professors and how helpful it was to them, as shown in Table 2.3.

It is interesting that students think encouragement to discuss spiritual matters is less helpful to them than opportunities to discuss the purpose and meaning of life. Perhaps a closer look at differentiating these two areas is warranted.

Everyone, including faculty and students, needs to have the psychological safety to explore, question, confide, and share with others. Thus, it is essential to keep in mind that student exploration and self-critical reflection will occur only if the class environment is considered safe. This respondent's statement captures many students' sentiments: "There is no problem sharing religious beliefs in the classroom or elsewhere as long as these beliefs are not imposed on others. It very much depends on not when, but *how* professors are talking about their religious beliefs."

TABLE 2.3
Students' Perceptions on Feedback From Faculty and Degree of Helpfulness

Professors have frequently or occasionally provided:	*% offered*	*% thought it helpful*
Advice/guidance about your educational program	77	85
Intellectual challenge or stimulation	62	94
Opportunities to discuss course work outside of class	70	89
Emotional support and encouragement	74	91
Help in achieving professional goals	72	73
Opportunities to discuss the purpose/meaning of life	61	53
Encouragement to discuss spiritual matters	64	20

Professors influence students more than they know sometimes, and it's important that a professor be very careful when and where he or she talks about religion. Many students thought that faculty "did a good job of respecting the separation between the education they are giving and religious education . . . respecting where everyone is coming from type of thing." One male respondent, an engineering major, remarked:

> Most of the time I see that the professors are trying to separate this moral life and the academic life. I don't even know what their religion is or if even they have a religion. I think it would be a good learning experience if I was just able to learn their religion . . . and what it is about. I think those types of discussions may be helpful in class.

Many students expressed that professors should be able to use "their own discretion . . . to express their beliefs. They should [in doing so], however, not openly negate or belittle the beliefs of students." In fact, if a religious discussion comes up, "let it happen to let people feel comfortable to share and let them know they're not being judged . . . that's part of the reason that people don't speak up in class. You feel like you're being judged."

Some students reported that sometimes they are silent about their religious views in class, because religion is a private matter or intimidating and not something they want to discuss in class. Other students had different opinions on where religion should be discussed. Many mentioned social events organized by religious groups, but many also mentioned certain courses, but not just "any class." Many of these students mentioned that religion classes were "definitely the places . . . to discuss different religious topics from an academic perspective."

"Academic perspective" is key for looking past dualistic patterns of thinking, as one biology/psychology first-year further explained:

> I can't say that I don't believe in this [Islamic studies] or [that] what the professor is saying [is wrong], just because I think [my beliefs] are right . . . like in the beginning of September, but then I kind of understood that even if you're in a religion class you have to kind of look at it from an academic perspective. I can still talk about religion and ask these questions, but I can't be just outright biased or judge everything by my standards.

Furthermore, one religion major said, "My academic studies of religion have brought me along spiritually . . . and some classes and professors have taught me other religious beliefs which have made me examine my own and come up with my own unique spirituality." In general, the students on this campus wanted more religion classes.

Besides religion classes, others mentioned courses that discussed religion, including ethics and morality issues in philosophy, communications, engineering, and chemistry classes; Spanish classes that taught the history of Spain and Latin American countries with the Catholic Church; and English literature classes. One student mentioned "a class on the black power movement/era . . . that focused solely on Malcolm X as a historical civil rights activist rather than his role in the nation of Islam . . . that was intentionally done rather than just coincidence." This was perhaps a missed opportunity to learn more about Islam, especially in light of growing religious illiteracy (Prothero, 2007).

Additionally, a few students mentioned specific projects they found meaningful. For example, a theater major mentioned experiencing a final theater project:

> I really incorporated a lot of religious things . . . into my performance. I wasn't trying to indoctrinate or convert my class . . . I ended up performing an encyclical that the Pope had written . . . it's interesting to see how people respond and what they associate with what you're doing. I feel like there are opportunities as a performer to express your own beliefs and weave them into what you're doing.

Although, some students find these types of discussions ample, others want still more discussion and opportunities focused on religion and morality. These students think faculty do not want to talk about these issues because they "are not aware of the issues with different religions" and/or they think religion clashes with their own discipline (e.g., "science and religion can be combative" on the subject of stem cells). These students want these issues "discussed in class, too, if it's part of the class." Some students suggested setting up more classes or seminars that could specifically discuss these religious and morality issues and, more important, alert the students that these courses are being offered. Also, the students encouraged "more emphasis on interfaith education and dialogue."

Students also commented on other meaningful events that involved student-faculty interaction and allowed for more discussion—office hours, advising meetings, and special trip and/or experiential learning opportunities. For example, one student went on an alternative spring break trip: "It wasn't religious at all in any aspect, but . . . we ended up having these religious discussions, and it was just a really enriching experience, getting different perspectives."

Implications of the Role of Faculty: Challenges and Strategies

This section discusses challenges for faculty who help students search for purpose and meaning and suggests some strategies for faculty to address faith and religious issues in the classroom and encourage faculty-student interactions. Additional data gathered from in-depth institutional case studies of 10 church-related institutions, including in-depth interviews with faculty, are used as well. Church-related institutions have a history of addressing fundamental issues such as the roles of faculty and how their curricular and co-curricular practices reinforce learning and development and intentionally integrate faith and learning (Dovre, 2001; Dykstra, 1999). *Putting Students First: How Colleges Develop Students Purposefully* (Braskamp et al., 2006) presents a comprehensive overview of the research project.

Faculty grapple with their course content and teaching methods with regard to assisting students in their search for meaning making. Even at church-related colleges, debates about the role of faculty are intense and personal. Faculty want to connect with students, but often are concerned about including personal perspectives in the classroom and blurring boundaries with issues of faith—influencing students too much or silencing them (Braskamp et al., 2006).

Curricular Content and Pedagogical Strategies in the Classroom

Faculty are providing more developmentally tailored experiences for students (e.g., first-year, sophomore, senior experiences) to help address curricular content. First-year experiences are usually small, highly interactive, and focus on students beginning their journey of self-discovery, engaging in reflection and critical thinking, and acquiring a body of knowledge or set of skills. The goal is for students to get to know faculty on a personal level and become socialized into the campus community. On the other hand, senior or capstone experiences tend to integrate knowledge and understanding, delineate the practice of particular worldviews in the real world, and encourage reflection and applying knowledge to personal life. For example, Hope College's senior seminar, described as "stressing personal assessment of one's education and life view," allows all senior students to express their understanding of their faith in a senior seminar taught by a variety of professors. One philosophy professor's senior seminar course is titled, "Saints, Heroes, and Ordinary People." Students read a number of biographies, novels, and stories that illustrate how various people have lived their lives, some Christian and some not, to "stimulate their thinking." Each student writes a Life View Paper that "articulates a philosophy for living in a coherent, disciplined, yet personal way." In this class, religion is not studied as an object or as a scholarly exercise, but rather, the students have an opportunity to apply their faith and use it to guide them.

Many argue that faculty not only should engage with students in values clarification, but also assist students to make commitments in life by taking a position, while still advocating that one needs to remain open to change and growth (e.g., Baxter Magolda & King, 2004; Parks, 2000). This is not easy to do. Faculty struggle with their own authority and expertise when teaching such issues, and a number of trends have influenced the notion that all ideas are equally valid in the classroom (Nash, 2002; Weisser, 2005). Faculty members generally try to help students avoid increasing relativism, where every thought/idea/proposition is a personal one and thus worthy of equal consideration and validity even though it involves insufficient intellectual reasoning or content.

To address these challenges, faculty members use different pedagogical strategies to assist students to become more accepting of others and guide them in discerning faith and religious issues (e.g., Braskamp et al., 2006). These strategies may include

- conducting question-and-answer sessions in class;
- playing the role of devil's advocate;
- providing role-playing among students;
- requiring position papers, essays, and written arguments of different worldviews;
- using books as references and authoritative sources to illustrate how students can discern multiple views from books and writings;
- encouraging personal journal assignments;

- appointing small-group discussions about a topic;
- using experiential and service-learning projects;
- using one-on-one sessions in the lab or studio; and
- using campus events (e.g., forums, plays).

Faculty-Student Interactions Outside the Classroom

Students develop and learn outside the classroom as well. Often faculty members are expected to be good mentors and role models for students. Getting to this point calls for frequent and in-depth interaction between faculty and students beyond the classroom. From the students' perspective, informal interactions they have with faculty in such places as retreats, dining areas, residence halls, and office hours are very important. Faculty have found that students are more apt to discuss their life goals and their struggles with the "big questions" of life, for example, when the discussion flows more naturally and, thus, is less threatening.

It is not surprising that respondents reported office hours as by far where the most meaningful interactions take place (Braskamp et al., 2006). Office hours provide students with the opportunity to receive extra help on class problems and allow them to feel free to ask faculty about life's big questions. Faculty also report they are more willing to reveal personal information and expand on classroom discussions in their offices, including addressing the intersection of faith and learning on various topics (e.g., gay marriage, abortion, presidential elections, race relations). Both students and faculty believe the rapport developed during office hours precipitates greater involvement in the classroom. Additionally, sharing meals and department/orientation retreats, immersion/community service trips with faculty as guides, public forums/presentations, and close proximity of faculty offices to labs or student carrels help students develop rapport with faculty.

Conclusion

This chapter shows that many undergraduates are open and willing to discuss spirituality and religion in the classroom and beyond. Students do not develop intellectually and morally separately, nor should they. Faculty relationships with students are important. When faculty are active in linking cognitive, interpersonal, and intrapersonal dimensions of development, including diverse beliefs and backgrounds such as different faith and religious perspectives, students have opportunities to find meaning in life and seek careers and an existence that reflects who they are. Furthermore, Prothero (2007) argues that Americans' ignorance about their own religions and those of others is dangerous to society. It seems that many of today's undergraduates are asking for help to prepare them to be future leaders by better understanding the world's religions.

Faculty who assist students with their search for meaning making usually find it both challenging and rewarding, intellectually and personally; they are engaging students in integrating their faith with their learning. Faculty who teach classes and participate in events in which a diversity of views is examined have an opportunity to reflect and sharpen their own identity and character, along with their students. Getting involved in issues of faith and religion provides opportunities for everyone to learn how to be "judges" of perspectives and to avoid being "judgmental" of those with a different set of perspectives. In our pluralistic world, everyone can benefit from interacting with those whose perspectives differ—even in the classroom.

References

Astin, A. W. (2004). Why spirituality deserves a central place in higher education. *Spirituality in Higher Education Newsletter, 1*(1). Retrieved February 1, 2005, from http://www.spirituality.ucla.edu/newsletter

Baxter Magolda, M. B., & King, P. M. (Eds.). (2004). *Learning partnerships: Theory and models of practice to educate for self-authorship.* Sterling, VA: Stylus.

Braskamp, L., Trautvetter, L. C., & Ward, K. (2006). *Putting students first: How colleges develop students purposefully.* Bolton, MA: Anker.

Buley-Meissner, M. L., Thompson, M. M., and Tan, E. B. (2000). *The academy and the possibility of belief.* Cresskill, NJ: Hampton Press.

Chickering, A. W., Dalton, J. C., & Stamm, L. (2006). *Encouraging authenticity and spirituality in higher education.* San Francisco: Jossey-Bass.

Chickering, A. W., & Reisser, L. (1993). *Education and identity* (2nd ed.). San Francisco: Jossey-Bass.

Dalton, J. C., Eberhardt, D., Bracken, J., & Echols, K. (2006). Inward journeys: Forms and patterns of college student spirituality. *Journal of College & Character, 7*(8), 1–22.

Dalton, J. C., Russell, T. R., & Kline, S. (Eds.) (2004). Assessing character outcomes in college. *New Directions for Institutional Research, 122.* San Francisco: Jossey-Bass.

Dovre, P. J. (2001). *The future of religious colleges*. Grand Rapids, MI: Eerdmans.

Dykstra, C. (1999). *Growing in the life of faith*. Louisville, KY: Geneva Press.

Fowler, J. W. (1981). *Stages of faith: The psychology of human development and the quest for meaning*. San Francisco: Harper & Row.

Higher Education Research Institute (HERI). (2005). *Spirituality in higher education: A national study of college students' search for meaning and purpose*. Los Angeles: University of California.

Higher Education Research Institute (HERI). (2006). *Spirituality and the professoriate: A national study of faculty beliefs, attitudes, and behaviors*. Los Angeles: University of California.

Howe, N., & Strauss, W. (2003). *Millennials go to college*. Washington, DC: American Association of Collegiate Registrars and Admissions Officers and LifeCourse Associates.

Lageman, E. C. (2003). The challenge of liberal education: Past, present, and future. *Liberal Education, 89*(2), 6–13.

Love, P. G. (2002). Comparing spiritual development and cognitive development. *Journal of College Student Development, 43*(3), 357–373.

Marty, M. M. (2000). *Education, religion, and the common good*. San Francisco: Jossey-Bass.

Nash, R. J. (2002). *Spirituality, ethics, religion, and teaching: A professor's journey*. New York: Peter Lang.

Palmer, P. J. (1990). *The active life: A spirituality of work, creativity, and caring*. New York: Harper and Row.

Palmer, P. J. (1998). *The courage to teach: Exploring the inner landscape of a teacher's life*. San Francisco: Jossey-Bass.

Parks, S. D. (2000). *Big questions, worthy dreams: Mentoring young adults in their search for meaning, purpose, and faith*. San Francisco: Jossey-Bass.

Prothero, Stephen. (2007). *Religious literacy: What every American needs to know*. San Francisco: Harper.

Tisdell, E. J. (2003). *Exploring spirituality and culture in adult and higher education*. San Francisco: Jossey-Bass.

Weisser, S. O. (2005). "Believing in yourself" as classroom culture. *Academe, 91*(1), 27–31.

3

FAITH IN GRADUATE EDUCATION

Perspectives of Students and Faculty
in Student Affairs Preparation Programs

Judy L. Rogers & Patrick G. Love

The beginning of the 21st century in American higher education will be noted for its return to considering the spiritual development of students as once again central to learning. The push for this renewed emphasis is coming from the students themselves. *The Project on Spirituality*, a national study of first-year undergraduates conducted by the Higher Education Research Institute (HERI, 2005) reports that 75% of today's entering college students are "searching for meaning" in their lives. They have very high interest in both spiritual and religious involvement. In addition, they come to college *expecting* their institutions to help them develop values and explore purpose. Abdullah (1995) persuades that this search for meaning is in response to our society's individualistic, materialistic, and narcissistic values. These young people seek to fill a deep void in their lives— "a chronic hunger of the soul" (p. 20).

Concomitantly, Nash (2001) argues that, for many students, religio-spiritual identity is primary and influences all other identities (e.g., race, ethnicity, gender, class, sexual orientation, abilities). Thus faculty and student affairs staff should be literate about religion and spirituality and their impact on student learning just as they are about other forms of diversity.

While the spirituality movement in higher education has significant implications for faculty in all disciplines, it holds particular import for faculty and graduate students in the helping professions, that is, those who are preparing to work with students, clients, and patients in contexts where "Big Questions" (Parks, 2000) of meaning, purpose, and values are often engaged. All of these graduate students-in-training and their faculty increasingly need to be prepared to respond to the spiritual exploration of those they teach, mentor, and serve.

Recognizing the lack of research about spirituality in graduate education, we undertook a qualitative study to examine, first, how graduate students and faculty in college student personnel (CSP) graduate programs conceptualized spirituality and religion, and, second, how curriculum and pedagogy in preparation programs influenced graduate students' own spiritual development and their preparedness to work with undergraduates' spiritual questions (Rogers & Love, 2007a, 2007b). (College student personnel master's programs prepare professionals to serve as advisors and administrators in college and university student affairs offices.) In this chapter, we present our findings and discuss their implications for the place of spirituality and religion in the graduate classroom and, in particular, implications for graduate training in the helping professions.

The Study

We interviewed faculty and students of CSP programs in three differing institutional contexts—one program was at a state university (Secular State) and the other two were at religiously affiliated institutions (Christian University and Catholic College). In each program we interviewed four faculty members and held individual and focus group interviews with graduate students. At Secular State we interviewed 9 students; at Catholic College, 12 students, and at Christian University, 11 students.

CSP Graduate Student and Faculty Conceptualizations of Spirituality and Religion

Students' conceptualization of spirituality included several dimensions. First, while some experience religion and spirituality as analogous, for the majority of students in our study, spirituality and religion were separate phenomena. One student from Secular State described the spirituality/religion distinction in this way:

I think both can help you make meaning of things, but looking at spirituality is an internal process, and religion is an external process. I look at spirituality as a kind of defining who you are and finding your purpose in life, but also, it helps you understand your capabilities and kind of works with your intellectual and physical intelligence.

Another student at Secular State offers a less clear-cut distinction between religion and spirituality:

I find religion as a community-oriented expression of faith where spirituality is the innermost search, the innermost passion for a belief structure, and the two can certainly be separate but they can also be very much linked.

A student at Catholic College captured the dominant belief among those interviewed, that all people have an innate spiritual dimension while religion is learned.

I think of religion as sort of like spirituality in a structural sense, and it's just sort of giving you rules to define your spirituality and practice in an ordinary setting. Spirituality to me is just something that wells up inside of you. I feel like religion is something you practice and something that's taught to you.

The prevailing theme of the graduate students' definitions of spirituality was connection. A student at Christian University put it this way: "I believe spirituality to be a fundamental connection with all things and people." There were differences among students about the role of God in one's spirituality. For some, "belief in the Divine" was central, particularly among those students for whom religion and spirituality were synonymous. For others, God was not part of the definition. However, for most, spirituality included a connection with something beyond oneself, as described by a student from Christian University:

I think spirituality is an acknowledgment of your soul, however you answer that for you, and I think that spiritual people mix beliefs a lot . . . they will take a little bit from this [religion] or a little bit from that . . . to create their own spiritual beliefs. They acknowledge that there's a power higher than them in the universe, whatever that power may be, and maybe it is the universe.

A dichotomy arose in our interviews with students at Christian University. Several who identified as fundamentalist evangelical Christians made a distinction among Christianity, spirituality, and religion. In their view, "Christianity is more focused on a personal relationship with Jesus Christ" while spirituality is more open to everything rather than built on a specific belief system. In contrast, "a religious person is someone who has a book of rules . . . do this and this and this and these good things could happen to me."

These student notions of spirituality and religion mirror the conceptualizations of the faculty we interviewed. Like the students, the majority of the faculty distinguished spirituality from religion. For several among them, this distinction was a relatively new insight. As one faculty member from Christian University explained,

> Coming out of a Christian faith tradition, I certainly have historically viewed spirituality [as synonymous with religion] . . . I no longer think of spirituality in terms of religious expression . . . I think of it more broadly than that.

Another faculty member from Catholic University said she had to think about spirituality inclusively. In doing so she had two definitions—one secular, in which "spirituality is about the relationship you have with your authentic self," and the other, which she uses in speaking with someone who comes from a faith tradition, in which she talks about "spirituality being that relationship we share with the Divine." Or as one faculty member from Christian University who blends the secular and religious in her definition states, "spirituality is about meaning as well as my belief in Jesus Christ." Thus, similar to student conceptualizations, it was the presence of a higher power or God in the conversation that seemed to create the dividing line between what comprised spirituality and what comprised religion. In addition, each faculty member recognized that spirituality may not include religion for some of his or her students, and it was important to honor that distinction when facilitating dialogue about spirituality in the classroom or in informal conversations with students.

These student and faculty constructions of spirituality represent the debate in the literature about the definitions of these two concepts. Scholars such as Parker Palmer (1996) and Chickering, Dalton, and Stamm (2006) argue that there is a difference between spirituality and religion, and their distinctions are captured in the faculty and student perspectives detailed above. Other writers, such as Robert Nash (2001), see the two dimensions as intertwined, and in fact he uses "religio-spiritual" to underscore the view that they are one and the same. Understanding the definitions of spirituality and religion that students and faculty bring with them to the college classroom has real implications for what each thinks appropriate to include in classroom talk, curriculum, and pedagogy.

Student Perspectives on Spiritual and Religious Talk in the Classroom

Students expressed differing views on the content of spiritual talk that was considered "legitimate" in the classroom. Some of this variation, though not all, was correlated with institutional type (Rogers & Love, 2007b). Not surprisingly, it was at Christian University where "God talk" was more prevalent and expected in the classroom—though even in this context there were varying levels of comfort with just what this should comprise. For example, the students who identified as fundamentalist evangelical said their faith was just a natural part of their lives, and they felt free to talk about it with no "push back" from faculty. However, these students wanted even more explicit discussions in class settings about the integration of faith into their practice. And despite the fact that the mission of Christian University is grounded in religious belief, with faculty and undergraduates (though not graduate students) required to sign a faith statement (i.e., a statement that specifies particular religious beliefs and perspectives that are to be upheld by faculty and undergraduates), some graduate students still felt hesitant to reveal fully how central God and Jesus were to their philosophy. This concern was candidly expressed by one student:

> I felt embarrassed when I wrote my paper and I was like, "Oh, I hope I didn't tell too much about Jesus in my paper." . . . Honestly, I had that thought. . . . I so remembered this distinct time in class [when] I felt like such a moron, but the professor asked what's the number one relationship on campus, and I was like your relationship with God . . . that's the number one thing, everything else is secondary. . . . Everyone laughed. . . . I couldn't believe I said that answer out loud.

Alternately, the non-Christian graduate students at Christian University at times felt silenced and marginalized by the religious talk in the classroom, which assumed all were of the same beliefs. One student described her experience this way:

> I get to the point sometimes where I can feel my blood pressure rising and my heart will be pounding fast and I'll try not to say anything about an issue [that I disagree with on religious grounds] and not go there, and other times my hand just shoots up and I can't stand it any longer. But . . . I keep my mouth shut most of the time.

The quotations above indicate that Christian University students at either end of the continuum, from evangelical Christian to non-Christian, have widely divergent opinions about what is appropriate religious talk in the classroom. The Christian University students who identified as moderate evangelical, that is they engaged in a wider range of questioning about their religious beliefs than did fundamentalists, seemed satisfied with the amount and focus of faith talk that occurred in their courses. One student described what this appropriately religious class environment comprised for him:

> We start each class with a devotional and prayer, sometimes led by students and sometimes led by the instructor. So there's that, and then sometimes the way some of the questions are approached, some of the case studies, are kind of a little more from a Christian perspective . . . Since we discuss case studies within the courses, the class members also offer up their comments, and some students will choose to refer to certain Christian beliefs.

Another student shared what he valued in the class dialogues: "There is no sense of 'as a Christian you must respond this way or be this way.' Rather, we have a faith at our base and discuss difference from that base."

While at Christian University there was a wide variety of views on what kind of spiritual/religious talk was legitimate and desired in the classroom, at both Secular State and Catholic College, the range of what was considered appropriate was much narrower. For example, the curriculum at Secular State required a great deal of reflection to the extent that the students referred to "a culture of reflection." The point of constant critical assessment was for students to gain a clear sense of their beliefs, identities, and relationships. There was an emphasis throughout the program on seeking personal authenticity, transcending one's ego and belief system, developing connection and community with others, and deriving meaning and purpose in life. Some recognized that these four elements embodied Love and Talbot's (1999) definition of spiritual development and found these curricular emphases appropriate and valued in the program. However, when students perceived a shift from these spiritual foci to a discussion that included a higher power and/or God, they expressed discomfort. Invoking the Divine was not considered acceptable in the Secular State program because it was religious and crossed the public/private line. Those students who identified as religious felt they would be "outliers" if they shared this aspect of themselves, despite the program's stated value of openness. These students were hesitant to bring their faith perspectives into the class dialogues. As one observed, "I think that [it] is still hard to be fully open and honest [about one's religious beliefs] because we are still feeling everyone out and we don't want anyone to judge us."

There were crucifixes in the classrooms at Catholic College, and many instructors introduced class with a prayer. But despite the school's religious tradition and these religious practices, CSP graduate students did not expect or really desire much talk about God and religion in their classes. If it came up, it was not considered unacceptable because of the college's Catholic affiliation. Nor did students feel as if religion was "thrown in your face." They saw spirituality as more implicit—emanating from the social justice and vocation emphases in the program. One stated emphatically that religion would not be welcome by his peers in the classroom "because they think you are going to be preaching or proselytizing," and clearly that was not appropriate for this CSP program's curriculum. However, it is important to note that Catholic College students did feel they could have conversations about their own spirituality with their faculty; as one stated, "I think here at Catholic I would feel very comfortable talking about my spirituality just because all of the teachers seem to be open to spirituality."

What emerged from our findings was that, for most of the graduate students in our study, when spirituality was recognized and explored as distinct from religion it was accepted and even desired in the curriculum and classroom (Rogers & Love, 2007b). Further, the students' own spiritual development, defined by Love and Talbot (1999) as seeking connection, authenticity, transcendence, and purpose, was an important aspect of their professional preparation. It was when God or a higher power entered into the dialogue that most of these students became uncomfortable and drew the line about including that in their graduate work. In contrast, the evangelical Christian students, both fundamentalist and moderate, could not envision learning without Jesus at the center. Their religious beliefs were completely interwoven with their learning. It was difficult for them not to bring God into their professional preparation because the Divine is at the center of all they do. They wanted and expected class conversations to include references to their religious foundation. Obviously, context was critical here—at Christian University, evangelical Christian students could voice these beliefs more readily, at Secular State they hesitated to do so.

Creating the Context for Spirituality/Religion in the Classroom

The Faculty Role

We discovered that CSP faculty at each of the institutions identify examining ultimate questions of meaning, purpose, and values as critical elements in the curriculum (Rogers & Love, 2007a). They believe it is part of their students' professional development to be engaged in exploring these issues. In the context of classroom discussions, course assignments, and individual advising, faculty raised issues of vocation; personal and professional values; developing an authentic identity; advocating for social justice; and ethical dilemmas centering on abortion, sexual orientation, religious diversity, and so on. As one professor at Catholic College shared, "I think that programs like ours should not be preparing professional technicians. . . . Throughout the curriculum we should be asking big questions." The focus on developing authenticity, transcendence, community, and purpose were themes in all three of the programs we researched. These comprise elements in Love and Talbot's spiritual development framework and indicate that an emphasis on the spiritual dimension is considered important in the education of emerging student affairs professionals. So faculty were not reluctant to engage with students around these ultimate concerns; indeed, they saw it as part of their role.

The pedagogy these CSP faculty used to explore ultimate questions with their students involved creating "safe spaces" for these at times risky and deeply personal dialogues to occur. They expressed dedication to protecting and nurturing the voices of those who might be marginalized because of their minority viewpoint in a particular context. As one professor at Christian

University offered: "I try to make it safe in class. For example, Catholic students feel marginalized here so I try to weave Catholicism into the conversation where appropriate. It makes it okay to raise the topic."

They also emphasized the value of hearing others' stories and of having a space to share one's own. A faculty member at Catholic College described how she achieved this:

> I very consciously make an effort to use inclusive language that will help de-stigmatize students' experiences . . . and to make it clear that I know and accept that there are those among us who may have family members in jail, who may have had problems with drugs and alcohol themselves or in their families, or may have grown up in different types of parenting situations, or have been through traumatic experiences.

At Secular State, all four faculty interviewed discussed the emphasis they placed on creating space for students to develop identity in the context of the learning community. One of them said, "The program has an explicit focus on encouraging students to connect with self and others and balancing their focus on self and others." Also at Secular State, while religious or spiritual talk is not part of classroom norms, students have the opportunity to select important issues on which to reflect. As one professor shared, "There are a lot of students who when they can choose what to write about will write about the spirituality part of it . . . so I would argue that there is a space."

A final insight from our interviews with faculty was their recognition that if they push students to examine these issues of meaning and purpose, they (faculty) needed to share their struggles with these big questions, too. They had to be vulnerable in discussing these ultimate concerns with students. As one faculty observed, "They need to know that we didn't arrive fully formed either."

Student Response

Students in the study corroborated what faculty intuited—teachers do need to create a safe space for discussing spirituality/religion and to be authentic in "putting themselves out there" in sharing how they make meaning in their own lives (Rogers & Love, 2007b). These graduate students made it clear that a safe classroom environment was necessary if they were to bring this aspect of their identity to the learning context. A safe space for students was one where they could be vulnerable in sharing their spiritual and religious questions and beliefs and where these revelations were accepted with respect. The instructor's role was critical in this as one student explained: "I think it is how the professor creates a context for risk-taking, that is, offering a framework—a safe space [that dictates our willingness to explore these deep questions]." Students did not expect that everyone would agree with their views; in fact, some were eager for the constructive critique as it would help them clarify and deepen their faith/spirituality. But there was a pervasive sense that their faculty must deem it legitimate to bring these conversations into the classroom, and then faculty must carefully craft an arena where differing perspectives could be voiced and contrasting stories shared. And the parameters of what this negotiation of space entailed were mediated by the institutional and program context. For example, at Christian University, faculty needed to engage a pedagogy that welcomed the voices and views of non-Christian students, while at Secular State, the religious dimensions of students' meaning-making had to be brought from the margins of the dialogue to the center.

Finally, students felt faculty authenticity was a crucial influence in their exploration of big questions of meaning and purpose. A student at Catholic College captured this sentiment by observing how influential it was to see professors "in a light where they experience challenge and difficulty, too." Students at Christian University described how one professor modeled his faith in how he made ethical decisions and by openly sharing his thinking and decision-making process. Perhaps the most compelling statement about the significance of faculty being authentic came from a student at Christian who believed that, when discussions revolve around these questions of ultimate concern, faculty have "to be and do" what they want students to learn.

Relevance of Spirituality and Religion in Other Professional Disciplines

While the spirituality movement is a primary impetus for the student affairs profession to consider this dimension in its graduate students' education, other professions are including the spiritual in their professional training programs as well. There are a number of reasons for this, and they coincide with what we discovered in our investigation. They are:

- Spirituality/religion is increasingly recognized as a legitimate form of diversity in client/student populations.
- Professionals such as nurses, counselors, and social workers (along with student affairs professionals) deal with questions related to the meaning of life, each in distinct, but some overlapping, ways.
- If we treat clients/students from a holistic perspective, we cannot ignore their religio-spiritual needs and issues (Rogers & Love, 2004, p. 3).

We now examine each of these points in more depth. In particular we draw implications for faculty in other professional education arenas.

Religious/Spiritual Diversity

Just as we value and celebrate diversity of race and ethnicity, social class, sexual orientation, and abilities, we need to honor religion and spirituality as a valid form of diversity (Nash, 2001). What that means for faculty is that we become literate in the language and metaphors of religion and spirituality. We are making it a priority to educate ourselves about issues of White privilege, racial identity development, the impact of social class on student learning, and understanding the needs of students with disabilities. In a similar vein we to need to know more about our graduate students' religious/spiritual frameworks. Primarily, we have to understand how our students make meaning through these religio-spiritual lenses. As was evident in the CSP student interviews, for many students, their religio-spiritual identity is at the core of who they are. They cannot divorce their learning from their spiritual/religious definitions of self, others, and the world. As faculty, we need to realize this and educate ourselves about how the content we teach is filtered through and shaped by this powerful identity lens. Even a beginning knowledge of this form of diversity can help temper our fear of and discomfort with religio-spiritual talk emerging in the classroom. We then understand it as an aspect of identity and recognize it as not necessarily promoting a particular sectarian perspective but, rather, as how our students make meaning about themselves, the universe, and each other. Perhaps, given this new frame, religio-spiritual talk in the classroom becomes less intimidating or foreign.

Spirituality in the Helping Professions

Other helping professions, including counseling, nursing, and social work, have incorporated exploration of the spiritual dimension in training their emerging professionals. For example, the nursing profession was founded on the notion of holistic care of the patient, so spirituality has been part of the conversation from Florence Nightingale to the present. It appears to be the field with the most advanced and extensive work on the role of spirituality in professional practice (Wojnar & Malinski, 2003).

In counseling training, incorporating spirituality within a wellness paradigm can help counselor educators value and address spirituality as an integral component of optimum human functioning. "By distinguishing between religiosity and spirituality and operationally conceptualizing spirituality as a life span developmental phenomenon that is essential for achieving wellness, counselor educators can more readily incorporate spiritual issues within the philosophy of the counseling profession" (Myers & Williard, 2002, p. 142).

Besides the helping professions, we argue that spirituality can be incorporated appropriately into the sciences, the humanities, and the arts. This is evident in the perspectives of other authors in this book who discuss the place of faith in law, biology, psychology, English, and philosophy. Every field of study has its unique ways of making meaning, and these ways include variations on spiritual themes. Thus, faculty across the professions are influenced by the spirituality movement and must consider the implications, not only for what they teach but how they teach. As was evident in our study, faculty play a powerful role in mediating the learning context so discussions of spirituality and faith in a particular discipline can be explored. Faculty must attend to ensuring that all voices join the dialogue in the classroom, and they have to set aside their own views in allowing opposing beliefs to be aired. Nash (2001) provides insights about raising issues of spirituality in the classroom and includes a practical guide to assist in structuring successful dialogues that include spiritual/religious diversity. His six principles of a moral conversation can serve as a compass for successfully engaging these issues when they arise in the college classroom.

Holistic Learning

In *The Courage to Teach*, Parker Palmer (1998) argued that, "To educate is to guide students on an inner journey toward more truthful ways of seeing and being in the world" (p. 6). This perspective recognizes that learning involves the intellectual, emotional, and spiritual dimension of students. Emphasizing the holistic development of students is gaining increasing credence in higher education as we shift from an instructional to a learning paradigm (American

College Personnel Association & National Association of Student Personnel Administrators [ACPA & NASPA] 2004; Baxter Magolda, 2001). Particularly in graduate education, so long entrenched in the German model focusing solely on intellectual development, this represents a sea change in faculty identity and pedagogy. Yet, given the current research on holistic learning, faculty in graduate programs need to expand their teaching methods to include engaging the whole student. This includes students' religio-spiritual dimension. For example, Wojnar and Malinski (2003) offer a compelling argument from the perspective of nurse preparation that

> [s]pirituality, healing, and caring are intertwined human experiences for both nurse and client. If we do not teach and demonstrate caring to our students, they will not be able to demonstrate caring for clients. If we do not value and encourage a diverse expression of students' spirituality, they will have a difficult time providing spiritually relevant care for clients. (p. 297)

There is much wisdom in this perspective. The recognition that students bring their whole selves to the learning environment means that all faculty in professional education need to attend to the spiritual and emotional development of graduate students as well as to expanding their intellectual capabilities.

Our conclusion from listening to graduate students and faculty is that the religio-spiritual dimension of development has a valid place in our professional education programs. Further, these big questions of meaning and faith are not only legitimate in graduate coursework but also, according to Chickering, Dalton, and Stamm (2006), considering them in the classroom does not breach the church/state divide established in the U.S. Constitution. Including these conversations about faith and spirituality in graduate education is a new frontier. We are on the edge of a shift in how faculty define their professional identity and their role with students. Any change of this magnitude comes with discomfort, some reticence, and the realization that new skills are needed in one's teaching repertoire. But embedded in this change as well is a sense of homecoming. When faculty can legitimately bring their spiritual selves into the academy, they no longer have to live divided lives. Our full humanity has a place in the ways we teach, in the questions we explore with our students, and in the developmental growth we prompt for them. It is a new day in higher education and one that promises a more fulfilling, authentic learning experience for both faculty and students.

References

Abdullah, S. (1995, Winter). Feeding our hunger for the sacred. *Noetic Sciences Review, 35*, 18–23.

American College Personnel Association (ACPA) & National Association of Student Personnel Administrators (NASPA). (2004). *Learning reconsidered.* Washington, DC: Author.

Baxter Magolda, M. B. (2001). *Making their own way.* Sterling, VA: Stylus.

Chickering, A. W., Dalton, J. C., & Stamm, L. (2006). *Encouraging authenticity and spirituality in higher education.* San Francisco: Jossey-Bass.

Higher Education Research Institute (HERI). (2005). *The spiritual life of college students.* Project on Spirituality. Los Angeles: University of California at Los Angeles.

Love, P. G., & Talbot, D. (1999). Defining spiritual development: A missing consideration for student affairs. *NASPA Journal, 37*(1), 361–375.

Myers, J. E., & Williard, K. (2002). Integrating spirituality into counselor preparation: A developmental, wellness approach. *Counseling and Values, 47*, 142–155

Nash, R. J. (2001). *Religious pluralism in the academy: Opening the dialogue.* New York: Peter Lang.

Palmer, P. J. (1996). Spirituality and leadership: A conversation with Parker Palmer. *Concepts & Connections, National Clearinghouse for Leadership Educators, 4*(3), 1, 3–4, 14.

Palmer, P. J. (1998). *The courage to teach.* San Francisco: Jossey-Bass.

Parks, S. D. (2000). *Big questions, worthy dreams: Mentoring young adults in their search for meaning, purpose, and faith.* San Francisco: Jossey-Bass.

Patton, M. Q. (2001). *Qualitative research and evaluation methods* (3rd ed.). Thousand Oaks, CA: Sage.

Rogers, J. L., & Love, P. G. (2004, June 24). Preparing professionals to respond to students' search for meaning. *Journal of College and Character, 2.* Retrieved August 15, 2006, from http://www.collegevalues.org/articles.cfm?a = 1&id = 1279

Rogers, J. L., & Love, P.G. (2007a). Exploring the role of spirituality in the preparation of student affairs professionals: Faculty constructions. *Journal of College Student Development, 48*(1), 90–104.

Rogers, J. L., & Love, P. G. (2007b). Graduate student constructions of spirituality in preparation programs. *Journal of College Student Development, 48*(6), 689–705.

Wojnar, D., & Malinski, V. (2003). Developing a nursing perspective on spirituality and healing: Questions and answers following a letter to the editor. *Nursing Science Quarterly, 16*(4), 297–301.

PART THREE

CONSIDERATIONS

BLINKING IN THE SUNLIGHT

Exploring the Fundamentalist Perspective

Dr. Peggy Catron

I n the well-known allegory of the cave, Plato asks us to imagine the plight of a man who had spent his entire life within the confines of a cave in the muted light of a flickering campfire. What will be the response of this man when he is liberated and allowed out of the cave, into the sunlight? This man will experience perplexity at the sight of the sunlit world, Plato suggests, and pain in his eyes as he blinks in the sunlight.

I often hear stories from faculty about "confrontations" with zealous fundamentalist students who refuse to read or consider certain texts they see as offensive or anti-Christian or who express intolerance for other viewpoints or lifestyles (including gay/lesbian). Often these encounters are chalked up to a lack of critical thinking skills, closed-mindedness, irrational thinking, or hostility toward objective investigation. The student can interpret this frustration on the part of the faculty member as hostility, which can lead to a rift in the faculty student relationship, a confrontation in the office of the department chair, or, at worst, the student's disengagement from the learning process—a retreat from the sunlight that pains his eyes. By looking more closely at the fundamentalist perspective, we can understand the challenges these students sometimes face. Often, what appears to be hostility and closed-mindedness may really be fear—fear of new ideas and the potential for personal loss these ideas represent.

I have been working in higher education for more than 15 years, serving on the faculty, in administration, and as a faculty developer. I began my college teaching career as a licensed minister at a ministerial training college within a fundamentalist denomination. I am now a communications faculty member at a large land-grant university and have long since left my ministerial credentials behind. While my faith is still central to my life, it looks very different now from the way it did when I began teaching. I have found an expression of faith that is compatible with and complementary to my academic life through a lot of learning and unlearning, and with the help of compassionate mentors along the way.

Writing this chapter is more for me than just a pedantic exercise; it is an act of composing the narrative of my life, interpreting my experiences from a fundamentalist past and my interactions with fundamentalist students within the framework of various theories. In the following pages, I attempt to lead you through an exploration of the nature of fundamental Christianity and some of the meanings of faith within fundamental Christian communities that can pose challenges to learning. These challenges are often compounded by certain characteristics of today's millennial students; I explore these as well. Finally, I suggest five attitudes that may help these students face the learning process with courage and an open mind instead of retreating into the safety of inherited truth alone.

What Is Fundamental Christianity?

Between 1910 and 1915, conservative religious scholars and writers from both Britain and America produced a 12-volume set of work, known as *The Fundamentals*. The goal of this collection of essays was to reaffirm the authority of scripture over the authority of science in an increasingly secularized world (Marsden, 2006). While the origin of the term "fundamentalist" was forgotten, the dialectical tension between scripture and science became a defining characteristic of the movement. The source of this tension lies in the fundamentalist claim that the Bible is the inerrant, literal word of God and the ultimate authority on all matters. This view is still widely held. According to a 1990 Gallup poll, 31% of Americans believe "the Bible is the actual word of God and is to be taken literally, word for word" (Noll, 1994, p. 231).

The insistence on a literal interpretation of scripture put early fundamentalists on a collision course with science and secular education. A literal reading of the Bible led many fundamentalists to espouse a creation story that (a) held that the world was created approximately 6,000 years ago and that (b) man was created in his modern form at the beginning of time. Fundamentalists saw the teaching of the evolution of man over hundreds of thousands of years as a direct attack on the faith, and dialectical tension became outright war when rural congregations, primarily in the south, rallied to fight the teaching of evolution in the public schools. During the 1920s, the scientific community came to view fundamentalism as "pseudo-science and false philosophy" (Marsden, 2006, p. 218), and by 1930, "not only were the nation's universities alien territories for evangelicals, but fundamentalists, the most visible evangelicals, had made a virtue of their alienation from the world of learned culture" (Noll, 1994, p. 211).

Just as the view of the inerrancy of scripture is still very much alive, so also is the view of *Genesis* as a historical record; Noll cites a recent survey of *Christianity Today* readers that revealed that 70% of those surveyed held that "if we believe in an inerrant scripture, we must take the creation stories of *Genesis* one and two as literal history" (Noll, 1994, pp. 231–232). Also alive is the felt enmity between fundamentalists and secular higher education. One author, relating his own experience of attending graduate school as a fundamentalist believer, recounts, "enrolling in Harvard was like walking into the belly of the beast" (Carpenter, 1997, p. 192).

While the experience of early fundamentalists was one of disenfranchisement from institutions of secular learning, this did not affect its popular appeal. In fact, the "outsider pose" became a defining characteristic of embattled fundamentalists (Carpenter, 1997, p. 5). Heeding scriptures such as *Colossians* 2:8, "Beware lest any man spoil you through philosophy and vain deceit," alienation became separatism, and separatism became a badge of spirituality readily donned by the warriors of righteousness.

According to Marsden (2006), the 1950s and 1960s were a time of redefinition for many fundamentalists. It was during these years that fundamentalist evangelist Billy Graham began to challenge the extreme separatist mentality. Seeking to soften the separatist edge and move away from the somewhat stigmatizing term "fundamentalists," all but the hard core separatists began to call themselves "evangelicals." Yet, the change in terminology did not necessarily lead to a change in culture. While evangelicals distanced themselves from the fundamentalist label, their faith remained "fundamentalistic" at its core.

By the time I got to high school in the mid-1970s, fundamental Christianity had become cool. The Baby Boomers were becoming the Jesus Generation, and the long-haired, sandal-clad "Jesus freaks" were breathing new life into fundamental religion. This new breath was called the charismatic movement, and by 1979, 19% of the American population identified themselves as either charismatic or Pentecostal (Marsden, 1991, p. 78).

In the current age, fundamentalism has become ubiquitous in the land-scape of Protestant religious culture, and the tension with higher education, inherent in the fundamental worldview, remains pervasive as well. The main tenets of fundamentalism, including the inerrancy doctrine and the literal interpretation of scripture, are grounded in a dualistic worldview, and since a primary goal of higher education is to help the student move beyond sim-plistic dualism into higher levels of intellectual development, the tension is not likely to go away.

Fundamentalism and Dualism

In 1968, William Perry published a groundbreaking work on student devel-opment, *Forms of Ethical and Intellectual Development in the College Years: A Scheme*. Based on the results of a study conducted at Harvard University, Perry posited a model of student intellectual development that suggests stu-dents move through a number of stages on their way to thoughtful intellec-tual/moral commitment. The beginning stage is the position Perry called "Basic Dualism." In the position of dualism, students see the world as a dichotomy: "authority—right—we, as against the alien world of illegiti-mate—wrong—others" (Perry, 1968/1999, p. 66). Perry suggests that depen-dence on authoritarian structures (an essential feature of fundamentalism) leads to entrenchment in a dualistic view of the world. In this world, moral-ity means unquestioning obedience.

The next major position after dualism is "Multiplicity," a position where students come to realize there are many different and perhaps valid perspectives that must be examined. To reach the position of multiplicity, the student must be able to extend "potential legitimacy to 'otherness'" (Perry, 1968/1999, p. 79). This is a difficult step for students who have known only the world of fundamental dualism. Having witnessed a faith based on obedience to an external code of belief and conduct, they can barely conceive of the potential legitimacy of other views. Perry suggests that "a salient characteristic of [dualism], and the source of its innocence, is its lack of any alternative or vantage point from which a person may view it" (p. 69). This difficulty is compounded by the tendency to view anyone who offers an alternative vantage point as blind to the truth and a moral threat.

It is easy to see why the threads of anti-intellectualism and hostility toward secular learning run consistently through the fabric of fundamentalist history. For students who remain in the dualistic orientation nurtured by fundamentalist religion, higher education presents a considerable challenge for growth.

The Fundamentalist Family

Citing Wuthrow's 1998 work, *After Heaven: Spirituality in America Since the 1950s*, Hood, Hill, and Williamson (2005) classify fundamentalists as "dwellers" rather than "seekers." While seekers are always looking for new "spiritual vistas," "Dwellers" find safety in inhabiting a familiar religious space (p. 18). For fundamentalist dwellers, faith is about sharing a space—a very familiar, protected space—with others who see the world in the same way. These spaces are havens of familial relationship, close-knit communities where the outside world is kept at a safe distance.

When I think back over my childhood, almost all of my rites of passage and moments of self-definition happened within the context of my faith community. We went to church twice on Sunday and on Wednesday night. I was "born-again" at six years old and baptized soon after. Social events and holiday celebrations revolved around the church, and the youth group offered an array of activities that buffered teenagers from the outside world. My friends were from the church, or from other fundamentalist congregations, and I was admonished to date only fellow believers. My faith was not an aspect of my life, it was my life, and the "brothers and sisters" in the congregation closely guarded these parameters. For me, as for fundamentalists in general, the faith community was the ground from which all "meaning and purpose" arose; the context within which all life experiences were interpreted (Hood et al., 2005).

When I began to consider college, I remember being fearful of the unholy influences of the secular campus. I was warned that universities were filled with liberal professors, and opening my mind to the "ideas of men" would jeopardize my salvation. Feeling a "call" to ministry, I opted out of the university experience and went to a ministerial training college instead. According to Hood and colleagues, my experience is typical within a fundamentalist framework, where "education and vocation are good only to the extent that they facilitate the divine intention. . . . Should, for example, higher education or career advancement undermine these higher purposes, they become tools of the devil, which protestant fundamentalists interpret literally" (p. 32).

For many people who haven't been raised in a fundamentalist culture, it seems odd that one would adhere to such a system. Iannaccone (1994) suggests that the "psychological staying power" of fundamentalist religion in a postmodern age lies in its "ability to create a unifying philosophical framework that meets personal needs for meaning and provides coherence to an existence that may otherwise seem fragmented" (Iannaccone as cited in Hood et al., 2005, p. 16). It is not surprising, he concludes, that "the most successful religions, in terms of growth and maintenance of membership, are those with absolute, unwavering, strict, and enforced normative standards for behavior" (p. 16).

For those born within such a system, the dichotomized world of "us" and "them" is all too familiar, and although the isolation can restrict growth and development, the fear of leaving is often greater than the pain of confinement. This may be especially true for millennial students, whose identities are intimately interwoven with those of their parents and extended family.

Millennials, Family, and Religion

In the 1960s and 1970s, America was in the midst of a social revolution. According to Howe and Strauss (2000), adults didn't have a lot of time or attention for the children. This was the world into which generation "X" arrived (birth years 1962–1981). This was the generation of latchkey kids and a treacherous economy; cuts in education funding, and widespread use of drugs. Generation "X" saw its world fragment before its eyes, and grew into individualistic, street-smart, addiction-prone adults. In 1989 Ohio governor George Voinovich suggested that the only way to address the violence, substance abuse, and poverty plaguing society was "to pick one generation of children, draw a line in the sand, and say 'this is where it stops'" (p. 37), and that is just what society did.

America fell in love with children again in the 1980s. The millennial generation, birth years 1982–2001, has seen more legislation written for their benefit and protection than any generation before them. As a result, they are more trusting of government and the police than are Boomers or Gen Xers (Howe & Strauss, 2000). They grew up in a world where Disney was the biggest draw at the box office, trophies were awarded for effort, and adults were their kids' biggest champions. In a 1997 Gallup poll, 9 in 10 children attested to having close and satisfying ties with parents, and, when asked to identify their "heroes," most named their parents or other adults (p. 187).

Being very sheltered and intimately tied to parental support and approval, it is no surprise these students are as tied to their religious communities as their parents are, if not more so. Howe and Strauss tell us that religion is an important part of the school culture, and, according to the *Los Angeles Times*, religion has even become the basis of "a new teenage social caste" (2000, p. 234).

These characteristics—close ties to parents, roots set deep in faith communities, and a need for parental approval—can make the inherent tension between fundamentalism and secular higher education particularly threatening for millennial students.

Potential Costs of Dualism Lost

> It is an odd thing to fall out of a myth. It is like standing on the shore and looking back in astonishment at the myth from which you've so recently emerged, a beached whale lying in the summer sun. Only yesterday you were in the belly of the whale, with no idea just how contained you really were, just how much larger the vast sea could really be. Seeing your life now from outside the myth, everything on which you formerly stood is revalued, in an instant. And great sadness, like waves rolling along the sand, washes over the realization that such a living body, such a thing of beauty, should lie in silent rigor, exposed to time and long decay until the tide seeks the moon and beats away the bones to untold depths. (Bond, 1993, p. 27)

I walk into the classroom on the first day of classes and survey my new freshman charges. Their eyes are bright, their faces eager, although they are a bit shy and reticent to speak. We begin with an introduction session, and students share their names, towns of origin, and one interesting fact about themselves. One student offers that his goal is to "follow Christ more closely in all he does." Another student states as an interesting fact that Jesus Christ is the center of his life. On hearing these statements, many others smile approvingly. In a moment of déjà vu, I feel like I'm back in the 1980s, teaching at a Bible college. I wonder how those faculty who insist religion should stay out of the classroom would respond. Since this is a communications class and we'll soon be talking about contexts of communication, I ask how many have, as a primary context of interpersonal communication, a community of faith to which they are committed. More than 75% of the students raise a hand. They look at me with apprehension; I know that look. They're wondering if I'm one of those liberal professors they've been warned about.

After all of the students have introduced themselves, I make my introduction. I state my slate of degrees and summarize my experience in higher education. Then I mention that I was a minister at one time. Eyebrows are raised, and students become markedly more interested in what I have to say. I also share that, through the process of education, my faith has been pushed, pulled, and rearranged, but it remains an important part of my life. After class a student hangs back, one of the guys who made a profession of faith a part of his introduction. "So, I'd be interested to know how education has affected your faith. Do you still believe?" I recognize his question as an inquiry into the state of my soul, and I smile. "It's a long story. Come by during office hours and we'll talk about it."

Some suggest that such dialogue in a secular classroom is inappropriate, but I have come to believe it is very useful to open the possibility of such dialogue early. I know we will talk about a lot of issues that will challenge a fundamentalist attitude: issues of gender identity, respect for diversity, and the need to maintain a provisional, as opposed to dogmatic, attitude. I know that even to open one's mind to a new perspective, when the person comes from a fundamentalist viewpoint, feels like dancing on the rim of the abyss, and it helps to know that your guide is not hostile to your plight and has danced on the rim of the abyss as well—and survived.

Perry (1999) suggests that a dualistic mindset is not displaced, but modified out of existence, and that for these necessary modifications to be made, there must be modeling by a respected mentor or authority. When students perceive faculty as closed-minded and dismissive of students' views, this modeling cannot occur. Relationship with a respected authority creates a "safe space" where students have the courage to step out of the safety of dualism, a step that ultimately may put their views at odds with family, friends, and their faith community. Especially for millennials, this step may appear too costly. If the fear of moving beyond dualism is too great, and no "safe space" is available, the student may simply shut down and retreat.

Awakening from dualism is never an easy thing. While some fundamentalists may reach stage 5 in Perry's model of intellectual development (1999), and may thoughtfully commit to a fundamentalist myth as an expression of faith, this is a very different thing from seeing fundamentalism as singular truth. The naïveté of inherited dualism must give way to a broader view from outside the belly of the whale if growth is to occur, and this giving way can feel like expulsion from the Garden of Eden all over again.

According to Fowler (1996), transition to a new mindset first requires disengagement from the old. This begins when we "give up a significant connection to some context of relationship and shared meanings that has helped to constitute our sense of self" (p. 73). This loss of old connections and meanings can bring a sense of "liberation and empowerment," according to Fowler, but it can also bring feelings of "grief, loss, guilt, shame, lostness, and confusion" (p. 73). Faculty need to remember that moving out of dualism can be a frightening proposition for fundamentalist students, and there's no guarantee that, with the beach in sight, they will have the courage to step out of the whale and into the sunlight.

Perry (1999) suggests there are three options for growth open to the student who faces expulsion from the garden of dualism: temporizing, retreat, and escape. Temporizing is the process of pause, a step back from the process, "quite aware of the step ahead," to "gather his forces" (p. 198). A student making this choice may decide to take a year off from school, or stay in school and just disengage intellectually and emotionally from the learning process. This might manifest in a sudden and uncharacteristic preoccupation with partying, socializing, or any other nonacademic pastime.

Some students may choose the escape route, finding "detachment" in a "middle position on the scale" (Perry, 1999, p. 198), thus avoiding complete alienation from a dualistic myth. This is as much a state of limbo as temporizing; the student cannot experience total immersion in the dualistic myth (often a requirement for good standing in the fundamentalist community), yet will not take the step forward into a new vista of intellectual development.

If the student perceives the presence of an enemy force, the student may go into fight mode and turn back to the earlier dualistic position. In the "retreat" response, the student fortifies him or herself with "anger and hatredness of otherness." In the act of retreat, the student tightens his or her boundaries against any pressure to change that comes from the hostile other (Perry, 1999, p. 198). The role of the faculty member is crucial here: if the faculty member is perceived as being hostile to the student's beliefs, this perceived attitude may become the very impetus that pushes the student into retreat.

While the responses are clear-cut in definition, they may be very hard to recognize in day-to-day interaction with students. The student on the verge of intellectual growth may simply be seen as the partygoer who isn't serious about learning if he or she is in the process of temporizing. The student whose fundamentalistic views seem militant may actually be fighting a change in perspective by attempting to retreat. The quiet, unquestioning student may actually be a polite dualist who affords no possible validity to the ideas he or she obediently regurgitates. Often there's no way to tell what's really going on in the mind of the student, as long as the faculty member is "the other" looking in. If, however, the student has been able to develop a sense of identification with the faculty member, the boundaries of "us" and "them" may dissolve, and the faculty member may get an inside view from which to understand and guide the student.

For one fundamentalist graduate student, the discovery that his "liberal mentors were admirable people" was an important discovery. "For conservative graduate students reared on stories about believers being ridiculed and browbeaten in university classrooms, this was something of a revelation," the author relates. "Some suspected they were being treated more kindly in liberals' home institutions than the liberals would be in theirs" (Carpenter, 1997, p. 192). It may be that the "fundamental issue" in creating a safe environment where students from a dualistic religious tradition can find the courage to grow comes down to the professor's attitude and openness.

Attitudes That Foster Growth

If our goal in the classroom is really to foster intellectual development rather than quiet compliance among all students, what attitudes will help us achieve our goal? Research and experience suggest the following attitudes may be helpful when dealing with fundamentalist students:

- *A holistic approach to student development and learning.* It is necessary to understand that, for students from a fundamentalist background, all aspects of life find meaning in and are interpreted by their community of faith. We know from deep learning theory that new knowledge must be related to prior knowledge for deep learning to occur. To immediately exclude any discussion of religion from the classroom negates the student's entire life experience and severely limits the perspectives from which new knowledge can be approached and appropriated.

- *Willingness to reveal our own struggles with faith and intellectual development.* Perhaps for some of us, reluctance to allow discussions of religion and faith in the classroom springs from our own deep ambivalence about the issues. Academics have often been accused of hiding from religion in the ivory towers of intellect. In matters of faith, there is no right answer, no objective proof, and for academics who swim in the water of objectivity and rationalism, discussions concerning these matters may throw us off balance and make us unsure of our footing. Ironically, it is that tentativeness and provisionalism that may be most inviting and make the deepest impression on fundamentalist students who have too long been fettered by dogmatism. When we become vulnerable and honest about our own uncertainty, we may cease to be perceived as the enemy.

- *Acceptance of students and their views, wherever they are on the development scale.* To express hostility openly toward a fundamentalist viewpoint in the classroom is to immediately identify yourself as "the other." In the mind of the fundamentalist student, this invalidates you and the knowledge you have to offer. These students have many scripts to refer to when dealing with the enemy, but encountering an open-minded, accepting mentor on the "outside" may be a new experience that opens up brand-new possibilities for interaction.

- *Patience; realize growth may be slow and painful for students entrenched in fundamentalism.* Perry (1999) cautions:

> In our records, however, innocence is not lost in a single moment of realization. Indeed, the entire development may be looked upon as a drama in which a persona apprehends, step by step, the extent of his loss and then learns how to affirm his own responsibilities in a world devoid of Eden. (p. 68)

Growth is not a neat, lock-step process. Often, a momentary regression to an old position is the precursor to a breakthrough—and to a new level of functioning. Remember: antagonistic expressions of intolerance for new ideas may actually be fearful attempts to fend off growing doubts.

- *Willingness to engage in dialogue with fundamentalist students.* For many students, and especially for fundamentalist students, relationship often precedes learning. While it is impractical to suggest faculty form close relationships with all students, certain students seem to gravitate to you. Attempts to "witness" to you may actually be a great opportunity to open a life-changing dialogue. Learn to listen; in listening you may find opportunities to lead the student into a critical analysis of long-entrenched views. It was one graduate professor who was willing to engage in discussion over coffee who gave me the courage to question my views and, ultimately, move to a place of greater understanding. This professor never attempted to change my beliefs; he simply posed questions that led me into objective critique of those beliefs. Within the safety of a relationship with a respected mentor who was willing to serve as a fellow seeker, I found the courage to open my eyes and stand blinking in the sunlight.

References

Bond, D. S. (1993). *Living myth: Personal meaning as a way of life.* Boston: Shambhala.

Carpenter, J. A. (1997). *Revive us again: The reawakening of American fundamentalism.* New York: Oxford University Press.

Fowler, J. W. (1996). *Faithful change.* Nashville, TN: Abingdon Press.

Hood, R. W., Hill, P. C., & Williamson, W. P. (2005). *The psychology of religious fundamentalism.* New York: Guilford Press.

Howe, N., & Strauss, W. (2000). *Millennials Rising: The next great generation.* New York: Vintage Books.

Iannaccone, L. (1994). Why strict churches are strong. *American Journal of Sociology, 99*, 1180–1211.

Marsden, G. M. (1991). *Understanding fundamentalism and evangelicalism.* Grand Rapids, MI: Eerdmans.

Marsden, G. M. (2006). *Fundamentalism and American culture.* New York: Oxford University Press.

Noll, M. A. (1994). *The scandal of the Evangelical mind.* Grand Rapids, MI: Eerdmans.

Perry, W. G. (1999). *Forms of ethical and intellectual development in the college years: A scheme.* San Francisco: Wiley. (Original work published 1968)

5

WHAT I THINK I BELIEVE

Using the CHANGE Method to Resolve Cognitive Dissonance

Tamara H. Rosier

My class looked at me, waiting. Some stared at me, others looked down at their notes. They were waiting. I had just finished explaining constructivism as an educational theory and pedagogical approach to preservice teachers. "Any questions?" I asked. They sat, waiting. I could feel the uneasiness in the room, but I had no idea why it was there. They seemed to be waiting for me to say something. "We need to understand this theory before we can apply it," my voice trailed off.

After a long, uncomfortable silence, a student raised her hand, "What do you think about this approach? Do you *believe* it?"

The silence, the uncomfortable feeling in the room, and the averted looks made sense with that question. I had unknowingly caused them considerable dissonance, and they did not know how to reduce it. I was teaching at a Christian university that endorsed the idea of absolute truth, that is, truth considered to be universal and valid in all times and places. I had just spent 20 minutes discussing an approach to learning that emphasizes that individuals actively construct knowledge and understanding. Students were confused; I shared their beliefs, they trusted me, yet I was presenting a theory that seemed to contradict a basic tenet of our faith. The honest conversation that developed because of that question fueled my interest in cognitive dissonance. That experience reminded me to acknowledge and tend to students' personal worlds when I teach. Because of that day, I teach many topics even more constructively.

Students enter their classes with a personal world created from a collection of views of their context: their experiences of people, relationships, preferences, philosophies, and values. Since their professors teach topics and ideas that challenge their personal world, students feel uncomfortable or dissonant. To reduce their dissonance, they spend a great deal of energy regaining consistency or consonance in their personal world (Geen, 1995; Piaget, 1969). Because of the nature of learning in higher education, cognitive dissonance is often present in a classroom. Professors can create environments that encourage students to become better thinkers and manage conflicting information (Barr & Tagg, 1995; Conrad & Haworth, 1995). It is important for the leader in a classroom environment to understand the importance dissonance plays in learning, and to develop strategies for creating it and then reducing it. Educators who can use cognitive dissonance effectively in their classes can affect student learning, motivation, and retention (Burns & Gentry, 1998; McFalls & Cobb-Roberts, 2001).

According to the National Research Council (1999), expert learners approach uncomfortable learning situations by actively analyzing and evaluating the information using effective metacognitive strategies. Many learners, however, have not sufficiently matured in the use of metacognitive processes to sort the information effectively. These students most likely will use several unconscious strategies to reduce the dissonance they feel in academic situations. Unfortunately, the unconscious strategies they use are not always beneficial to their learning process. When challenged with new information, students with weaker metacognitive skills may deny the information, reduce its importance, or accept it unquestioningly to reach a sense of consistency or consonance. As students develop as thinkers, they need to become aware of these unconscious strategies and manage their learning and decision-making process.

Cognitive Dissonance Theory

Dissonance theory applies to situations involving attitude formation and change. It is especially relevant to decision making and problem solving. Dissonance theory provides a useful framework for understanding and monitoring learning in the academic setting because learners need to make decisions regarding the new information that challenges their opinions and attitudes.

New information (or cognition) that conflicts with an individual's ideas creates cognitive dissonance. Cognitive dissonance theory contends that when dissonance occurs, the situation resolves by either discarding the new evidence or discarding the old idea (Festinger & Carlsmith, 1959; Mills, 1999). Simply stated, learners expect consistency. Inconsistency creates a state of dissonance, and this feeling of dissonance drives learners to restore consistency. Students experiencing dissonance respond in one of five predictable manners to reduce dissonance: (1) reject the new information; (2) reduce the importance of the information; (3) add the new information to what they already know; (4) change the dissonant personal beliefs or information so the information is no longer inconsistent; or (5) change their personal beliefs or information to reflect the information.

The first two responses to reducing dissonance are less likely to incorporate critical thinking. In the first response, where students reject the information taught, they may respond by thinking, "This is not correct. We will not learn this." When students reject the information based only on dissonance, critical reflection has not occurred. When students disagree with the information presented in class, it is important that they have carefully analyzed and evaluated the material first. In the second response to dissonance, students reduce the importance of the inconsistencies. Students with this strategy are likely to think, "We don't need to learn this because it is not important." This decision is deadly for learning because the student has decided to remain unchallenged and, therefore, will not engage in an analytical process. Again, the basis for rejecting the new information is not a critical analysis of the validity or evidence. These first two responses reduce dissonance but do not nurture learning or an attitude change.

The remaining three dissonance-reducing options offer opportunities that are more likely to encourage deeper thought. In the third option, students evaluate the new knowledge, adopt the new cognition, and add it the old information. If students choose to add the new information to their personal world, they may think, "We can add this to what we know." The fourth option for resolving dissonance occurs when students modify their dissonant belief so it aligns with the new information. In this situation, students may think, "We can change and accommodate what we thought previously with what we have now learned." The final option occurs when students change their previous belief and accept the new information. When students apply that strategy, they may think, "What we previously thought was not accurate; we need to change our thinking." With each of these dissonance-reducing options, professors can lead students through a process that enhances deeper learning.

Professors can create and manage dissonance in their classes so meaningful learning develops. Their task is to guide students through a process so the students will carefully analyze new information. CHANGE is an acronym for the process professors use when they want students to evaluate new information (see Figure 5.1). The six steps in the CHANGE method, designed to lead a process of creating and managing dissonance, are (1) creating cognitive dissonance; (2) helping students express their dissonance; (3) aiming to resolve dissonance as information is presented ; (4) noticing the students' levels of dissonance; (5) giving students an opportunity to clarify thinking; and (6) ending the session with a metacognitive experience.

Assumptions in Learning and Motivation

The CHANGE method assumes two theoretical tenets of learning and motivation to be true: (a) the learner constructs learning, and (b) the psychological state of the learner is important to the learning process. The first assumption is based on how the learning occurs. Individuals actively construct knowledge and understanding (Piaget, 1969; Vygotsky, 1987). In a constructivist's view, professors should not attempt to pour information into

FIGURE 5.1
The CHANGE Method for Resolving Dissonance

Create cognitive dissonance.

Help students express their dissonance.

Aim to resolve dissonance as you present information.

Notice students' dissonance levels.

Give students an opportunity to clarify their understanding.

End the lesson with a metacognitive exercise.

the learners as if they are empty vessels. Rather, students should be encouraged to discover knowledge, explore theories, reflect, and think critically (Ambrose, 2004; Brooks & Brooks, 2001). In classrooms, social contexts of learning often create an environment for students to build learning mutually (Bearison & Dorval, 2002). Professors who create learning environments that approach learning in this manner stress social interaction with peers and constructing a collaborative meaning (Oldfather, West, White, & Wilmarth, 1999). Professors of these classes closely monitor students' perspectives, thinking, and feeling while guiding students' thought processes.

The second assumption of learning recognizes the impact of the psychological state of learners on cognitive processes. If students do not feel safe emotionally or physically, the learning environment is compromised because they will focus on survival-related cues (Franken, 2002). In addition to safety, the level of curiosity affects students' motivation to learn. Loewenstein's (1994) curiosity model argues that motivation tends to increase as students realize a gap exists between their current knowledge level and a desired state of knowing. At this optimal level, students find it satisfying to resolve the gap between what they do not know and what they should know. Loewenstein cautions that, if the informational gaps are too great, students consider the new level too great and are likely to be deterred from attempting to gain the new knowledge. Similarly, if the gaps are too small, learners are apathetic to the challenge (1994). Students need an optimal level of tension to be motivated to learn, and the CHANGE method suggests a process for creating and managing optimal tension.

Setting Goals When Approaching Dissonant Topics

When approaching topics I think may cause dissonance, I set four goals for myself. First, I remind myself of my role in the class for that topic. I am there to facilitate learning, thinking, and decision making. Because of this role, I construct activities that encourage learners to participate actively. When I teach the topic of constructivism now, I ask students to read the definition from their text and write a response about whether this theory complements their religious worldview. Then I divide them into groups according to responses: those who think the theory does fit with their worldview and those who think it does not. I let them discuss and build their arguments with others who agree with them.

The next goal I set for myself is to allow students to struggle with their thoughts. As an educator, I am often too quick to rescue my students with the "right" answer or to make complex situations simple so they can feel good about learning. When I approach subjects that may create dissonance, I reassure students that I will continue to support them as they learn, but accompanying learning is often an uncomfortable feeling. Learning becomes uncomfortable when discussing controversial topics because emotions such as uncertainty, confusion, and misunderstanding are involved. When I teach the topic of constructivism now, I ask the students to form groups consisting of one person who shares their opinion and two who have a different opinion. Students who felt bolstered from their earlier discussion may feel a bit more challenged in their thought process at this point.

My third goal is to use techniques that encourage students to ask questions. I ask more honest and authentic questions and I speak less. When I teach constructivism, I ask my students at two different times during the class to write down three questions they have. These often provide fodder for deeper small-group discussions.

Finally, I set the goal of leading my students through the process of managing their cognitive dissonance. I developed the CHANGE method to provide a framework for me as I plan to approach sensitive topics.

Create Cognitive Dissonance

The first step in the CHANGE method is to *create cognitive dissonance* using strategies designed to show learners the discrepancy between what they know and what they want to know. Remember: learners are very motivated to resolve the uncomfortable feeling of dissonance. When teaching ideas that relate to religious ideology, it is very important to bring students' assumptions and prior knowledge to the forefront of their minds. This often means that professors need to create cognitive dissonance intentionally. To introduce a topic, a professor may consider using knowledge ratings, authentic problems, or student predictions.

Knowledge ratings evoke a metacognitive dissonance because the strategy asks students to evaluate what they know and what they do not know. Students often unconsciously spend mental energy resolving the dissonance by attempting to reach a higher knowledge rating. I use this strategy to discover what my students already know and to show them they have increased their knowledge during the session. I ask students to rate their knowledge about a topic on a scale of 0 to 3 at the beginning of the lesson (0 = no knowledge; 3 = very knowledgeable). Then, after I teach some of the lesson, I ask students to rate their knowledge again. As I see the increase in the mean rating, I ask them to write down questions they still have about the topic. Most of the time students write questions that show they are analyzing, synthesizing, or evaluating. By asking them to write questions, I evoke dissonance for the second time. They have acknowledged they do not know all of the information and are motivated to fill in the gaps as we progress through the lesson.

Beginning the class with an authentic problem is another easy way to create dissonance. Minds actively seek uncertain situations in which they can solve problems (Hebb, 1949; Loewenstein, 1994). If students are given a problem similar to one that occurs in the "real" world, they are likely to engage in a problem-solving process to reduce the dissonance they feel with an unresolved challenge. Students who are directed to consider a situation using their current knowledge are more likely to attempt a metacognitive process of asking themselves to look for additional information they need to solve this problem. Case studies or problem situations produce dissonance, especially when they are introduced before students learn the information that applies to the problem or case study. Students search for consonance while their professor teaches the information necessary to solve the problem.

For example, a professor may begin the class by presenting a situation and related questions: Students have been known to sue their school district over issues related to religion. Consider a situation where, every year, students are elected by their classmates to give pregame prayers at high school football games over the public address system. Why would a number of students sue the district because of this practice? What would they argue? How might the district counter their arguments? What would you decide? After providing time for students to wrestle with the issues presented, the professor discusses the Establishment Clause and the facts of *Jones v. Clear Creek Independent School District* (5th Cir. 1992), an example where a student sued a district because of a pregame prayer tradition. As students observe the details of the Establishment Clause and the court case, they actively search for information to support their original opinions and are more likely to actively engage in the topic. They will want to resolve any dissonance between what they are learning and what their first ideas were about the issues. In my experience, students are more eager to discuss, even argue, the judgment in greater detail than they would be if the case were merely presented without the dissonance-creating situation and questions.

Like the previous strategy for creating dissonance, predictions ask students to make a series of guesses about the information they will learn, while often exposing preconceived notions. For example, in a social work class, a professor may ask students to list the issues they consider important when counseling individuals who are exploring end-of-life options. A professor then would want to ask students why certain items are on their lists. A discussion of what appears on the students' list may clarify students' personal bias. The professor then would discuss a list of issues the literature has identified as potentially influencing what particular end-of-life decisions are made and the process by which options are selected.

The important component of this first step of the CHANGE method is to create dissonance intentionally to motivate students to engage a learning process. Some professors may not even need to manufacture a dissonance experience; instead, the very topic they teach provokes dissonance in many students. For example, a science professor approaching the topic of evolution theories may notice a degree of discomfort or confusion in the class because the ideas presented seem to contradict students' personal beliefs or religious paradigms. Once the professor identifies the presence of cognitive dissonance, he or she must move to the second step in the CHANGE method. It is critical to address and discuss dissonance because, when students identify the source of their uneasiness and sort through their ideas, they are able to resolve some of their initial dissonance and learn.

Help Students Express Dissonance

The second step in the CHANGE method is *helping students express dissonance*. When students voice their dissonance in class, they become aware of it and engage in actively seeking consistency. Feelings of confusion and frustration usually emerge at this point as students say, "But I thought . . ." or "I know that . . ." The role of the professor for this time should be that of a facilitator. Taking a step away from direct instruction is critical so the professor can listen to students' ideas, questions, and concerns. As a facilitator, the professor should avoid correcting any misconceptions at this point, but should tell students to note their ideas or feelings about the topic. Reminding students that learning is a process not only of acquiring information, but also of sorting information is very important because it validates their personal learning process.

It is very important to have students record their thoughts or feelings at this point because, as the class proceeds, they often do not remember they felt dissonance at the beginning and may minimize the quality of thinking they experienced. To think critically, students should be mindful of how their thinking developed on a particular topic or issue. Many strategies accomplish this quickly and easily. For example, a professor may ask students to turn to the person next to them and describe their thoughts, beliefs, or confusion. Another way of accomplishing this is to ask students to write a few sentences about their current thoughts or confusion. Using completion phrases such as "I'm wondering if . . ." or "I don't understand   " provides a place for students to note their confusion. The important component of this step is met when students begin a metacognitive process regarding their dissonance.

Aim to Resolve Dissonance

Once dissonance is present, and students are aware of it, they are highly motivated to resolve this struggle. The next step in the CHANGE method is *resolving the dissonance*. The goal of this step is to resolve the dissonance created by guiding a thinking process. Knowing the strategies students use to rid themselves of the dissonant feelings, the professor needs to intentionally lead a process that seeks to resolve the students' dissonance. The professor needs to focus students' attention on how to assimilate or accommodate the new information because if he or she does not, students may reduce the importance of the new information, or even reject it. Because students in dissonance are at an alert phase in learning and are actively sorting the information they are receiving (Franken, 2002; Loewenstein, 1994), this is an opportunity to show them how to adjust their thinking to include the new cognition or how to incorporate new cognition into an existing cognition.

If a topic cannot be resolved easily, such as a controversial issue where there is no correct answer, it becomes the professor's responsibility to provide a framework for how an educated person approaches such an issue. For example, when I discuss approaches to learning in an undergraduate educational psychology class, I create with the class a graphic organizer of five approaches that delineate the benefits and challenges for each approach. Then I ask my students to write in their journal about the two approaches that fit their academic evaluation of the approaches, their teaching context, and their personal style.

Notice Students' Dissonance Levels

As a professor presents information, it is important to notice the level of dissonance in the room, remembering that, if the dissonance becomes too great, learning is likely to decrease. Students who feel too dissonant will satisfy their dissonance by rejecting the new information without analyzing it. It may be helpful for the professor to remind students that learning is an active process of constructing understanding. It may also be useful for the professor to say, "I notice many of you are feeling very dissonant about this subject," and then provide the students with another opportunity to voice their dissonance. This time, however, the professor emphasizes the need for individuals to monitor, manage, and regulate their thought process.

If dissonance is no longer present, students may have simply accepted the new information without thinking critically about it (Franken. 2002). If this occurs, student should be reminded of their earlier dissonance, which should challenge students to reconcile the two cognitions by using higher-order thinking skills such as analysis or synthesis.

Give Students an Opportunity to Clarify Their Understanding

Once dissonance has been introduced, students have been encouraged to express their dissonance, and professors have attempted to guide students through a thinking process, then students need an opportunity to clarify their understanding. This step encourages students to begin to restore consistency before leaving the class. Professors encourage students to ask questions because learning new information involves making a decision about its relevance and significance.

To promote conversation, students may be asked to return to their first thoughts: What has changed in their minds? What should they do with the new information? What do they still need to know? This provides a natural opportunity for small-group or partner discussion. Students are, in a sense, deciding if they should assimilate, accommodate, or reject the information. If students are reluctant to ask questions, a professor may ask such questions as, "If you had to ask a question, what would you ask?" or "If someone was just learning this information, what questions would he or she ask?" Students find this step in the CHANGE method the most satisfying because it gives them a sense of accomplishment or competence.

End the Lesson with a Metacognitive Exercise

Metacognition, thinking about one's own thinking, brings the dissonance to a settling closure. Metacognitive strategies involve monitoring and reflecting on one's current or recent thoughts. These thoughts include both factual knowledge, such as how to apply the information learned, and strategic knowledge, such as how and when to use specific learning strategies. Students should participate in a closing exercise that allows them to retrace their learning journey so they can understand and appreciate their learning process. It is important to use metacognitive strategies to help students resolve the dissonance they felt during their learning experience. A simple strategy is to ask students to discuss in pairs their learning process during this class. Another successful strategy has students completing an exit slip (Kirby & Liner, 1988). For example, I ask students to complete the following sentence, "At the beginning of class, I thought . . . ; now I think . . . because . . ." Or I ask my students to summarize their learning using the questions, "What happened?" "What does this mean for me?" and "What should I do with this information?" This last step is important because it encourages students to summarize, paraphrase, and transform their thoughts.

Conclusion

Understanding cognitive dissonance and the CHANGE method enables professors to gain further insight into the processes individuals experience when presented with information designed to change attitudes. If professors can create dissonance effectively, help their students express dissonance, aim to resolve it, notice the level of frustration during learning, and end their classes with metacognitive exercises, they can establish a need to learn with their students, provide opportunities for learners to interpret and understand information in a different way, and initiate active learning in their classes.

In turn, students' approaches to learning by analyzing and evaluating new information in an effective manner will mature.

Because of my experiences with dissonance-producing subjects, I have learned to be much more aware of my students' internal struggles. I have learned to explore their personal philosophies before I begin a topic. I concentrate on the process of learning and how the material I teach affects the learners in my course in hopes of producing better thinkers. Creating and managing dissonance has energized my teaching and stimulated thoughtful interaction in my classes. I anticipate the dissonance now; I no longer need to wait during the awkward silences for a student to raise his or her hand and hesitantly ask, "Do you believe this?"

References

Ambrose, D. (2004). Creativity in teaching. In J. C. Kaufman & J. Baer (Eds.), *Creativity across domains* (pp. 45–64). Mahwah, NJ: Eerlbaum.

Barr, R. B., & Tagg, J. (1995). From teaching to learning: A new paradigm for under-graduate education. *Change*, November/December, 16–25.

Bearison, D. J., & Dorval, B. (2002). *Collaborative cognition*. Westport, CT: Ablex.

Brooks, J. G., & Brooks, M. G. (2001). *In search of understanding: The case for constructivist classrooms*. Upper Saddle River, NJ: Merrill.

Burns, A. C., & Gentry, J. W. (1998). Motivating students to engage in experiential learning: Tension-to-learn theory. *Simulation & Gaming, 29*(2) 133–151.

Conrad, C. F., & Haworth, J. G. (Eds.). (1995). *Revising curriculum in higher education*. Needham Heights, MA: Simon and Schuster.

Festinger, L., & Carlsmith, J. M. (1959). Cognitive consequences of forced compliance. *Journal of Abnormal and Social Psychology, 58*, 203–210. Available at http://psychclassics.yorku.ca/Festinger/

Franken, R. E. (2002). *Human motivation*. Belmont, CA: Wadsworth/Thomson Learning.

Geen, R. G. (1995). *Human motivation: A social psychological approach*. Pacific Grove, CA: Brooks/Cole.

Hebb, D. O. (1949). *The organization of behavior*. New York: Wiley.

Kirby, D., & Liner, T. (1988). *Inside out: Developmental strategies for teaching writing*. Portsmouth, NH: Boyton/Cook.

Loewenstein, G. (1994). The psychology of curiosity: A review and reinterpretation. *Psychological Bulletin, 116*(1), 75–98.

McFalls, E. L., & Cobb-Roberts, D. (2001). Reducing resistance to diversity through cognitive dissonance instruction. *Journal of Teacher Education, 52*(2), 164–172.

Mills, J. (1999). Improving the 1957 version of dissonance theory. In E. Harmon-Jones & J. Mills (Eds.), *Cognitive dissonance: Progress on a pivotal theory in social psychology* (pp. 25–42). Washington, DC: American Psychological Association.

National Research Council. (1999). *How people learn.* Washington, DC: National Academy Press.

Oldfather, P., West, J., White, J., & Wilmarth, J. (1999). *Learning through children's eyes: Social constructivism and the desire to learn.* Washington, DC: American Psychological Association.

Piaget, J. (1969). *Psychology of intelligence.* New York: Littleton.

Vygotsky, L. S. (1987). Thinking and speech. In R. W. Reiber & A. S. Carton (Eds.), *The collected works of L. S. Vygotsky* (pp. 28–39). New York: Plenum.

6

BRINGING FAITH AND SPIRITUALITY INTO THE CLASSROOM

An African American Perspective

Mark S. Giles, Odelet Nance, and Noelle Witherspoon

Throughout the history of American higher education, themes of religion and spirituality have shaped institutional structure, curriculum, leadership, and student life (Thelin, 2004; Rudolph, 1990). For many African American college students, the legacy and meaning of faith, religion, and spirituality, and how it affects their ability to persist and graduate, takes on a contextually unique phenomenon that deserves specific attention. Tapping into the deep well of spiritual legacy that shapes the African American experience and the personal strength derived from spiritual awareness can add to these students' persistence to degree attainment and commitment to excellence. Just as issues of race are relevant in educational settings (Ladson-Billings & Tate, 1995), religious and spiritual socialization in the African American faith tradition becomes central as they engage in the higher education learning process (Mattis & Jaegers, 2001). Therefore, faculty members, especially at predominately White institutions (PWIs), are encouraged to reexamine their pedagogical lenses, practices, and curricular developmental premises to meet the complex needs of students who openly embrace their spirituality (Cherry, Deberg, & Porterfield, 2001; Collins, Hurst, & Jacobsen, 1987; Jablonski, 2001).

This chapter provides a discussion for faculty members to link their methods of teaching and advising with the ways some African American college students might construct meaning regarding their religious and spiritual beliefs and practices that affect formal learning settings. Are there ways to connect classroom learning, faculty approaches to advising, and student retention to church or nonchurch-related faith traditions and spiritual beliefs?

If faith is hope in the unseen, and we understand spirituality as a personal inward journey toward higher self-knowledge and relationship to a God-force and holistic belief system, then how African American students make meaning of their collegiate experience has significance to their persistence and success. How we define and understand such terms as spirituality, religion, and faith helps to clarify our dialogue on these topics and places arguments and issues in particular context. Elizabeth Tisdell (2003) identifies seven assumptions about spirituality, some of which find resonance in our definition; she states, "[S]pirituality is about an awareness and honoring of wholeness and the interconnectedness of all things . . . spirituality is fundamentally about meaning-making . . . spiritual development constitutes moving toward greater authenticity or to a more authentic self" (pp. 28–29).

We agree with a growing number of scholars (Dennis, Hicks, Banner-jee, & Dennis, 2005; Hindman, 2002) who define spirituality as a transcendental personal notion of meaning and purpose. Some scholars draw the line between spirituality and religion by arguing, "Spirituality involves fully living a meaningful, purposeful life while religion entails engaging in traditional practices, ceremonies, and dogma in religious institutions" (Dennis et al., 2005, p. 135). The personal and holistic aspects of spirituality versus the institutional-structural-operational characteristics of religion can help us understand how many college students find favor with the loosely coupled idea of spirituality. Church attendance or membership is not required to have a strong sense of spirituality. To be "religious" implies close ties to a church or religious organization/tradition. Within the African American historical context, spirituality and religion represent tangible mechanisms related to the struggles for collective freedom, personal fulfillment, and personal relationships to a higher power (Cone, 1986); but, for the purposes of our work here, some distinctions add clarity to the discussion.

James Fowler's work (1995) on the parameters and implications of the stages of faith development connect with traditional cognitive and psychosocial theories. Fowler's theory contributes to college student development theory through the inclusion of a dimension beyond the more popular theories. Fowler noted, "Faith is not always religious in its content or context," and

"Faith is a person's way of seeing him- or herself in relation to others against a background of shared meaning and purpose" (p. 4). These definitions create an image of personal purpose and meaning-making taking center stage in how we might understand the characteristics and beliefs students bring with them into the classroom.

Research indicates that religion and spirituality have strongly influenced the way most African Americans view public service (Lincoln & Mamiya, 1990); health and wellness (Ellison, 1993); politics (Stewart, 1999); the role of community in educational aspiration (Giles, 2003); psychological well-being and coping mechanisms (Ellison, 1993; Markstrom, 1999); school leadership (Dantley, 2003; Dillard, 1995); and institutional religious organizations (Frazier & Lincoln, 1974; Lincoln & Mamiya, 1990). Studies have even linked academic achievement and spirituality within the African American culture (Hoffman, 2002; Zern, 1989). However, few studies have directly addressed the role of religion in the lives of African American college students (Herndon, 2003; Hoffman, 2002; Stewart, 2002). This focus might help address our understanding and concerns regarding the low retention rates of African American college students at PWIs (Hoffman, 2002). By examining faith as a link to retention and persistence, we hope to open the conversation that advances educational theory and practice of faculty regarding African American student success in educational settings and their involvement in religious institutions.

African American Religion and Education

According to W. E. B. DuBois (1968), Black religion has been a means of survival and identity for African Americans throughout their sojourn in America. Some research indicates that African Americans are broadly religiously affiliated. One study found that 84% of all African Americans attend worship services and pray consistently (Dyer, 1999). Indeed, understanding the history of African American faith traditions is necessary to examine the role of spirituality in the lives African American youth. Many scholars, including historians, sociologists, and theologians, posit that the African American spiritual experience is unique and so deeply interwoven with any aspect of Black history that one cannot be examined without examining the other (DuBois, 1968; Frazier & Lincoln, 1974). Since slavery, African Americans have embraced spirituality and religion as forces of liberation and power

(Stewart, 1999) in both informal (e.g., family, community) and formal (e.g., church, social/fraternal organizations) settings.

The Black church is largely known for its participation in the fight for equal rights and racial uplift, especially during the civil rights movement. One consistently powerful tool of liberation for African Americans has been literacy and formal educational achievement. Slaves had a strong desire to learn, and many learned to read using the Bible as a primary text; they believed freedom was linked with education. Immediately after the Civil War, northern white missionaries and newly freed slaves undertook major efforts to open schools throughout the South to provide educational opportunities for the Black community. These schools were designed to cultivate morally responsible individuals while providing literacy and vocational skills (Lincoln & Mamiya, 1990).

For many Black churches, early educational experiences began in Sunday school classes, youth programs, and mentoring activities. Churches have also instituted formal precollegiate programs to encourage youth to adopt attitudes of academic excellence and aspire to attend institutions of higher education. There are rich examples of church and college partnerships that encourage the success of African American college students.

Spirituality as a Critical Factor in African American Student Success

One cultural component that holds historical and contemporary significance for African American students is religion (Stewart, 2002), which is known to be an important source of social support for African American students (Markstrom, 1999). Research suggests that those students who attend religious services have a more positive college experience than those who do not, which may lead to retention (Zern, 1989). Studies indicate that religious involvement can maximize a student's potential to excel academically (Zern, 1989). According to Robbie Steward and Hanik Jo (1998), students who identified themselves as religious used their spirituality as a means of coping in college settings. Their quantitative study revealed that religious students are well adjusted and have high academic performance and may support the findings of the ongoing UCLA-HERI research. In addition, findings by the Higher Education Research Institute (HERI) at the University of California, Los Angeles (UCLA), revealed that African American college students reported higher levels of religious commitment and engagement than did other groups (HERI, 2005). This national report indicated a clear need for deeper specificity and greater consideration of cultural, racial, and gender distinctions in this area (Garner, 2004; Stewart, 2002; Watt, 2003).

We argue for broadening perspectives to include diverse voices and unique cultural experiences as conceptual tools for faculty and student affairs practitioners who wish to better understand how religion and spirituality might shape African American student learning. Of course, we recognize the rich diversity of religious and spiritual beliefs and backgrounds African Americans represent; the African American community is not monolithic in its views or practices. At the same time, common social and cultural antecedents can inform faculty and the teaching and learning process when working with groups of African American students (Tatum, 2003). For example, many African American students often relate their educational journeys at PWIs to a sense of struggle and further link notions of struggle and overcoming obstacles with their spiritual selves, a way of connecting the practicalities of education with broader ideas of purpose, prayer, and a higher power.

Theoretical Considerations and Perspectives

This chapter highlights theoretical perspectives from scholars who understand and are sensitive to the African American historical and cultural context learning for so-called marginalized groups. We argue for more attention to the often undervalued voices and experiences of African American college students regarding how their faith traditions and spirituality sustain and stimulate their learning.

The lenses of critical spirituality (Dantley, 2003), and Black theology (e.g., James Cone, Carlyle Fielding Stewart III, Cornel West, Deloris Williams, Katie Cannon, Vincent Harding, and Cheryl Sanders) relate to a uniquely African American–centered perspective and reconceptualize how faculty and student affairs practitioners might better understand and help African American college students stay in college and succeed (Herndon, 2003; Hoffman, 2002; Stewart, 2002; Watt, 2003). Recent spirituality-focused studies by higher education scholars such as Dafina Stewart (2002) and Sherry Watt (2003) emphasize the importance of understanding African American college students' experiences regarding religion and spirituality.

In the introduction to *Education as Transformation: Religious Pluralism, Spirituality, and a New Vision for Higher Education in America*, Diana Chapman Walsh (2000) notes the holistic value of recognizing education as a transformative process:

> To support our students in this process of transformational growth, we need learning environments that integrate into the educational process all of student experience: curricular, extracurricular, residential, social, inter- and intra-personal. And we must address the central question of how to find greater coherence, meaning, and purpose in academic life. (p. 4)

Parker Palmer (1993) argues that some in the academy oppose attempts to include insights from spiritual traditions: "rather than welcome it in all its forms" (p. xi). David Hindman (2002) recognizes the need to advance and support students' spirituality, and those institutions must make an "explicit, overt, public commitment . . . to assist students in acquiring a particular set of values and attitudes about themselves and the larger community" (p. 175).

Michael Dantley (2003) identifies the importance of "critical spirituality" to the African American experience and educational leadership: "[T]he acknowledgement of one's spiritual self has served as the very bedrock of African American life" (p. 6). Black theology stands in opposition to forces deemed exploitative and oppressive to African Americans and offers a critique of religious views and practices that are not grounded in notions of liberation and true democratic principles (West, 2002). Based on the African American experience from slavery to the 21st century, theories of liberation and self-agency find significant resonance.

Patrick Love and Donna Talbot (1999) note, "By failing to address students' spiritual development in practice and research we are ignoring an important aspect of their development" (p. 362). If we are to accept the premises and findings of these researchers, then faculty are well served to develop a sense of students' whole selves and find ways to connect the faith and spirituality students bring to the classroom with pedagogy. Perhaps these issues gain an additional degree of relevance when applied to African American students. Bryan Warnick (2004) suggests that education must engage religious thought or it risks becoming extraneous to the field and alienating those to whom religious thought matters. Many people look to their faith traditions for meaning and guidance, and education is not exempt from that process. Warnick argues for a "religious criticism" approach that asks what a religious tradition means, not whether that tradition is true (p. 347). This approach could shape activities faculty might introduce to students as a way to get students to consider the meaning of their traditions for educational success and prevent them from becoming defensive about the "truthfulness" of their views.

According to Odelet Nance (2005), students attributed their retention in college to their spiritual and religious beliefs and church involvement. The findings affirm the need to acknowledge and understand the role of the church as a support system in the lives of these students to expand emerging student development and retention theories. The respondents indicated that the church provided support in the following four areas: scholarships, tutorial services, mentoring, and personal counseling, which in turn aided in their retention and persistence in college. Faculty must realize that churches can play a direct role in helping African American students succeed in college settings if bridges are built and partnerships are developed.

Faculty as Mentors of Faith?

Faculty members and curriculum developers should be aware of cultural and spiritual interests (Marty, 2000) and explore ways of opening space in the classroom for students' spiritual selves to find expression. Many African American students find outlets for informal mentoring through involvement with local and campus ministry, Bible study groups, and campus religious organizations. These mentoring relationships provide support networks, a sense of belonging, and space for dialogue and identity development, all of which are critical acknowledgments of cultural relevancy.

By affirming these same acknowledgments, university professors become part of this same community of faith mentoring, whether the faculty share the students' faith traditions or not. A part of this interaction involves becoming transparent when dealing with students. For example, religious courses, campus forums, and the space we create in classrooms allow students to be treated as multidimensional and affirm their cultural and spiritual identity. Students need to have forums to explore their positions and beliefs further, along with oppositional perspectives; classrooms present an interesting space for constructed dialogues and writing assignments to promote this type of interaction (Moody, 1997). For example, in English classes, writing assignments could focus on negotiating faith in the classroom and follow up with small-group discussions of how and why faith is important to them and how it might enhance their learning experience. In an American history class, students could discuss and write essays that explore the religious and faith-based origins of particular organizations and institutions such as philanthropic agencies or colleges. Since written assignments and projects are the primary mode of expression in the university classroom, these types of assignments could find relevance in many social science and humanities courses.

Indeed, bell hooks (1994) encouraged all to break the silence about the connection between spirituality and education in the academic classroom. To have true multiculturalism in the curriculum of education, religious identity must be included (Light, 2001). Faculty should grapple with their own sense of religious, spiritual, and faith-based perspectives and understand that, to embrace the holistic model of teaching and learning fully, these elements must be included. Faculty members are encouraged to demonstrate transparency with students and open dialogue regarding issues of faith with intentionality and inclusiveness in mind. One suggestion is to begin a semester with an "I am" poem exercise. Following the lead of the instructor, this allows students to write short poems describing their identity from a holistic perspective and begin to think about their spiritual selves. As an icebreaker exercise, this provides multiple opportunities to share brief autobiographical sketches and create self-expressionistic space for the students to think about and discuss their multiple identities and beliefs. Another suggestion is to have faculty introduce resources to students (e.g., books, videos, campus religious leaders, faculty from other disciplines—Black studies) that recognize the African American religious experience.

Rather than a 12-step instrumentalist approach to integrating religion and faith into the classroom, we believe faculty should refrain from reductionism and avoid oversimplifying how we might engage these experiences. There is no one basic or defining framework exemplifying what culture or faith is for everyone. In the same vein, no essential pedagogical practices are appropriate for every classroom. However, faculty can develop dispositions that engage them toward pluralistic practice. In working with African American students, it is important to review the historical context of the role of religion and faith within the African American experience and apply culturally relevant practice in creating and assessing classroom assignments. This may involve reframing assignments to integrate culturally specific phenomenon and then applying the same approach for students of other diverse backgrounds. What we can do is allow our students to grapple with big questions and big answers (Parks, 2000) rather than dismiss faith traditions and spirituality as having no place in the classroom.

Dillard, Abdur-Rashid, and Tyson (2000) state, "the silencing of the spiritual voice through privileging the academic voice is increasingly being drowned out by the emphatic chorus of those whose underlying versions of truth cry out, we are a spiritual people!" (p. 448). In addition, according to Nash (1999):

> Religion must find an educationally appropriate voice in the schools and colleges; not one that promotes, proselytizes, or practices, but rather a voice that teachers and students can explore for its intellectual (narrative) strengths and weaknesses, just as they would any other kind of "voice" in the curriculum. (p. 14)

Religious beliefs should not be ignored in curriculum development, pedagogy, and methodologies but acknowledged and encouraged in the classroom and in student life.

Conclusion

As African American students continue to struggle, persist, and succeed in academia, many of them hold to cultural parameters that incorporate issues of religion and spirituality important to their personal, interpersonal, racial, and intellectual development. This dynamic can create tensions *and* opportunities for difficult dialogues among students, faculty, and student affairs staff. If African American college students are expected to embrace the social and cultural environments of diverse college campuses and universities, the institutions should acknowledge the students' whole selves (i.e., historical, cultural, and political realities), and should consider their unique religious and spiritual perspectives through the use of transformative, culturally, and spiritually responsive instructional strategies, content, and materials in the classroom. Faculty play a critical role in connecting with students' authentic selves based on what students bring to the classroom and campus settings (Chickering, Dalton, & Stamm, 2006), including knowledge of and feelings about personal faith and spirituality. Faculty members should construct ways to learn how best to advance the students and their own holistic development, which includes finding ways to acknowledge and connect with the issues of faith and spirituality (humanity) that exist on both sides.

References

Cherry, C., Deberg, B. A., & Porterfield, A. (2001): *Religion on campus*. Chapel Hill: University of North Carolina Press.

Chickering, A. W., Dalton J. C., & Stamm, L. (2006). *Encouraging authenticity and spirituality in higher education*. San Francisco: Jossey Bass.

Collins, J. R., Hurst, J. C., & Jacobsen, J. K. (1987). The blind spot extended: Spirituality in higher education. *Journal of College Student Personnel, 28*(3), 274–276.

Cone, J. (1986). Black theology in American religion. *Theology Today, 43*(1), 6–21.

Dantley, M. E. (2003). Critical spirituality: Enhancing transformative leadership through critical theory and African American prophetic spirituality. *International Journal of Leadership in Education, 6*(1), 3–17.

Dennis, D. L., Hicks, T., Bannerjee, P., & Dennis, B. G. (2005). Spirituality among a predominately African American college student population. *American Journal of Health Studies, 20*(3/4), 135–142.

Dillard, C. B. (1995, November). Leading with her life: An African American feminist (re)interpretation of leadership for an urban high school principal. *Educational Administration Quarterly, 31*(4).

Dillard, C., Abdur-Rashid, D., & Tyson, C. (2000). My soul is a witness: Affirming pedagogies of the spirit. *International Journal of Qualitative Studies in Education*, 447–462.

DuBois, W. E. B. (1968). *The souls of Black folks*. Greenwich, CT: Fawcett Publications.

Dyer, E. (January 1, 1999). Black generation Xers take a broad look at religious experience. *Pittsburgh Post-Gazette*. Retrieved from: http://www.postgazette.com/re gionstate/19990101genx3.asp

Ellison, C. G. (1993). Religious involvement and subjective well-being. *Journal of Health and Social Behavior, 32*, 80–99.

Fowler, J. W. (1995). *Stages of faith: The psychology of human development and the quest for meaning*. San Francisco: Harper.

Frazier, E. F., & Lincoln, C. E. (1974). *The Negro church in America. The Black church since Frazier*. New York: Schocken Books.

Garner, R. (2004). *Contesting the terrain of the ivory tower: Spiritual leadership of American American women in the academy*. New York: Routledge.

Giles, M. S. (2003). *Howard Thurman: A spiritual life in higher education.* Unpublished dissertation, Indiana University, Bloomington.

Herndon, M. (2003). Expressions of spirituality among African American college males. *Journal of Men's Studies, 12*(1), 75–84.

Higher Education Research Institute (HERI). (2005, October 5). Spirituality in higher education: A national study of college students' search for meaning and purpose. Retrieved March 21, 2006, from http://www.spirituality.ucla.edu/news/2005–10–06.html

Hindman, D. M. (2002, Spring). From splintered lives to whole persons: Facilitating spiritual development in college students. *Religious Education, 97*(2), 165–182.

Hoffman, J. L. (2002). The impact of student cocurricular involvement on student success: Racial and religious differences. *Journal of College Student Development, 43,* 712–739.

hooks, b. (1994). *Teaching to transgress: Education as the practice of freedom.* New York: Routledge.

Jablonski, M. A. (Ed.). (2001, Fall). The implications of student spirituality for student affairs practice. *New Directions for Student Services, 95.*

Ladson-Billings, G., & Tate, W. F. (1995). Toward a critical race theory of education. *Teacher's College Record, 97*(1).

Light, R. J. (2001). *Making the most of college: Students speak their minds.* Cambridge, MA: Harvard University Press.

Lincoln, C. E., & Mamiya, L. H. (1990). *The Black church in the African American experience.* Durham, NC: Duke University Press.

Love, P., & Talbot, D. (1999). Defining spiritual development: A missing consideration for student affairs. *NASPA Journal, 37*(1), 261–375.

Markstrom, C. A. (1999). Religious involvement and adolescent psychosocial development. *Journal of Adolescence, 22,* 205–221.

Marty, M. E. (2000). *Education, religion, and the common good: Advancing a distinctly American conversation about religion's role in our shared life.* San Francisco: Jossey-Bass.

Mattis, J. S., & Jagers, R. J. (2001). A relational framework for the study of the religiosity and spirituality in the lives of African Americans. *Journal of Community Psychology, 29,* 519–539.

Moody, J. (1997). Professions of faith: A teacher reflects on women, race, church, and spirit. In K. M. Vaz (Ed.)., *Oral narrative research with black women* (pp. 24–37). Thousand Oaks, CA: Sage.

Nance, O. (2005). *First year journey: Spirituality and religion in lives of five African American Christian students.* Unpublished dissertation, University of Illinois at Chicago.

Nash, R. J. (1999). *Faith, hype, and clarity: Teaching about religion in American schools and colleges*. New York: Teachers College Press.

Palmer, P. (1993). *To know as we are known: Education as spiritual journey*. San Francisco: Harper & Row.

Parks, S. D. (2000). *Big questions, worthy dreams: Mentoring young adults in their search for meaning, purpose, and faith*. San Francisco: Jossey-Bass.

Rudolph, F. (1990). *The American college & university: A history*. Athens, GA: The University of Georgia Press.

Steward, R., & Jo, H. (1998). Does spirituality influence academic achievement and psychological adjustment of African American urban adolescents? [ERIC document, ED417248].

Stewart, C. F., III. (1999). *Black spirituality and Black consciousness: Soul force, culture and freedom in the African American experience*. Trenton, NJ: Africa World Press.

Stewart, D. L. (2002). The role of faith in the development of an integrated identity: A qualitative study of Black students at a White college. *Journal of College Student Development, 43*, 579–596.

Tatum, B. (2003). *Why are all of the Black kids sitting together in the cafeteria together? And other conversations on race*. New York: Basic Books.

Thelin, J. (2004). *A history of American higher education*. Baltimore, MD: The Johns Hopkins University Press.

Tisdell, E. J. (2003). *Exploring spirituality and culture in adult and higher education*. San Francisco: Jossey-Bass.

Walsh, D. C. (2000). Transforming education: An overview. In V. H. Kazanijan Jr., & P. L. Laurence (Eds.), *Education as transformation: Religious pluralism, spirituality, and a new vision for higher education in America* (pp. 1–16). New York: Peter Lang.

Warnick, B. R. (2004). Bringing religious traditions into educational theory: Making an example of Joseph Smith Jr. *Educational Theory, 45*(4), 345–364.

Watt, S. K. (2003). Come to the river: Using spirituality to cope, resist, and develop identity. *New Directions for Student Services, 104*, 29–40.

West, C. (2002). *Prophesy deliverance: An Afro-American revolutionary Christianity*. Louisville, KY: Westminster John Knox Press.

Zern, D. S. (1989). Some connections between increasing religiousness and academic accomplishment in a college population. *Adolescence, 24*, 141–154.

7

RELIGION IN THE CLASSROOM

Legal Issues

Barbara A. Lee

T he increasing diversity of college campuses has led to tensions over the role of religion in the classroom. While some faculty would prefer to exclude religion completely from their curriculum and assignments, others wish to discuss religious views or doctrines, sometimes in courses that have no apparent relationship to religion. Students may object to assignments that require them to address issues or perspectives that run counter to their beliefs. Other students may be uncomfortable if a professor discusses issues of faith or religious doctrine in class. This chapter addresses the legal rights and responsibilities of both students and professors when religious issues arise in the classroom.

The chapter begins by discussing basic legal concepts related to religion in higher education. The source of legal protections (and prohibitions) depends on whether the college or university is public or private (and, for private institutions, whether they are secular or religious). It then discusses the legal rights of students and faculty when students object on religious grounds to classroom discussion, assignments, or other requirements. The discussion then turns to the rights of faculty to inject religious issues into their classroom discussion or assignments, the right of the institution to limit discussion of religious issues in the classroom or prohibit it altogether, and the right of faculty at religious institutions to differ from the official doctrine of the college's religious sponsor. Finally, the chapter suggests several strategies for avoiding legal problems related to religion's presence in—or absence from—the classroom.

Basic Legal Concepts Related to Religion in Higher Education

Most legal challenges to the presence (or absence) of religion in the classroom arise at public colleges and universities. First Amendment claims have been made by both students and faculty who either wish to embrace religion in the classroom or to exclude it. Other legal issues arise when a religious college or university attempts to regulate classroom speech or conduct of a faculty member based on the official doctrine of the religious group that sponsors the college. These claims may be brought under nondiscrimination laws or under contract law.

Public colleges and universities are bound by the U.S. Constitution, and the constitutions and laws of their states. The U.S. Constitution (and state constitutions as well) prohibits the government from "establishing" religion (called the "Establishment Clause" of the First Amendment), which means that a government body, or in this case a college funded by the government, may not prefer one religion over another and may not be related to any religious denomination. The First Amendment also has a "Free Exercise Clause" that protects from government interference all individuals who wish to exercise their religious freedom. These portions of the U.S. Constitution require public institutions to be neutral toward religion—they cannot support one or more religions, nor can they forbid religious exercise (such as prayer groups or religious services) on campus. "Neutrality" is not an easy concept for college administrators to ascertain, however. For example, the U.S. Supreme Court has ruled that public universities must allow religious student groups to hold prayer meetings on campus if they allow other student groups to use campus facilities (*Widmar v. Vincent*, 1981), and public institutions must recognize and support religious student groups if they provide such support for secular student groups (*Rosenberger v. Rector and Visitors of the University of Virginia*, 1995). But if a public institution provides financial or other support for a religious group or activity beyond what other student groups receive, or appears to advocate the ideas or doctrine of such a group or activity, that action could be a violation of the Establishment Clause. In particular, if a public institution *appears* to be coercing students (or faculty) into embracing the doctrine of a particular religion, that action clearly violates the Establishment Clause.[1]

Students and faculty at public institutions also have free speech rights under the First Amendment of the Constitution. Institutional administrators or government officials may not violate the free speech rights of faculty and students as long as their speech is germane to the curriculum or a matter of public concern.

Private institutions are not regulated by the U.S. Constitution (although some state constitutional provisions may apply to private institutions, and state laws may as well). Private religious institutions are, for the most part, protected from government "interference" with their hiring, curriculum, and admissions decisions (unless they are accused of discrimination on the basis of some unlawful reason other than religious discrimination—such as sex or race). Federal courts have ruled that they are not constitutionally permitted to review such decisions by private religious institutions because that would entangle the government with the affairs of the religious college, thereby violating the Constitution's Free Exercise Clause. On the other hand, if institutional documents such as faculty handbooks, collective bargaining agreements, or other institutional policies promise faculty and/or students certain rights, such as the protection of academic freedom, then violations of these handbooks or policies could result in contract claims, which the courts entertain, unless they require the court to review matters of religious doctrine. Private secular colleges are not answerable to the U.S. Constitution, but they also do not enjoy the protection religious colleges have with respect to judicial deference to decisions grounded in religious doctrine.

Faculty at both public and private colleges and universities may argue that academic freedom protects their right either to insist on teaching certain subjects or to engage in discussions of religion in class or at official college functions. In public institutions, faculty typically file claims under the First Amendment's free speech clause, and, if academic freedom guarantees are included in faculty handbooks or other policy documents, they could also file breach of contract claims if they believe the institution violated their academic freedom rights. Faculty at private colleges could state breach of contract claims if the institution's handbook or other policy documents promises academic freedom for faculty.

Students are beginning to use contract claims to seek remedies for alleged violations of their own academic freedom rights. Although student academic freedom rights are not as well developed in the legal arena as are faculty academic freedom rights, student academic freedom rights (particularly the right to speak, the right not to speak, and the right to receive information) are developing in the courts, and faculty and administrators need to understand them.[2]

Students With Religious Objections to Curricula, Assignments, or Events

There have been several lawsuits in which students object to assignments or other course requirements because the topic is offensive to their religious beliefs or they are not allowed to address the topic from the perspective of their religious beliefs. These cases have occurred in public universities, and the courts have generally upheld the institution's right to control the curriculum as long as it does not discriminate on religious grounds against students who raise objections to assignments or classroom discussion.

The latter problem was an issue in *Axson-Flynn v. Johnson* (2004), which involved a student enrolled in the University of Utah's actor's training program. She was a devout Mormon, and objected to using certain words in the scripts that she was assigned to read aloud. Although she told her instructors she would not "take the name of Christ in vain" or use words she considered offensive, she was admitted to the selective program and had been allowed to omit certain "offensive words" earlier in the semester. In fact, she omitted any language she found offensive throughout the semester. At the end of the semester, her instructor told her she would either have to read the script as written and "modify your values" or leave the program, stating that she should "talk to some other Mormon girls who are good Mormons, who don't have a problem with this."

The student sued the university for free speech and free exercise violations under the First Amendment, claiming that "forcing her to say the offensive words constitutes an effort to compel her to speak in violation of the First Amendment's free speech clause." She also claimed that "forcing her to say the offensive words, the utterance of which she considers a sin, violates the First Amendment's free exercise clause" (*Axson-Flynn v. Johnson*, 2004, p. 1283). The university argued that requiring students to read scripts accurately, even if they contained offensive language, was a legitimate pedagogical approach to teaching acting. The court concluded that the words the student objected to were "school-sponsored speech" and a legitimate part of the curriculum (thus she did not have the academic freedom right to refuse to say the words).

The court said that the university "may exercise editorial control so long as its actions are reasonably related to legitimate pedagogical concerns" (*Axson-Flynn v. Johnson*, 2004, p. 1286) and as long as it was reasonable. It also said that "schools must be empowered at times to restrict the speech of their students for pedagogical purposes" and that "schools also routinely require students to express a viewpoint that is not their own in order to teach the students to think critically" (p. 1290). But, said the court, if the pedagogical concern was pretextual, and the faculty members were really motivated by religious discrimination, then the court would not defer to the faculty members' actions. The court also stated that if the faculty members had given students exemptions on religious grounds in the past, to refuse such an exemption in Axson-Flynn's case was a constitutional violation. The court remanded the free speech and free exercise claims to the trial court, but the university settled the case before it proceeded further.

In some cases, members of the public and even legislators become involved when a public university decides to sponsor an event to which some individuals object on religious grounds. The University of Indiana–Purdue University at Fort Wayne decided to present a play, *Corpus Christi*, which was selected for production as the senior project of a drama student. This play portrayed Christ as a homosexual who engaged in sexual activities with his disciples. Several Indiana taxpayers and state legislators sued the university, attempting to halt the production because they considered the play to be blasphemous. They asserted the play was an "undisguised attack on Christianity and the Founder of Christianity, Jesus Christ," arguing that performing it at a public university violated the Establishment Clause of the First Amendment. In *Linnemeir v. Board of Trustees, Indiana University–Purdue University, Fort Wayne* (2001), the appellate court affirmed the trial court's denial of an injunction. The appellate court said that "school authorities and the teachers, not the courts, decide whether classroom instruction shall include work by blasphemers," and added "[a]cademic freedom and states' rights alike demand deference to educational judgments that are not invidious" (p. 760).

Other cases involving student objections to course content on religious or moral grounds have involved claims of sexual harassment. For example, in *Cohen v. San Bernardino Valley College* (1996), Professor Cohen taught remedial English at a community college. He required students to discuss in class or write papers on pornographic subjects as well as on cannibalism, obscenity, and consensual sex with children. He read some articles he had written for *Playboy* and *Hustler* magazines to the class. When he assigned the students a paper in which they were required to define pornography, a female student objected and asked for an alternate assignment. Cohen refused to allow her to submit a different assignment, and the student filed a claim of sexual harassment against him. The college disciplined Cohen, and he sued the college for First Amendment free speech violations. Although the trial court sided with the college, the appellate court reversed that decision, ruling that the sexual harassment policy was unconstitutionally vague, and Cohen, who had been using these topics as paper assignments for years, had no notice that they were suddenly a violation of college policy. In a similar case, *Silva v. University of New Hampshire* (1994), a federal trial court ruled in the professor's favor, finding that his use of sexual imagery in a writing class was pedagogically appropriate and not a violation of the university's sexual harassment policy. Although neither of these cases involved explicit claims of religious discrimination by the students, their concepts are applicable to such claims.

The cases suggest that, as long as faculty have legitimate pedagogical reasons for choosing topics for classroom discussion or assignments, and the topics are relevant to the subject matter of the course, the courts will uphold the faculty member's right to insist that students participate in the assignment, discussion, and so on. But the courts have also said that the institution itself, and the faculty as a collective, have the right (and the obligation) to ensure a faculty member's course content is appropriate, germane, and pedagogically sound. The next section discusses conflicts when faculty assign topics or engage in classroom discussion of a religious nature.

Faculty Rights to Discuss Religious Topics in the Classroom

Cases at Public Institutions

Over the past several years, some colleges have required first-year students to read a particular book and attend a mandatory discussion session about the book during the fall semester or as part of an orientation program. At the University of North Carolina at Chapel Hill, the faculty established such a requirement for incoming freshmen to give them a common intellectual experience during orientation. The faculty task force recommended for the summer of 2002 that students read *Approaching the Qur'an: The Early Revelations* by Michael Sells. Several anonymous students and a group of named taxpayers sued the university, claiming that requiring students to read the book, which they labeled "Islamic propaganda," violated their rights under the Free Exercise Clause of the U.S. Constitution.[3] The university defended its actions on the grounds of academic freedom, stating that the choice of the book was "entirely secular, academic, and pedagogical." A faculty member who submitted an affidavit in the university's defense questioned: "Would next year's committee be forbidden to require incoming students to read *The Iliad*, on the grounds that it could encourage worship of strange, disgraceful gods and encourage pillage and rape?" (Euben, 2002, p. 86). In *Yacovelli v. Moeser* (2002), the trial court denied the plaintiffs' request for an injunction and found no constitutional violation. The court said, "[T]here is obviously a secular purpose with regard to developing critical thinking, [and] enhancing the intellectual atmosphere of a school for incoming students" (Euben, p. 86). On the day the freshman seminar was scheduled to take place, the federal appellate court affirmed the trial court's ruling, and the seminars went forward.

In a few lawsuits, faculty members have been disciplined or discharged for injecting their religious views into classroom discussion. For the most part, the courts have upheld the right of the institution to limit or forbid a faculty member from discussing his or her religious views in class. The leading case is *Bishop v. Aronov* (1991). Bishop was a professor of exercise physiology at the University of Alabama. According to the court,

> Dr. Bishop occasionally referred to his religious beliefs during instructional time, remarks which he prefaced as personal "bias." Some of his references concerned his understanding of the creative force behind human physiology. . . . He never engaged in prayer, read passages from the Bible, handed out religious tracts, or arranged for guest speakers to lecture on a religious topic during instructional time. (p. 1067)

Shortly before final examinations, Professor Bishop organized an optional meeting after class during which he discussed "evidence of God in human physiology" and his religious beliefs with respect to divine creation. Five students and a faculty member attended the meeting. In a memo to Bishop, the department head told him to refrain from references to his religious beliefs in class and to cease holding the "optional" after-class meetings because he believed students could feel coerced into attending them. Bishop sued the university for First Amendment violations of his free speech and free exercise rights. The university had been careful to distinguish between Bishop's rights of religious expression in and outside the classroom and made no attempt to regulate his speech except during class time.

The court created a balancing test that weighed the institution's need to avoid violating the Establishment Clause by appearing to endorse a particular religious viewpoint against the professor's rights under the Free Exercise Clause and free speech clauses. Said the court:

> First and foremost, we consider the context: the university classroom during specific in-class time and the visage of the classroom as part of a university course in an after-class meeting. This context also leads us to consider the coercive effect upon students that a professor's speech inherently possesses and that the University may wish to avoid. The University's interest is most obvious when student complaints suggest apparent coercion—even when not intended by the professor.
>
> Second, it follows, we consider the University's position as a public employer which may reasonably restrict the speech rights of employees more readily than those of other persons. As a place of schooling with a teaching mission, we consider the University's authority to reasonably control the content of its curriculum, particularly that content imparted during class time. Tangential to the authority over its curriculum, there lies some authority over the conduct of teachers in and out of the classroom that significantly bears on the curriculum or that gives the appearance of endorsement by the university.
>
> Last and somewhat countervailing, we consider the strong predilection for academic freedom as an adjunct of the free speech rights of the First Amendment (*Bishop v. Aronov*, 1991, pp. 1074–1075).

The court ruled that the university's concern that "personal religious biases" not affect the course content was a valid one and entitled the university to forbid such discussions in courses. Second, the court agreed with the university that students could perceive the "optional" religious meetings as coercive, since they took place before the course was over.

The court concluded:

> In short, Dr. Bishop and the University disagree about a matter of content in the courses he teaches. The University must have the final say in such a dispute. Though Dr. Bishop's sincerity cannot be doubted, his educational judgment can be questioned and redirected by the University when he is acting under its auspices as a course instructor, but not when he acts as an independent educator or researcher. The University's conclusions about course content must be allowed to hold sway over an individual professor's

judgments. . . . We have simply concluded that the University as an employer and educator can direct Dr. Bishop to refrain from expression of religious viewpoints in the classroom and like settings. (*Bishop v. Aronov*, 1991)

In rejecting Professor Bishop's claims that the university's prohibition violated his religious freedom, the court distinguished between freedom of religion and freedom in teaching. The university, said the court, was attempting to maintain a "neutral," secular classroom, and Professor Bishop was free to write about religious subjects, to organize university-wide meetings on religious subjects, or to answer student questions about his religious viewpoints.

Although most litigation concerning faculty academic freedom in the classroom involves nonreligious issues (such as using profanity, refusing to administer student course evaluations, or insisting on discussing controversial departmental matters that are not germane to the course topic), most of the cases have upheld the institution's right to limit the subject matter and faculty's pedagogical treatment in their teaching. For example, in *Edwards v. California University of Pennsylvania* (1998), a tenured professor was disciplined when he refused to conform to the department's standard syllabus for that particular course. The court characterized the academic freedom right as belonging to the university rather than to the faculty member and said, "a public university professor does not have a First Amendment right to decide what will be taught in the classroom" (p. 491). The *Edwards* court relied, in part, on cases from the early 1970s in which faculty members clashed with university administrators over teaching methods. In *Hetrick v. Martin* (1973), for example, the contract of a nontenured faculty member whose teaching philosophy differed from that of her departmental superiors was not renewed. The court upheld the nonrenewal, saying the university had the right to determine its pedagogical philosophy and to require adherence to that philosophy.

Religion in the Classroom at Religious Institutions

Faculty who discuss religious issues at religious colleges are usually on safe ground unless they differ from or oppose the doctrine of the college's religious sponsor. Religious colleges and universities are not required to comply with the free speech or religion clauses of the First Amendment and can regulate the speech and classroom teaching of faculty. They are, however, required to comply with nondiscrimination laws and contract law. If the court determines that it must interpret or rule on matters of religious doctrine, it may decline on the grounds that the government (e.g., the state or federal court) may not become entangled in matters of religious doctrine because of the prohibitions of the Establishment Clause of the First Amendment. So, in a dispute involving a religious college, the court must first determine whether resolution of the claim turns on matters of religious doctrine. If it does, the court dismisses the case. If only secular issues are involved, the court interprets the contract. For example, if the faculty handbook promises academic freedom to faculty in teaching, and a lay faculty member is disciplined or discharged for speaking freely on relevant religious issues, the faculty member may bring a breach of contract claim, and a court would very likely entertain such a claim.

When the issue of a faculty member's fitness to discuss religious matters at a religious college arises, however, the issue typically involves matters of religious doctrine. For example, in *Curran v. Catholic University of America* (1987), Curran, a Catholic priest, was a tenured professor of theology at Catholic University, an institution authorized by the Vatican to confer ecclesiastical degrees. Professor Curran had publicly disputed several of the Catholic Church's teachings, and the university's board of trustees withdrew his "ecclesiastical license," which was required to teach in certain departments of the university (such as the theology department). Although university administrators offered to place Curran in a department that did not require an ecclesiastical license, he refused the offer and sued for breach of contract and constructive discharge.

The court determined that the parties to the employment contract had intended to be bound by canon law (the law of the Catholic Church), and that the university had the right to require faculty who taught theology courses to meet the Vatican's requirements for an ecclesiastical license, since the university's own right to award ecclesiastical degrees could have been threatened. Therefore, the court dismissed Professor Curran's lawsuit on constitutional grounds.

In a similar case, *McEnroy v. St. Meinrad School of Theology* (1999), Carmel McEnroy, a Catholic nun and professor of theology at a seminary that prepares individuals for the priesthood, signed a statement opposing Pope John Paul II's teachings on the ordination of women as priests. She was one of more than 1,500 signers. The president of the seminary dismissed McEnroy after learning that she had signed the statement, whereupon McEnroy sued the seminary, claiming breach of contract and a variety of other claims. Again, the court concluded that it could not review the seminary's actions because they were based on ecclesiastical grounds.

Faculty Rights at Private Secular Colleges

The primary protection for a faculty member who wishes to discuss religious issues in the classroom is academic freedom. But such freedom is not automatic, and it is not a license to discuss any topic for any reason.

Private secular colleges typically promise academic freedom to faculty (and, to a lesser extent, to students) in handbooks, catalogues, or policy statements. If the faculty handbook says faculty are protected by academic freedom, then a faculty member may file a breach of contract claim should that faculty member believe his or her academic freedom has been abridged. But academic freedom is not absolute. The "1940 Statement of Principles on Academic Freedom and Tenure" of the American Association of University Professors (AAUP, 2001, pp. 3–8), which courts have ruled is the national normative statement on the protections of academic freedom, says that academic freedom includes responsibilities. With respect to academic freedom in the classroom, the Statement says:

> Teachers are entitled to freedom in the classroom in discussing their subject, but they should be careful not to introduce into their teaching controversial matter which has no relation to their subject. Limitations of academic freedom because of religious or other aims of the institution should be clearly stated in writing at the time of the appointment. (p. 3)

Therefore, the limitation on academic freedom is that the topics discussed be germane to the subject matter of the course. A private institution (or a public one) may discipline a faculty member for repeatedly discussing religious topics or religious opinions in a course that is unrelated to religion. But if religious topics or beliefs are relevant to the subject matter of the course, and if the faculty member does not attempt to coerce the students into agreeing with his or her beliefs or to punish those students who disagree, such religious topics and discussions are probably protected by academic freedom.

Suggestions for Avoiding Legal Problems

This section draws implications from the litigation reviewed and discusses strategies faculty can use to include relevant, germane topics related to religion without running afoul of institutional or legal prohibitions on religion in the classroom. It also discusses strategies for dealing with students who have religiously based objections to classroom discussion, assignments, or tests.

1. If a faculty member intends to include topics that students may find controversial because of their political, personal, or religious views, the syllabus should make this clear.

2. A faculty member should give individualized consideration to student requests for alternate assignments or exemption from certain course activities (e.g., requiring an Orthodox Jewish student to eat forbidden foods in a cooking class or rejecting a student's request to be excused at a certain time for a specific religious exercise requirement). Although not all such requests must be honored, the request should be considered carefully and a reasoned explanation for any rejection of the request should be given.

3. A faculty member should not inject personal religious opinions or beliefs into courses in which religion is either irrelevant or of tangential relevance (e.g., some science courses, certain business courses, physical education courses).

4. If a faculty member believes his or her personal opinion on a religious topic is relevant to the course, it is permissible to express it as long as the faculty member makes it clear that it is a personal opinion and students are permitted to disagree without fear of retaliation.

5. A faculty member should never make fun of a student's expressed statement of belief or a student's objection to a statement made by another student or by the faculty member. It is certainly appropriate for a faculty member to disagree with a student, or to point out inconsistencies or errors in the student's statement, but ridicule is not

appropriate and is likely to lead to student complaints and/or to litigation.

6. A faculty member should treat students respectfully, even if he or she disagrees with the student's point of view or with what the student says or writes.

7. If a faculty member is unsure whether a particular topic is appropriate for classroom discussion or how to respond to a student's question or statement, it is prudent to say the matter will be taken up at the next class meeting. This will give the faculty member time to consult with a department chair, other colleagues, or fellow disciplinary experts.

Despite the perpetual possibility of disputes concerning the presence or absence of religion in the classroom, a faculty member who focuses on germane topics, treats opposing views with sensitivity and respect, and maintains control of the class discussion should prevail if complaints are filed or in the unlikely event of litigation.

Summary

In both private and public colleges and universities, faculty and students have the right to discuss matters of religion in class when religion is relevant to the course. The courts have made it clear that the institution itself has the legal right—and legal responsibility—to determine curricular content and to decide whether certain topics—religious or otherwise—are germane to the subject matter of the course. Although the courts do recognize the protections of academic freedom, particularly when academic freedom is explicitly incorporated into faculty handbooks or other policy documents, academic freedom has boundaries and does not protect faculty who inject religious topics or religious beliefs and opinions into courses in which religion is not a relevant topic. This is particularly true at public institutions. Religious colleges have a clear legal right to insist that faculty who are members of religious groups, particularly those who teach theology or other religious subjects, adhere to the doctrine of the religious sponsor of the college. Respecting the perspectives and beliefs of one's students, and insisting that fellow students follow that example, should help prevent disputes over religious and moral differences in college classrooms from being played out before a judge.

References

American Association of University Professors. (2001). *Policy documents and reports.* Washington, DC: Author.

Axson-Flynn v. Johnson, 356 F.3d 1277 (10th Cir. 2004).

Bishop v. Aronov, 926 F.2d 1066 (11th Cir. 1991).

Cohen v. San Bernardino Valley College, 92 F.3d 968 (9th Cir. 1996).

Curran v. Catholic University of America, Civ. No. 1562–87, 117 *Daily Wash. Law Review* 656 (D.C. Super. Ct., February 28, 1987).

Edwards v. California University of Pennsylvania, 156 F.3d 488 (3d Cir. 1998).

Euben, D. (2002). Curriculum matters. *Academe, 88*(6), 86.

Hetrick v. Martin, 480 F.2d 705 (6th Cir. 1973).

Kaplin, W. A., & Lee, B. A. (2006). *The law of higher education* (4th ed.). San Francisco: Jossey-Bass.

Lee v. Weisman, 505 U.S. 577 (1992).

Linnemeir v. Board of Trustees, Indiana University–Purdue University, Fort Wayne, 260 F.3d 757 (7th Cir. 2001).

McEnroy v. St. Meinrad School of Theology, 713 N.E.2d 334 (Ct. App. Ind. 1999).

Rosenberger v. Rector and Visitors of the University of Virginia, 515 U.S. 819 (1995).

Silva v. University of New Hampshire, 888 F. Supp. 293 (D.N.H. 1994).

Widmar v. Vincent, 454 U.S. 263 (1981).

Yacovelli v. Moeser, Case No. 02-CV-596 (M.D.N.C. 2002), *affirmed,* Case No. 02-1889 (4th Cir. 2002).

Notes

1. See, for example, *Lee v. Weisman* (1992), which ruled unconstitutional a prayer at a public high school commencement.

2. Student academic freedom is discussed at some length in Kaplin and Lee (2006, pp. 737–747).

3. For a fuller discussion of this case and challenges to other institutional attempts to require students to read a book with controversial content, see Euben, 2002, p. 86.

PART FOUR

DISCIPLINARY APPROACHES

8

EXPLORING RELIGION AND SPIRITUALITY THROUGH ACADEMIC SERVICE-LEARNING

Kent Koth

We were midway through the first class session of the quarter, and I thought things were going well. As is typical of most first sessions, students seemed somewhat reserved, but they also appeared engaged in learning about the course objectives, the service-learning component, the assignments, and the grading rubric. As instructor of the upper-level required liberal studies seminar, Leadership for Community Engagement, I hoped I could set a tone in this first session for the examination of intellectual ideas as well as the exploration of matters of the spirit.

With this second goal in mind, I invited the students to sign up to share a short "Moment of Meaning" at the beginning of one of the future class sessions. In my previous courses, some students had used these moments to read poetry, others presented photographs of loved ones, and still others shared personal experiences. Through this exercise, I hoped students would see each other not just as classmates in an academic context but also as seekers of authenticity in the realm of spirituality.

I could tell several students seemed excited about this opportunity, but I also noticed the incredulous expression on the face of one student, Daniel. At this early point in the quarter I had clearly lost him. I had my work cut out for me if I expected to engage all of the students, including Daniel, intellectually *and* spiritually throughout the remainder of the course.

Fast forward 10 weeks to the end of the quarter. In addition to a comprehensive paper, I asked students to write a reflection on what they had learned during the course and, more specifically, what they would remember from the course in five years. Somewhat to my surprise, Daniel's reflection referenced his thoughts about the course at the beginning of the quarter. He observed:

> The first week of the quarter, I had convinced myself that I would never get anything out of a class like Leadership for Community Engagement. I assumed that any class that had "moments of meaning" and explored "spiritual aspects of service" would be a waste of my time.

Even more surprising, Daniel then revealed a significant change of perspective. He continued:

> I am so glad that I was so wrong. I tend to be judgmental about difference, specifically difference in beliefs. It was really this quarter that I have begun to not be so quick to judge people who have highly specific religious beliefs.

While not all of my teaching experiences have provided such a clear example of profound student learning, this vignette does reveal the potential to weave together service-learning experiences, intellectual inquiry, and spiritual discovery. Admittedly, making these connections does not come without some risk. Even though I teach at a Jesuit Catholic institution, I have found this pedagogical approach can frequently lead to unpredictable, contentious, and messy situations. But it also can lead to deep moments of enlightenment and hopefulness. I believe the opportunities far outweigh the risks.

Two recent trends in teaching offer significant promise for college and university faculty who are interested in engaging their students in holistic and authentic educational experiences. The first trend is the increase in the number of faculty using academic service learning as a pedagogical strategy. The second trend is the emerging movement among faculty to develop lessons that connect academic learning with spiritual and religious exploration. Separate and distinct from each other, these trends offer many opportunities for faculty to deepen student learning. Yet, thoughtfully integrating the best practices from both can offer faculty an even more powerful way to create transformational educational environments.

In this chapter I present a short overview of both of these trends. In addition, I examine the theory, benefits, and challenges of connecting academic service learning with spiritual and religious formation. Finally, I offer practical examples of how to make this connection in both religious and secular classroom contexts.

Academic Service Learning on Campus: An Absence of Spirit

In the summer of 1984, recent Harvard graduate Wayne Meisel embarked on a symbolic walk. Carrying a letter of support from Harvard President Derek Bok, Meisel walked 1,500 miles, visiting 70 college campuses from Maine to Washington, D.C., and calling on students to address critical social issues by serving in their communities. Meisel's walk, and many less notable actions by other college students and recent graduates, soon led to a nationwide campus movement (Liu, 1996). Thousands of students began to serve meals at homeless shelters, tutor at local schools, participate in environmental restoration projects, assist at health clinics, build affordable housing, mentor young children, organize recreational activities at child care centers, and participate in government internships. As the number of students involved in the community continued to rise, student leaders, administrators, and faculty began to connect the students' service activities to formal and informal learning opportunities. The movement gained momentum and soon engaged millions of students in what became popularly known as service learning.

Today the service-learning movement has gained national prominence. College presidents have embraced service learning and formed coalitions to institutionalize programs on their campuses. Political leaders, such as former Senator John Glenn, have taken leadership roles in developing a vision to invigorate the national democracy through service learning. Federal funding and grants from large foundations have helped programs engage thousands of additional students. A wide array of literature has evolved that shares best practices for service learning and documents the positive effects of service on students and universities as a whole.

In developing programs and crafting legislation, service-learning practitioners and policy makers have used many theoretical models, including those of John Dewey, Kurt Lewin, Jean Piaget, and Paulo Freire. More recently, the experiential learning model of David Kolb has provided a strong framework for service-learning programs. Kolb's cyclical model moves from a concrete experience to reflective observation on the experience. The reflection leads to the formation of abstract concepts and, finally, to testing these concepts in new situations through active experimentation. The model repeats itself as the learner tests new theories through experiences and reflection. Recognizing that learning is an ongoing process, Kolb explains that the goal of experiential education is for one to learn how to transform experiences into practical knowledge for oneself and one's society (Kolb, 1984). For Kolb, "reflective observation" on experiences is the action that begins the cycle of learning. Figure 8.1 illustrates Kolb's experiential learning model.

Drawing on Kolb's experiential learning model, Jacoby (1996) defined service learning as:

> A form of experiential education in which students engage in activities that address human and community needs together with structured opportunities intentionally designed to promote student learning and development. Reflection and reciprocity are key concepts of service-learning. (p. 5)

FIGURE 8.1
Kolb's Experiential Learning Model

1. Concrete Experience
"Service Activity"

4. Active
Experimentation

2. Reflective Observation

3. Abstract Concepts

While this definition includes both co-curricular and curricular-based service learning, in this chapter I focus on service learning in academic courses, or what has commonly been called "academic service learning."

In their comprehensive bibliography of service-learning research, Eyler, Giles, Stenson, and Gray (2003) highlight the positive role academic service learning can play in students' academic learning, career explorations, moral development, and a better understanding of those who may be different from them. They also underscore the central role service learning can play in helping students explore their spirituality and religious identities.

Unfortunately, while research has shown that academic service learning can play a positive role in the development of spiritual and religious identity, faculty use of academic service learning to help students explore their spiritual and religious values remains underused (Koth, 2003). This is a missed opportunity for faculty to help students explore their personal meaning, question their spiritual values, discover their vocational "calling," and strengthen their long-term commitment to serve. This is particularly regrettable since there is a burgeoning effort on many campuses to reconnect higher education to spirituality and religion.

Spirituality and Faith Formation on Campus: An Emerging Movement

Teaching and working as an administrator at a Jesuit Catholic institution offers me a consistent opportunity to observe how a college campus chooses to draw on its distinct religious tradition. I am heartened by the requirement that students take courses in religion and philosophy to graduate. In addition, I am motivated by campus-wide gatherings and presidential speeches promoting the pursuit of the university's religiously inspired mission to lead for a just and humane world.

Yet, even on campuses with a strong religious identity, promoting a common vision for spiritual and religious engagement is not easy. With only a third of its students identifying themselves as Catholic, it has become increasingly challenging to express the university's religious tradition and mission in a coherent and inclusive manner. In addition, with fewer and fewer men becoming Jesuits, the question of what makes our institution distinctly Jesuit becomes more significant. Finally, the increasingly diverse student body has led to much more religious diversity. In many ways, these challenges are symbolic of the trends that have occurred on most college campuses over the past 100 years.

Over the past century we have seen a precipitous decline in the role that religion and spirituality have played in higher education. For example, during the early part of the century hundreds of small, private, religiously affiliated colleges slowly moved away from their initial mission to pursue more secular goals. In addition, vibrant campus ministry programs that attracted thousands of students in the 1950s ceased to exist by the 1990s because of major budget cuts (McCormick, 1987). While the rise of fundamentalism in the 1970s and 1980s attracted pockets of committed college students on many campuses, the focus on a rigid dogma tended to push an even more significant number of students away from religious participation altogether (Gould, 1998). By the 1990s, responses to questions about religious beliefs frequently led students to distance themselves from religion, stating, "I'm spiritual but not religious" (Cherry, Deberg, & Porterfield, 2001). As a result of these and other trends, by the early 1990s, religion and spirituality had been pushed to the margins of campus life at most institutions.

It is interesting that over the past 10 years there has been a resurgence of interest in the role that spirituality and religion play in higher education. National conferences have reenergized campus conversations. For example, organizations such as the National Association of Student Personnel Administrators (NASPA), the Institute for College Student Values, the Fetzer Institute, and the California Institute of Integral Studies bring together thousands of faculty and administrators to discuss the role of spirituality and religion on the contemporary college campus. One event alone, the Education as Transformation national gathering in 1998, attracted more than 800 people.

In addition to these national gatherings, significant research projects have offered growing data on spirituality and religion in higher education. For example, in their recent book, *Religion on Campus*, Conrad Cherry, Betty Deberg, and Amanda Porterfield (2001) conducted an intensive qualitative study on four diverse college campuses to determine what religion means to today's college students. In addition, the UCLA Higher Education Research Institute (HERI) also continues to conduct a national, multicampus study of college students' religious and spiritual beliefs and practices.

The recent proliferation of conferences, literature, and research supported by significant funding from several national foundations has led to an emerging movement among college and university faculty to develop lessons that connect academic learning with spiritual and faith exploration. In making these connections, most faculty are keenly aware of the need to address matters of faith and spirituality in pluralistic and inclusive ways. In many cases this means helping students explore new ideas without giving them simple explanations and easy answers. In this work is recognition that students can find meaning and clarity through the messy and complex explorations that engage them intellectually and spiritually.

Connecting spiritual and religious values, beliefs, and practices to academic inquiry is an important endeavor because it can allow students opportunities to explore what it might mean to lead integrated, authentic, and meaningful lives. Yet, how exactly does an instructor make this connection? The next two sections of this chapter present tangible ways for faculty to use academic service learning to deepen students' intellectual and spiritual understanding. While academic service learning is only one tool among many, it does provide much promise.

Using Academic Service Learning to Teach Religion

Teaching religion on contemporary college campuses is not an easy endeavor. The trend among students to distinguish themselves as "spiritual but not religious" makes it challenging for faculty to motivate them to want to explore religious traditions and scriptures. In addition, the sometimes contentious debates between religious fundamentalists and those with less dogmatic tendencies push many students away from engagement with religious traditions. After all, who goes to church, synagogue, temple, or mosque to fight? Finally, teaching many courses, let alone a course that focuses on texts, traditions, and practices that date back hundreds and thousands of years, proves difficult in the technologically oriented student culture of iPods, text messaging, and blogs.

While these are significant obstacles, using service learning to teach religion can offer faculty a thoughtful means to involve students in examining perceptions and beliefs about religion. Indeed, the experiential nature of service learning frequently disrupts students' preconceived notions and viewpoints, and in the process, students often find themselves hungry for fresh perspectives.

The historical and philosophical relationship in most religions between faith and service makes the connection between service learning and the study of religion a natural fit. For example, the Christian adherence to "faith and works" has prompted many churches to create social service organizations. In addition, the Jewish focus on *tikkun olam*, or repairing the world, has led to significant engagement with the wider community.

In using service learning to teach religion, faculty need to consider three important factors: (1) preparing students to serve; (2) structuring the service experience to complement the course objectives; and (3) drawing on campus resources to support the service-learning process.

Preparation to Serve

Preparing students to serve is an essential element of a high-quality service-learning experience. Faculty can prepare students to engage fully in service learning by providing a thoughtful overview of the service-learning assignment. In addition, by asking students what they think they will experience in the service-learning process, faculty can begin to engage students in exploring deeper questions and assess students' prior knowledge.

An exercise that explores definitions of service is one specific example of an activity that faculty can use to prepare students for service learning. I use this exercise to help students understand their preconceptions of service. In this exercise, I ask students to rank order 16 specific examples of "service" according to their personal definition. Examples range from "joining the armed forces" to "providing dinner once a week at a homeless shelter" to "chaining yourself to an old-growth tree as loggers enter the forest." After students have completed their rankings, I read the list and ask them to stand if I read an example they ranked as one of their top three. I also ask students to cross their arms if I read an example that is one of their bottom three.

This activity helps students to understand their personal criteria for serving and appreciate other perceptions and approaches to service. Faculty who use service learning to teach religion might want to modify this exercise to incorporate examples of religious service that may provoke interesting student discussions. For example, I include "attending a one-week meditation retreat" as a potential service activity. This example frequently sparks a lively debate among students who question its value as a service to others. Yet, observing that Mahatma Gandhi, Dorothy Day, Martin Luther King Jr., and other prominent leaders had strong religious practices often complicates this critique. Other examples of religious service to incorporate in this activity include "attending a prayer vigil," "teaching Sunday school," or "reading scripture during worship."

Structuring the Service-Learning Experience

Service-learning experiences should complement course objectives and ad-dress community needs. For faculty teaching religion courses, this is a partic-ularly important consideration. By encouraging students to serve in religiously affiliated community organizations, these professors can provide students with an experiential opportunity to explore course objectives. For example, a professor teaching a survey course on Christianity may have her students serve at several church-sponsored homeless shelters. Through their service experiences, students in this course may become more aware of how various Christian traditions connect faith and action. In addition, students may also begin to see the distinct variations in how different churches ap-proach the homeless people they are trying to assist. Indeed, some religiously affiliated homeless shelters require their patrons to worship before receiving a meal, while others do no require religious participation. The professor may use these distinctions to teach students about the widely varied interpreta-tions of frequently cited Biblical scriptures. Finally, the professor may invite representatives from each of the organizations to speak to the class, thereby providing additional means to explore the connection between religion and social action.

Campus Resources to Support Service Learning

Faculty who teach courses on religion may choose to take the lead in devel-oping a service-learning component in their courses. Yet, for many, this time-intensive process becomes a significant impediment. Fortunately, many campuses have resources to support faculty interested in service learning. Hundreds of campuses have professional staff available to assist faculty with all aspects of the service-learning process. In many cases, these professionals have strong relationships with local community organizations, which makes the development and coordination of service learning much easier and more effective. In addition, many campuses have websites with helpful informa-tion such as lists of community organizations and examples of service-learning course syllabi.

Campus-based religious offices such as Hillel or the Newman Center may be another resource for faculty interested in using service learning to teach about religion. Many of these offices have established relationships with local religious institutions that operate social service agencies. In addition, in some cases, campus-based religious offices have developed more formal programs to support academic service learning. For example, in the 1990s, Betsy Alden and Mark Rutledge developed and began disseminating *The Praxis Project: Campus Ministry and Service-Learning* (1997). Adopted on more than 100 campuses across the nation, the Praxis Project encourages campus religious leaders to coordinate service activities for faculty to weave into their courses. In some cases, the religious leaders also facilitate reflective sessions for students in the courses.

Using Academic Service-Learning to Enhance Spirituality

A key element of the pedagogy of academic service learning is reflection. As described above, Kolb's experiential learning model suggests that combining service with reflection creates a means for students to discover new understandings and insights about social issues and academic content. While this is important, weaving spiritual elements into these reflection activities could magnify the potential for student learning. These elements might have some links to religious traditions, but they generally arise from a broad definition of spirituality. With this in mind, a slight modification to Kolb's cycle may give faculty a better understanding of how spiritual development fits with service-learning pedagogy.

In this modified cycle, students engage in the concrete experience of service and then reflect on how these experiences connect to the academic course objectives. Yet, these reflections also involve spiritual explorations such as the examination of the meaning and mystery of life. In this way, the reflection on the service experience can be a gateway to significant personal explorations of values, vocation, and truth. Similar to Kolb's experiential learning model, in this model, reflection is followed by the development of new concepts and active experimentation. Figure 8.2 illustrates this model.

Incorporating spiritual reflection into service learning has the capacity to help students (1) explore personal meaning; (2) strengthen their commitment to serve; and (3) explore their calling.

FIGURE 8.2
Kolb's Experiential Learning Model with Spiritual Reflection

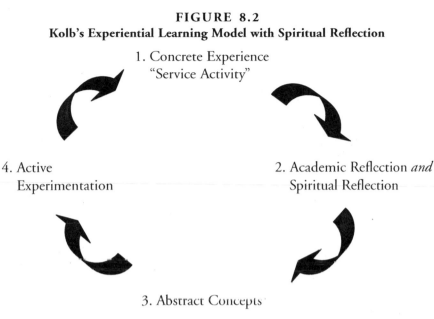

1. Concrete Experience
"Service Activity"

4. Active
Experimentation

2. Academic Reflection *and*
Spiritual Reflection

3. Abstract Concepts

Exploring Personal Meaning

Using spiritual components in service-learning reflection offers an important opportunity for students to explore questions of deep meaning. A few of the many questions that might arise from this process include, "what do I believe, how do I want to live my life, and what is success?" Examining such questions offers students the opportunity to embrace new perspectives and cultivate a more profound sense of spirituality. Noting the importance of this process, Sharon Parks (2000) writes, "[T]he promise and vulnerability of young adulthood lie in the experience of the birth of critical awareness and the dissolution and recomposition of the meaning of self, other, world, and 'God'" (p. 5).

Strengthening the Commitment to Serve

In addition to helping students make sense of their personal values, spiritual reflection provides new ideas and insights for future service experiences. As students explore the meaning of their lives, they are more likely to make long-term commitments to pursue positive social change. In other words, discovering greater personal meaning through spiritual reflection leads to more effective and stronger commitments to service.

Exploring a "Calling"

Through spiritual reflection, service-learning participants have the opportunity to explore their calling. Traditionally, in Western culture, the term *calling* has referred to a "call" from God to serve the church. Over the past several decades, another definition has arisen; this understanding implies that each person has a calling. Exploring one's calling while engaged in service has the added benefit of providing a living laboratory for trial and error. In a search for calling, difficult service experiences can provide as much instruction about oneself as can those that that bring great joy.

When I facilitate workshops on spirituality and service learning, I frequently ask faculty what obstacles they might face in using spiritual reflection in their classrooms. The most frequent responses include the challenge of giving up precious class time to activities that some might see as unscholarly; concerns about violating the separation of church and state; and the natural discomfort that faculty feel when leading students in a process that is often unpredictable.

I believe that the thoughtful use of specific spiritual exercises can mitigate most of these concerns. Hundreds of books and publications offer thousands of examples of spiritual exercises. Yet, because of their overtly religious overtones, most of these resources are not appropriate for use in the often secular and pluralistic environment of the college classroom. With this in mind, I provide several examples of spiritual reflection exercises that can be used in almost any service-learning context.

Nurturing the Spirit

Author and practitioner of monastic spiritual exercises, Debra Farrington (2000) describes this exercise as a means of demonstrating all the things one is already doing to lead a spiritual life (pp. 13–15). Drawing on Farrington's description, when I lead this exercise I give students 10 minutes to write down everything they do to nurture their spirits. I then ask them to share several things from their lists, and I record these responses on a marker board. After developing a lengthy list, I ask the class to look for themes among the list as well as what things are not on the board or on their personal lists. What is particularly interesting about this exercise is that students frequently do not include "serving the community" or other similar actions in their list. This provides a good opportunity for discussion and clarification. Farrington purposefully suggests asking the question, "What nurtures your spirit?" rather than "What nurtures your spiritual life?" because too often the word "spiritual" limits responses to religious activities such as prayer and worship. Asking the question in this way also addresses the concern about the separation of church and state.

Seeing All Beings as Enlightened

In my work with students engaged in service learning, I have come to notice a common pattern. After the initial visits to their service sites, students return bubbling with energy and enthusiasm. Yet frequently, after their fourth or fifth visit, they return frustrated and much less motivated because of something someone at the site said or did. In trying to redirect the students' energies in more positive directions, I have used a reflection by Jack Kornfield. Presenting this reflection as a means to change how we relate to difficulties, Kornfield (1993) writes:

> Picture or imagine that this earth is filled with Buddhas, that every single being you encounter is enlightened, except one–yourself. Imagine that they are all here to teach you. Whoever you encounter is acting as they do solely for your benefit, to provide just the teachings and difficulties you need in order to awaken. Sense what lessons they offer to you. Inwardly thank them for this. Throughout a day or a week continue to develop the image of enlightened teachers all around you. (p. 82)

Vocational Call

Earlier, I described how spiritual reflection offers service-learning participants the opportunity to explore their calling. I have used an exercise from Parker Palmer (2000) to help students in my service-learning course explore their call to serve. Initially, students write about two recent moments from their service-learning experiences—a moment when things went so well, they knew they were born to serve; and a moment when things went so poorly they wanted to give up. Next, students share their positive stories in small groups. The students who listen offer observations to the student who is sharing his or her story. This process helps students identify the gifts they possess that made the good moment possible; these gifts are often hidden because they are such an internal part of oneself. Finally, students share their stories of struggle and difficulty. The students who listen give feedback without offering judgment or advice. Palmer hopes that in sharing these types of stories, "We will become better leaders not by trying to fill the potholes in

our souls but by knowing them so well that we can avoid falling into them"
(p. 52).

Closing a Reflection

I have found that closing a service-learning reflection or course provides a
particularly good opportunity for deep student reflection. One example of a
closing activity I have used is what I have termed "Take One, Leave One."
In this exercise, I give every student two index cards. I ask students to reflect
on the class and think of one new personal commitment they can make to
create more just and compassionate communities. I ask participants to write
this on their first index card and then put it in a special place where they will
see it and remember to keep their commitment. Next, I ask participants to
write on the second index card a wish they have for other members of the
group. I collect all of these cards in a basket and ask every participant to take
an index card from the basket until all of the cards have been redistributed.
The exercise closes as each person reads aloud the wish for the group he or
she took from the basket. I have found this exercise helpful in honoring individual commitments and group connection. In addition, reading the wishes
gives everyone a role and avoids one person monopolizing the closing.

Don't Just Act, Sit There

If there is one lesson I take from my experiences of using academic service
learning to teach about spirituality and religion it is that students are hungry
to explore what it means to be authentic public leaders. The growing crisis
of global warming, the pervasiveness of poverty, the expanding AIDS crisis,
and the bitter divisiveness within the U.S. political system demonstrate the
need for this type of leadership.

Yet, in a culture of hyperactivity, students have few moments to make
sense of their lives and connect their academic studies to the rest of their
experiences. There is a Buddhist saying of which I am quite fond: "Don't
just act, sit there." Faculty use of academic service learning to explore spirituality, faith, and religion provides a chance for students to take action in their
communities. Perhaps more important, it offers students an invitation to
stop and reflect. Through this process, students discover how they can best
use their skills, gifts, and values to address the world's critical needs.

References

Alden B., & Rutledge, M. (1997). *The Praxis Project: Campus ministry and service-learning*. Nashville, TN: United Methodist Church.

Cherry, C., Deberg, B. A., & Porterfield, A. (2001). *Religion on campus*. Chapel Hill, NC: University of North Carolina.

Eyler, J., Giles, D., Stenson, C., & Gray, C. (2003). At a glance: What we know about the effects of service-learning on college students, faculty, institutions, and communities, 1993–2000 (3rd ed). In Campus Compact, *Introduction to service-learning toolkit* (2nd ed., pp. 15–19). Providence, RI: Brown University.

Farrington D. K. (2000). *Living faith day by day: How the sacred rules of monastic traditions can help you live spiritually in the modern world*. New York: Berkley.

Gould, J. S. (1998). On engineers and evangelism. In S. A. Kujawa (Ed.), *Disorganized religion: The evangelization of youth and young adults*. Boston: Cowley.

Jacoby, B. (Ed.). (1996). *Service-learning in higher education: Concepts and practices*. San Francisco: Jossey-Bass.

Kolb, D. A. (1984). *Experiential learning: Experience as the source of learning and development*. Englewood Cliffs, NJ: Prentice-Hall.

Kornfield, J. (1993). *A path with heart: A guide through the perils and promises of spiritual life*. New York: Bantam.

Koth, K. (2003). Deepening the commitment to serve: Spiritual reflection in service-learning. *About Campus, 7*(6), 2–7.

Liu, G. (1996). *To strengthen service-learning policy and practice: Stories from the field*. Stanford, CA: Haas Center for Public Service.

McCormick, T. (1987). *Campus ministry in the coming age*. St. Louis, MO: CBP Press.

Palmer, P. (2000). *Let your life speak: Listening for the voice of vocation*. San Francisco: Jossey-Bass.

Parks, S. (2000). *Big questions, worthy dreams: Mentoring young adults in their search for meaning, purpose and faith*. San Francisco: Jossey-Bass.

9

PHILOSOPHY AND RELIGIOUS DISAGREEMENTS IN THE COLLEGE CLASSROOM

Dona Warren

D isagreements about religion are potentially explosive. They require the touch of an experienced hand, and philosophy—a subject characterized by dissention—is nothing if not experienced when it comes to confronting radically divergent viewpoints. This is not to say, of course, that philosophers have given sufficient attention to the phenomenon of disagreement or that the attention philosophers have given to this subject has resulted in a universally accepted account of the phenomenon. Nor is it to say that philosophers are in a position to pronounce authoritatively on the subject of religious disagreements in the college classroom or that our opinions and advice are any more valuable than the opinions and advice of our colleagues in other disciplines. It is only to say that most teaching philosophers have, out of practical necessity, developed some techniques for addressing disagreements in our classrooms, and that some of us have, out of professional curiosity, reflected on the philosophical nature of disagreement itself. I've endeavored to do both.

I began teaching philosophy at the University of Wisconsin-Stevens Point, a public, teaching-oriented institution, in 1995, and I teach Introduction to Philosophy, Critical Thinking, Symbolic Logic, and the Philosophy of Religion on a regular basis. From the beginning of my teaching career, issues surrounding religious disagreements in the classroom have captivated my attention. As a philosopher, I'm interested in the rationality of religious belief; as a professor, I'm intrigued by the challenges posed by the demographics of my classes because UW-SP's approximately 8,700 students reflect a relatively diverse range of religious inclinations. Many of them have been raised Catholic and still identify with the religion. Many fervently identify themselves as "followers of Jesus Christ" in a nonsectarian, intensely personal, and (to my mind) vaguely evangelical way. A handful embrace Islam or Buddhism, and many are outspokenly atheistic or agnostic. One might expect such a religiously varied collection of individuals to pose serious pedagogical challenges for a discipline like philosophy, which addresses issues that are either explicitly religious or have obvious religious implications. Every semester, for example, my students and I discuss the existence of God, life after death, abortion, and homosexuality. Prima facie, one might predict that these issues raised with those students would generate routine conflagrations in the classroom. But strangely enough, they don't. Of course, my students disagree, often and openly, with me and with each other, about all of these topics. But seldom, if ever, do these disagreements rise to the level of confrontation. They've certainly never disrupted the lesson, nor (to the best of my knowledge) have they gotten in the way of student learning.

Nevertheless, I began to participate in campus events addressing conflict in the classroom, and through these gatherings, I learned that my colleagues in other disciplines routinely experienced the challenges I had anticipated but seldom or never faced. I started to wonder why, confident that the reasons resided in the nature of my subject rather than in my own pedagogical expertise because my colleagues were at least as gifted in the classroom as I.

I suspected that the explanation for our different experiences of religious disagreement lay in philosophy's fixation on *how* people think and in its relative disregard for *what* specific beliefs they hold. It's standard practice for philosophy professors to reassure their students that grades will be based on how well they argue for their positions, not on how neatly those positions tally with the professor's own. If accompanied by an appropriate and consistent classroom demeanor, this reassurance is usually effective, although I've never found it completely unproblematic from a purely philosophical point of view. If a student is arguing for a position with which I disagree, after all, logic dictates that I must either find an error in that student's reasoning or change my mind. Although I could revise my beliefs in the face of a student's argument, I'm unlikely to do so by virtue of my greater experience with the subject. Quite simply, I've already considered and discounted most of the arguments my students posit against my philosophical beliefs. From this, of course, it follows that when a student supports a position I reject, the probability that I'll find a mistake in that student's argument is very high. As a practical pedagogical matter, this doesn't pose great concern because some mistakes are more severe than others, and if I think an error committed by a student is relatively small, the sort that a rational person might make, I happily ignore it. The fact remains, however, that assessing the reasoning for a position and assessing the position itself are not quite as distinct from each other as we philosophy professors sometimes (with the best of intentions) lead our students to believe.

My reflection on religious disagreements in the classroom has been structured by the considerations I discussed above. Why don't religious disagreements disrupt philosophy courses as much as one might expect? Why do they pose greater challenges in other courses? And can we be quite so blithe about claiming to focus on the reasons for a position rather than on the position itself? This paper represents how I answer these questions at the moment. I begin by discussing how I, as a teacher of philosophy, address religious disagreements in my own courses. In the next section, I explore how other disciplines differ from philosophy, and I try to imagine some ways in which these disciplines can engage students whose religious beliefs oppose the starting assumptions or established results of the subject. Because I'm a philosopher, and not an expert in teaching those disciplines, my primary objective here is to map out some of the possibilities available, although I do comment on what I take to be the most obvious advantages and disadvantages of each approach. In the concluding section, I discuss what I see as an important unresolved issue that lingers behind every instance and examination of religious disagreement: how an inchoate awareness of this issue might lead some students to resist conversations that challenge their religious convictions. I also sketch how we might draw on our own experiences with disagreement to help these students develop coping strategies more conducive to growth and dialogue.

Religious Disagreements in the Philosophy Classroom

Philosophers disagree about everything, including the nature of philosophy. The account of philosophy I give my introductory students, however, isn't too controversial. I tell them philosophy is the activity of considering questions that can't be answered empirically and addressing these questions by thinking rationally. This account of philosophy has the benefit of carving out a domain of discourse and delineating a methodology for negotiating this domain. It also explains a salient feature of the subject: because philosophy questions everything, it has a vanishingly small set of starting assumptions and no established positions to speak of. After all, any prospective assumption or position is open to the question, "Why should we think this?" and is thereby transformed into a live philosophical issue, a status incompatible with that of a starting assumption or established result.

So, in philosophy we have a discipline that takes nothing for granted, accepts nothing as proven, and is devoted above all to the cultivation of reason. And this gives philosophy instructors a number of ways to address student challenges, whether those challenges are religiously motivated or not.

First, by virtue of philosophy's broad subject matter, absence of starting assumptions, and lack of established positions, virtually all challenges contain within them the seed of a philosophical claim that deserves to be taken seriously. A consequence of this is that practically no objection can place a student outside the realm of the discipline. Even objections to the method of rational inquiry have philosophical precedent and are the proper subject of philosophical examination, criticism, and defense. This enables philosophy instructors to acknowledge the philosophical insight and disciplinary relevance behind a student's challenge, even when the instructor is unable to devote much time to its examination. For example, if a student objects to the project of giving arguments for the existence of God, maintaining instead that religious beliefs don't require that kind of support, the student can be assured that his or her claim is philosophically intriguing, even though a serious examination of the issues involved is beyond the scope of the course.

Second, because there is no significant degree of consensus in philosophy, philosophy instructors seldom endeavor to convey a body of philosophical truths. Instead, they attempt to help students to understand different points of view and (just as important) to grasp and weigh the arguments that can be advanced in support of these positions. Ideally, students are brought to appreciate points of agreement, as well as points of disagreement, between themselves and individuals who hold beliefs they don't share. Students who object to particular philosophical positions can be assured that their *agreement* is not the issue; their *charitable comprehension* is. If, for example, a devout Christian objects to the argument from the existence of evil that's often advanced for atheism, a philosophy instructor can remind this student that his or her *acceptance* of the argument isn't necessary. The instructor can then help the student to appreciate more precisely the points at which he or she disagrees with the argument and the points at which he or she may agree with it.

Third, thanks to its emphasis on reason, philosophy devotes most of its critical attention to the support advanced for a position, significantly less to the position itself, and virtually none to the individual advancing the position. This places students behind a double barrier of protection. Because intelligent and morally good people have been mistaken about issues in the past, students can contemplate the prospect that some of their beliefs might be wrong without thereby jeopardizing their self-esteem. More important, by remembering that a true position can be supported by bad reasons, students are more receptive to a critical assessment of the reasons supporting the positions they accept, even if those positions are very significant to them. A student who believes in God, for example, can acknowledge the problems with an argument for God's existence without feeling compelled to conclude that God does not exist.

And, finally, philosophy's focus on slow and careful thinking helps students to detangle issues in a way that enables them to appreciate more clearly what is, and what is not, at stake in a discussion. It's not unusual, for example, for some of my students to assume that accepting evolution entails atheism, and it doesn't take much reflection as a class to help them see that this is not the case. Once they understand this, theistic students are significantly more open to a rational appraisal of the relative merits of evolution and creationism.

These four approaches to student challenges constitute a powerful set of tools for addressing the objections, religious or otherwise, that arise in philosophy classrooms. As philosophers, we can always acknowledge that a student's objection contains a philosophical insight worthy of attention; remind our students that we don't require them to accept specific claims but rather expect them to understand and engage positions and arguments; assure our students that a position they accept can be true even if an argument in support of that position is weak; and help our students distinguish between positions that are frequently conflated. What light, if any, does this set of techniques shed on how religious disagreements might be handled in other courses? Can other subjects simply transplant these methods from philosophy? I suspect not, because disciplines differ.

Religious Disagreements in Other Classrooms

Each academic subject is unique, so it's obviously impossible to say very much about the body of "disciplines-other-than-philosophy" as a whole. Furthermore, I'm a philosopher, so any claims I make about other subjects are subject to error. I'll nevertheless be bold enough to speculate about one significant similarity of other disciplines to philosophy and one important respect in which they differ.

Like philosophy instructors, college instructors across the disciplines tend to locate the true "meat" of their fields less in *what* they and the colleagues think than in *how* they and their colleagues think, in how they approach the questions posed by their subject, and in how they support their answers. Consequently, most courses taught at the college level do not simply require students to memorize a body of positions that are accepted by most experts in the field. Instead, these courses are designed to help students understand a bit about the evidence that's taken to support those positions and a bit about the sort of evidence that would be required to overthrow them. An emphasis on critical thinking and providing reasons is a thread that binds the disciplines together and constitutes what is probably the most important similarity between philosophy and other subjects.

Unlike philosophy, however, these other subjects *do* have a healthy set of starting assumptions and a body of established positions. The physical sciences, for example, need to assume that the external world exists and that our senses are reliable guides to truths about it. Biology takes evolution to be a currently established position, the best account we have at present for the origin of life on Earth. This is not to say that *every* physicist needs to believe our senses are trustworthy, that *every* biologist must accept evolution, or that these positions are forever protected from revision or rejection as the disciplines progress. It's only to say that, at the present time, accepting a healthy number of these starting assumptions and established positions is part of what constitutes doing and knowing the discipline in question.

It's this feature of disciplines other than philosophy that accounts, it seems to me, for the fact that student objections can pose *especially* vexing problems for these subjects. Because these fields have a reasonably robust set of starting assumptions and a body of established positions, students whose preexisting commitments contradict these assumptions or positions are forced to oppose the discipline. If a student studies physics but is unwilling to accept the experimental method, or takes a biology class but rejects evolution, it's difficult for the instructor to follow the lead of the philosophy faculty and recognize the relevance of these challenges, noting that they contain within them the seed of a disciplinarily pertinent insight. Instead of allowing students a form of access *to* the subject, such objections serve to alienate students *from* the field.

There are, I assume, degrees of alienation here. Students whose commitments prevent them from accepting a handful of relatively peripheral positions would probably be less alienated from the discipline than would students whose commitments prevent them from accepting positions that are more central to the subject because they serve to explain or justify other positions in the discipline, as, for example, the theory of evolution can help to explain various facts in biology and justify one interpretation of events over another.

Most alienated of all, perhaps, would be students who cannot accept the basic methodological presuppositions of the field. Nevertheless, all students who refuse to accept the starting assumptions or accepted positions of a subject have placed themselves, to varying degrees, outside the discipline in a way that it's impossible for students to place themselves outside philosophy. How, then, can instructors engage such students in their courses?

Naturally, as a philosopher, I cannot say. But, as a philosopher, I can reflect on the approaches available to an instructor faced with a student who refuses to accept the assumptions or positions of the field, and the first thing that occurs to me is that the instructor can either attempt to change the student's mind on these issues, or not. Both options open up potentially fruitful avenues of inquiry. If an instructor *does* hope to change a student's mind, for example, how might he or she go about it? And if an instructor *doesn't* hope to change a student's mind then what *is* he or she attempting to accomplish?

Let's first consider pedagogical approaches that aspire to change the student's mind, that endeavor, in other words, to bring the student to accept the assumptions or positions he or she is rejecting.

If this rejection is based on a student's preexisting commitments, religious or otherwise, the best we can hope for is that the contradiction the student perceives between his or her commitments and the positions in the discipline is merely apparent. I suspect this is sometimes the case. As noted above, some students tend to assume that evolution is intrinsically atheistic, so their commitment to theism leads them to reject evolution outright. For such students, noting that evolution is compatible with theism is sufficient to dissolve their resistance to the former.

Frequently, however, the student is correct in thinking that his or her preexisting commitments conflict with some positions of the discipline the student is studying, so, in attempting to have the student accept these positions, the instructor is effectively asking the student to abandon those commitments. How might the instructor go about this?[1] There are, it seems to me, two options: the instructor could ask the student to accept his or her word on the matter, or the instructor could attempt to convince the student by detailing the evidence supporting the positions at issue. Unfortunately, both alternatives face problems.

Although it's often proper for students to defer to their instructors on issues relevant to the subject, an approach to disagreement that asks students to accept a claim *simply* because the instructor endorses that claim fails to achieve one of the things that most college courses seek to do   it fails to help the student understand how the subject works, how claims within the subject are supported and defeated; it short, it doesn't make the student *think*.[2] On the other hand, it's often beyond the scope of the course to support a contested position from the bottom up. It may not be appropriate, for example, for an introductory anthropology course to establish the theory of evolution by reviewing the evidence in its defense; that would take too much time and divert attention from the material to be covered. Such a course may need to take evolution for granted, and if a student refuses to accept evolution on religious grounds, the instructor might correctly decide that it's beyond the range of the discussion to attempt to persuade the student otherwise.[3]

I fear, therefore, that if a student's preconceptions really *do* conflict with the assumptions or established positions of a discipline, approaches that attempt to change the student's mind will be unsatisfactory. And this means, of course, that the instructor must try to engage the student in the subject *without attempting to convince the student that the assumptions and positions the student rejects are true*. It's a bitter pill. If the instructor, as an expert in the field, believes the assumptions and established positions of his or her subject are very probably correct, is aware of the evidence to support these positions, and is devoted to helping his or her students understand these truths and the backing they enjoy, how can the instructor approach students who refuse to accept these assumptions and positions and whose refusal is fueled by reasons that have nothing to do with the discipline itself, so they can't be addressed in the subject's terms?

Obviously, in such a situation, the learning objectives have to be revised. If a student is unable to learn that certain claims are true, then the student must learn something else. Non-mind-changing approaches to teaching students who oppose the assumptions and positions of a discipline can be typed according to what they attempt to teach and the motivation for learning they endeavor to elicit.

The crudest example of such an approach encourages students to learn what the instructor wants to hear and motivates this learning by threatening a failing grade. This, of course, is one of the outcomes instructors most passionately want to avoid, incompatible as it is with every significant aspect of education. Under this arrangement, students learn only the shallowest of facts ("My instructor wants me to say X") for the shallowest of reasons ("I want to pass this class"). What other tactic is available? There are, I think, two closely related options.

First, in what I think of as the "Know Your Enemy" approach, students are encouraged to learn the course material to better understand their opposition. Students learn about positions that many people believe, learn about the reasons supporting these positions, and recognize this learning as important insofar as it will enable them to better defend themselves against people who actually think like that. The "Know Your Enemy" line is able to encourage significant comprehension of the material and bestow on this comprehension a rationale transcending artificial institutional requirements. However, this approach depends on both a generally adversarial perspective and the students' conviction that they possess the absolute truth. It isn't clear that this perspective or conviction is worth preserving, and it would be interesting (although beyond the purview of this paper) to argue that they are both somewhat antithetical to the objectives of higher education. It behooves us, then, to turn to the second option.

According to what I call the "Understand the Alternatives" approach, students are encouraged to learn the course material to better appreciate viewpoints they don't currently happen to share. They are motivated by the recognition that such appreciation will help them to respect those with whom they disagree, thereby enhancing their ability to communicate and cooperate with a variety of people. They are further inspired by the knowledge that appreciating the alternatives will enable them to understand their own positions better and allow them to modify these positions if they choose.[4] This tactic is similar to the "Know Your Enemy" approach in that it encourages students to understand how others think, but it differs from that approach insofar as it doesn't cast alternative viewpoints as the enemy or presuppose at the outset that students will never embrace the alternatives. I suspect, therefore, that this second approach is best. If the conflict students sense between their convictions and the subject is genuine, and if the prospects for changing their minds are limited by the practical impossibility of convincing them of the truth of the contested positions, we can at least encourage them to grasp the subject to understand those who think differently and to better negotiate their own beliefs. This, it seems to me, is far from a Pyrrhic victory.

But neither is it a unilateral success. A subset of students will remain intractably opposed to those disciplines that use assumptions or embrace positions conflicting with the claims of their religion. It may be the case that some of these students are so dogmatically sure of possessing the truth and so impatient with those who think differently that even a moderate call to understanding leaves them cold. But a far greater number of these students, I venture to guess, feel threatened, seeing the injunction to understand alternatives as a serpentine call to temptation: comprehending other viewpoints is the first step toward falling away from the truth, *especially* when those viewpoints are advocated by instructors who are diabolically able to make their positions sound so reasonable. Under such circumstances, it's best to rest secure in one's knowledge by refusing to entertain imposters.

It's easy to deride such an attitude; it seems so regressive and anti-intellectual. But it isn't stupid. There's an insight there.

The Paradox of Apparently Reasonable Disagreement

Suppose you and I disagree about an issue. If I think you're unaware of some relevant evidence, or if I think you're less able to reason from this evidence than I am, then I needn't be troubled by our disagreement. I have reason, after all, to think you're mistaken and that the evidence, properly considered, supports my view. But suppose we share the same evidence, and I think you are as able as I—most of the time at least—to appreciate the implications of the evidence. Suppose, to use the lingo, that we're "epistemic peers." *Now* I think I should be concerned. If someone at least as informed and as rational as I opposes me on an issue, why should I think my position is right and the other position is wrong? Whenever I disagree with an epistemic peer, I'm compelled to think that *someone* who's acquainted with the evidence and able to appreciate its force is committing a blunder. Why should I assume this unfortunate someone is the other person and not *me?* I could, of course, deny that my opponent *is* my epistemic peer, citing some unsharable evidence I possess (some intuitions, perhaps, that I can't communicate adequately) or appealing to some unusual ability I have to assess the implications of the evidence (some insight I enjoy, maybe, about where the evidence leads). Both options, however, provide only the illusion of escape because they both require me to attribute to myself some special intuitive capacities—either the ability to intuit special evidence or the ability to intuit the force of the objectively accessible evidence—and because my opponent can make exactly the same claims. Why should I think that *my* alleged intuitive abilities are reliable and the other person's are not? And so we are back where we were.

I call this "The Paradox of Apparently Reasonable Disagreement" and it vexes me greatly. I think it should vex us all as we reflect on how frequently we disagree with the opinions of our respected colleagues. It needn't vex us, however, when we contemplate the disagreements we've had with our students about matters relevant to our subjects, because with respect to our disciplines of expertise, our students aren't usually our epistemic peers.

Students, however, seldom avoid the full force of this paradox when they find themselves in conflict with their instructors over matters within the instructor's discipline, and they have only two ways to resolve it, neither of which is especially palatable. First, of course, students can change their minds, bringing their opinions in line with those of recognized experts in the field by rejecting the beliefs that conflicted with established positions in the discipline. As we've seen, however, it's difficult enough for the instructor to convince them to abandon their commitments, so it might be a bit much to expect the students to do it on their own. Second, students can retain their original beliefs and maintain that they enjoy epistemic privilege over their instructor. This would be a difficult move, one that involves explaining why the instructor is wrong about claims within that instructor's area of expertise. It *can*, however, be attempted. I've heard of students (possibly apocryphal) who maintain that their instructors are in league with the liberal elite, are committed to an anti-Christian agenda, or are otherwise compromised in their ability to seek and see the truth. As offensive as some of us might find these charges, we should see them for what they might be: the best attempts our students can make to claim the epistemic privilege they require to rationally sustain their beliefs despite the fact that their instructors believe otherwise.

Those are, I repeat, the only ways in which students can resolve the paradox generated by disagreeing with their instructors and other experts: either they think the experts are right and they change their minds, or they don't change their minds and think the experts are wrong. When religious commitments are involved, neither avenue is enticing. Is it any surprise, then, that some students try to evade this paradox by avoiding those situations that give rise to it, by dropping those courses that challenge their religious beliefs or, if that isn't possible, by shutting their minds to serious consideration of alternative points of view?

All we can do in this case, I suspect, is to help our students learn that paradoxes needn't be avoided or resolved, that they can be tolerated for a time, recognized for what they are as one awaits more light. Indeed, this is how I cope with the fact that I disagree with my epistemic peers on many issues. I acknowledge the oddity of the situation while continuing to be guided by the evidence as I see it. That's probably how most of us get through our thinking day. Maybe helping our students to cope like this, with honesty, patience, and inquiry, is the best we can do. Maybe it's enough.

Endnotes

1. "*Should* the instructor go about this?" is another question. Personally, I think that we sometimes should. If I have a student who thinks God told her to bomb the Gay and Lesbian Society on campus, I don't think I'd be wrong-headed in my attempts to change her mind—even if that meant trying to alter her religious beliefs. It's difficult, perhaps impossible, to delineate precisely the conditions under which it's acceptable to challenge a student's religious beliefs. As with so many issues related to the classroom, the instructor is probably the proper arbiter of this, the individual best able to be guided by the particulars of each circumstance.

2. This is an oversimplification. It isn't clear to me that a healthy recognition of expertise, a recognition informed by an understanding of how knowledge is dispersed and developed throughout a complex society, shouldn't be reason enough to accept a claim, even when that claim conflicts with one's previous commitments. A more extended examination of student disagreement might profitably focus on the

issue of beliefs passed down from experts, including the question of when it's justi-fiable, or even rationally mandatory, for a student to accept the instructor's word on a matter. However, because most of our troubling cases involve students who do *not* change their beliefs when the experts assure them they should, I don't examine this issue here.

3. There are also serious philosophical problems involved in appealing to the relevant evidence to convince a student to accept a position like evolution, because a student who rejects evolution and an instructor who accepts it might easily dis-agree about what *counts* as relevant evidence in this case. Under such circumstances, there might not be sufficient points of mutual agreement between the student and instructor to ground a reasoned argument in support of evolution, even if giving such a reasoned argument were within the scope of the course.

4. How, specifically, might students better understand their own positions by better understanding the alternatives? Among other things, they might discover that certain evidence allegedly supporting their viewpoint does not, in fact, serve this function very well. The theoretical feasibility of evolutionary accounts of ethics, for example, may be sufficient to undermine many moral arguments for the existence of God. An appreciation of this fact requires neither the acceptance of evolution nor the rejection of God and can help philosophically inclined theists to avoid many an unsound argument.

IO

WHEN FAITH AND SCIENCE COLLIDE

Mano Singham

Most high profile science-religion controversies tend to focus on biological topics such as evolution or medical-related topics such as stem cells. Isaac Newton's work, which forms the basis of an introductory physics courses that I taught for prospective science and engineering majors, does not usually ruffle religious sensibilities.

So it came as a surprise about 10 years ago when, just before he was about to graduate, a student came into my office to say goodbye and then, as he was leaving, said hesitantly, "Do you remember that stuff you taught us about how the universe originated in the Big Bang about 15 billion years ago? Well, I don't really believe all that." I must have looked surprised because he went on, "It kind of conflicts with my religious beliefs." He looked at me apprehensively, perhaps to see if I might be offended or angry or think less of him. But I simply smiled and let it pass because I instinctively felt that arguing with him would be the wrong thing to do.

But that conversation has stayed in my mind ever since, because it showed me how strongly people hold on to their religious beliefs even in the face of overwhelming scientific evidence and consensus to the contrary. To think in these days that the world is just 6,000 years old is to have a tenacity about one's beliefs that cannot be overcome by authority figures, such as teachers and textbook writers, simply dismissing them.

That encounter influenced how I prepared for a seminar, The Evolution of Scientific Ideas, for sophomore undergraduates, that I have been teaching for the last four years at Case Western Reserve University, a private research university with a strong science and engineering ethos. As a result of this planning, the discussions have been frank but devoid of friction and unpleasantness, even though we have dealt with very sensitive issues involving personal beliefs. The lessons I have learned about how to do this apply to anyone who teaches science-related courses. In essence, it requires creating a good classroom atmosphere and a deeper understanding of the purpose of education and the nature and goals of science.

My seminar deals with questions such as whether and how we can draw a line of demarcation between science and nonscience, and how scientific theories change and evolve over time (Popper, 1965, pp. 33–65). I knew this course would provide many occasions for students to confront challenges to their faith. After all, the question of whether "intelligent design creationism" is science squarely confronts the demarcation issue. The fact that natural selection is preferred over creationism as the paradigm for investigating the diversity of life, and scientists' adoption of methodological naturalism as a mode of operation, immediately raises the question of whether one has to be an atheist to be a scientist. The notion that science evolves without any preordained direction conflicts with the teleological notion of most religions that there is an existing plan that is unfolding toward a preordained goal. And then there is the big question: What is truth, and what should we do when "scientific truths" conflict with "religious truths"?

Since this would be a small seminar of fewer than 20, students would not be able to disagree silently, as they could in my large physics classes. Disagreements would be in the open and would occur frequently. And it would not just be between students and teacher but also among the students themselves, since our student body includes many different faiths as well as agnostics and atheists.

It is theoretically possible to avoid religion altogether and, if the topic should somehow sneak in, to deflect it or simply rule it out by fiat. This is a well-honed practice among scientists who do not want to get involved in exhausting, time-consuming, and frustrating discussions about science and religion, and is usually accomplished by claiming that science deals with the physical world while religion deals with the spiritual, and we should keep them separate. This sentiment is supported by a statement of the National Academy of Sciences (NAS): "Religion and science are separate and mutually exclusive realms of human thought whose presentation in the same context leads to misunderstanding of both scientific theory and religious belief" (NAS Committee on Science and Creationism, 1984, p. 6).

But I rejected that option for several reasons, one of which is philosophical. The argument that the physical world can be fenced off from the spiritual is glib and spurious and does not bear close examination (Singham, 2000). To invoke it would be to say something I strongly disagreed with for the sake of avoiding controversy.

The second reason was that I felt that a discussion of science and religion would be very illuminating for all concerned. Students are very interested in questions of religion and spirituality (Bartlett, 2005). For example, on the first day of my class, I ask my students what questions they are interested in examining. One offering was, "At what point in history did scientific thinking shift from a basic and universal belief in God and, more specifically, Christianity? Why did this shift occur?" Another question that clearly had a religious basis was, "What, if any, evidence is there proving that the evolution of man is false?"

Furthermore, science-religion issues have been very much in the news recently regarding whether schools should teach intelligent design along with evolution by natural selection. My students were only two years out of high school, and many had been engulfed by the passion of that debate. It would be a pity not to allow them to come to grips with that issue in a sophisticated way.

Finally, my seminar is designed to address deep philosophical issues. Since religion forms the basis for the worldview of many students, leaving it out would reduce the richness of the discussion by excluding the perspective of one of their biggest influences.

The next issue I had to address was the tricky one of what to do with my own views. Should instructors try and keep their own perspective a secret for fear of unduly influencing their students? Or should they reveal them freely? I opted for the latter for several reasons. One was that I was not sure how well I could keep my views a secret. And even if I could, students would know that I did have an opinion. I am an atheist, but I knew that most of my students belonged to various denominations of Christianity and Judaism, with a sprinkling of Muslims, Hindus, deists, agnostics, and atheists, and I thought it would be more distracting for them to constantly try to guess my perspective than to have them know it.

A second reason is that I believe instructors are models for students, and should behave in ways we expect our students to behave. Since I wanted the students to feel they could share their views freely, it would not be good modeling practice for me to hide my own. I discussed this point with the class, and the consensus was that, if relevant to the topic at hand, I should definitely share my views but not impose them on the class.

The third reason was that I wanted my students, instead of trying to defend their own beliefs from what they perceived as challenges posed by other beliefs (or lack of them), to view the discussions as a way to deepen their understanding of their own beliefs. Again, I felt that modeling why I believed what I believed, and how I arrived at that position, would help students to do the same for themselves. Self-reflective activities of this sort help develop metacognitive skills in students that are important in enabling them to become lifelong learners (Bransford, Brown, & Cocking, 1999).

I wanted to create a classroom atmosphere in which I was not overly dominant so my students felt somewhat equal with me and thus free to express ideas without worrying about conflicting with my views. Of course, true equality is never possible in a classroom where the instructor grades students, but it is possible to minimize the difference in formal power and make it less salient. I did so by delegating as much decision making as possible about the class (including how the students would be assessed) to the students. Of course, as the instructor of record, I was responsible for maintaining the integrity of the course, but I saw this as possible by laying out the framework and allowing students as much input as possible (Singham, 2005). Having students choose research topics; lead discussions; and decide due dates for assignments, grade distributions, grading rubrics, and so on, increases a sense of collective ownership of the course, thus reducing my dominance. Oddly enough, my conceding power to students resulted in their conceding power to me, in that none of them has challenged my assessments or the grades I assign.

The next question was establishing the tone of the discussions. The word "seminar" does not mean the same thing to everyone. For example, Salman Rushdie (2005) recently reflected on his own education:

> At Cambridge University I was taught a laudable method of argument: you never personalize, but you have absolutely no respect for people's opinions. You are never rude to the person, but you can be savagely rude about what

the person thinks. That seems to me a crucial distinction: You cannot ring-fence their ideas. The moment you say that any idea system is sacred, whether it's a religious belief system or a secular ideology, the moment you declare a set of ideas to be immune from criticism, satire, derision, or contempt, freedom of thought becomes impossible.

But it is good to remind oneself that not everyone enjoys this kind of argumentation on a *personal* level. Some revel in the verbal swordplay, the cut and thrust of ideas that the debating societies of Cambridge and Oxford are famous for. But not everyone is comfortable participating in a ferocious battle of wits.

Rushdie is perfectly right in saying that no ideas should be immune from criticism and that no one has the right to expect to be shielded from ideas they might find repugnant. In fact it is essential to challenge people's ideas if they are to learn. But how one scrutinizes ideas depends a lot on the situation. It seems to me that in the *private* sphere, which the classroom largely is, one should be circumspect about how one says things. Treating other people's ideas with derision or contempt is likely to shut down thought rather than stimulate it, since people can easily become defensive. People's ideas and their identities may be too closely intertwined to enable the neat separation between ideas and people that Rushdie envisages. In a classroom, I don't think you can be "savagely rude" about someone's ideas without also being seen as being savagely rude to that person.

Rather than unilaterally making rules about what can be said, I decided to focus instead on establishing a good atmosphere so people felt respected as individuals and thought of the whole group as friends. In such situations, people are not likely to word their ideas in ways that gratuitously offend, such as making flat declarative statements: "That idea is stupid" or "You are wrong." People were also less likely to feel offended if their cherished beliefs were critiqued and found wanting, because they would credit the speaker with good intentions.

As part of creating a good atmosphere for free and frank discussions, we addressed the Rushdie quote in the context of the science-religion conflict we would be discussing. If someone thought (as some in the class did) that all religious faiths, or any specific religious faith, was irrational, could he or she say that without religious believers feeling they were being labeled as irrational? On the other hand, believing that religion is irrational is a perfectly legitimate point of view, so if the speaker feels constrained not to say such things because of the conventions of politeness, then he or she is effectively being censored and the range of views in the discussion becomes artificially narrowed, depriving all participants of a growth opportunity. My classes decided to try not to offend others or to be offended easily, while at the same time not to avoid expressing unpopular or unpalatable ideas. I was heartened when the class arrived at this consensus because it seems like a good rule to live life by.

Considerable time was spent during the first two weeks of the class creating conditions whereby students got to know each other. This involved having name "tents" in front of each student, taking digital photos and distributing a contact sheet of faces and first names to the class, doing lots of small-group activities early on where the composition of the groups was changed each time so each student got to know every other student in a more intimate setting, and providing opportunities to share personal information and interests so we got to know each other as people.

Perhaps the most important question we discussed right away was the nature of the seminar and what educational purpose it is meant to serve. Students sometimes do not realize that different forms of instruction are meant to serve different pedagogical purposes and that the seminar has very different learning goals from a lecture, laboratory, or workshop. They also tend sometimes to overvalue the knowledge of the instructor and undervalue their contributions and those of their fellow students.

In the very first class I asked them what the point was of students listening to each other. After all, as the faculty member, I was presumably "the expert," and surely I had read and thought about the seminar topic for much longer than they had. Why was their time not better spent listening to me or reading the assigned books and papers written by scholars in the field? What was the point of discussing with each other?

Of course, the students knew I believed there was great value in students sharing ideas with each other, so they set about trying to find the reasons. A useful resource for this discussion was an unpublished article, "The Seminar," by Michael Kahn (1974) that I had shared with them before the first class. This essay discusses a hierarchy of seminar forms: the *free-for-all* (where each student tries to "win" by advancing his or her own perspective and attacking others'); the *beauty contest* (where each person ignores others when they are speaking and instead spends that time polishing his or her own idea before presenting it); the *distinguished house tour* (where students listen to and admire the various ideas put forward without really engaging with them); and *barn raising* (where the group pools their knowledge and ideas and tries to come up with a common, shared understanding). The class recognized that if we wanted a friendly yet frank discussion with everyone involved, then we should avoid the free-for-all (which is closest to the Rushdie model) and aspire to the barn raising, although the other two forms also had their place.

I suggested that one reason for avoiding the free-for-all format was that if the seminar was seen as a forum in which one sought to prove that one view was superior to that of others, then people's energies were devoted to hiding the weaknesses and exaggerating the strengths of their own position, while at the same time ignoring or minimizing the strengths of other views and emphasizing their flaws. And worse still, when we are in such a defensive mode, we tend to avoid those people who we feel might disagree with us and seek out only those who agree.

I suggested that it was more helpful to view the purpose of the seminar as not to change minds but *to help each person better understand why he or she believes whatever he or she believes.* If we see the purpose of discussion this way, then other perspectives or alternative views are actually encouraged because they are very helpful in achieving this greater depth of understanding. It is now to one's advantage to *seek out* alternative arguments that challenge one's own beliefs and even to make those arguments stronger, because that deepens one's own understanding. If someone's views do happen to change as a result, that is incidental.

This purpose of the seminar seemed to be quite eye-opening to students who, perhaps due to the nature of popular public discourse, seemed to start out with the idea that there must be one right position out there and were nervous that their own view was not it. This way of thinking inevitably leads to the free-for-all model that equates seminar discussions with debates, with identifiable winners and losers.

The approach we adopted has helped to avoid sterile arguments about right and wrong, which often lead to repetitious arguments and defensiveness, and instead has fostered a more collegial approach, where openness to other viewpoints is the rule.

Another issue I had to consider was what kinds of difficulties students of faith would have. In my discussions with students, I noticed (and this was confirmed in the private journals students e-mail me every week in which they can say anything they wish) that the level of comfort students had in expressing their views on faith and religion depended on whether they could assume that others were already familiar with their views. The divide was not between those who believed in a god and those who did not, or even between different religious faiths per se, but rather between those who could assume their peers already knew what they believed and those who felt they had to explain their beliefs.

The ones who had the least difficulty were what I call "liberal Christians," those who believed in some tenets of Christianity but did not go into specifics about their essential beliefs and were willing to concede that many things in the Bible were metaphors. This seemed to give them the flexibility to accept scientific findings about the age of the universe, evolution, and the like without any difficulty. Such views are common in higher education circles, and such students had the least trouble talking about their faith. But at the same time, since they tended to move in like-minded circles where any difficulties tended to be resolved somewhat glibly, they had never before had to grapple with difficult questions concerning the science-religion conflict.

Those students with beliefs that could be considered minority views in the immediate community (Biblical literalists, atheists, Jews, Hindus, Muslims, and so on) had a harder time speaking, not because of any hostility to those views, but because they could not assume others knew much about their beliefs at all, let alone the relationship of those views to scientific knowledge. Hence, they had to add clarifying remarks and explanations for whatever they said, and one can see how this could be tedious and inhibiting.

As the seminar progressed to a deeper philosophical level, it posed challenges to students of all religious faiths, one of which was the notion of truth. Many students at my institution have the view that science sees itself as providing "true" knowledge. They are uncomfortable when scientific discoveries and theories contradict some tenet of religious faith, since this runs the risk of their faith being shown to be not true.

Those whose faith favors intelligent design, for example, would like to see it considered part of science and are not comfortable with the NAS tenet that seems to relegate it to the spiritual realm and thus outside of science. Others have a more limited goal for their religious beliefs, not seeking to make them part of science but merely wishing to reassure themselves that science does not rule them out.

People of faith also tend to be concerned that science is an inherently atheistic enterprise, thus forcing one to choose between being a scientist (or at least scientific in one's outlook) and being religious. Since many of my students seek to pursue science-related careers, this idea that science requires an atheistic worldview can be unsettling. The challenge I faced was how to discuss these issues frankly in such a way that students would not feel defensive about their beliefs or hostile and dismissive of science. The strategies I developed involved several interwoven strands. One arises from recognizing that sophomore students tend to be at somewhat low levels on King and Kitchener's (1994) scale of reflective judgment and have a tendency to view knowledge in dualistic true/false, either/or, and right/wrong terms. Hence, they might take the course thinking in terms of either science being right or religion being right. Alternatively, in their desire to avoid disagreement with others, they may adopt the relativistic view that all views on such topics are merely matters of opinion and no judgments can be made about the validity of any particular view. So one of my key goals was to try and find ways for them to develop more sophisticated and nuanced views of knowledge, to have them advance along the path of reflective judgment.

Another strand was to deepen their understanding of the nature, history, and philosophy of science, since students tend to have naïve conceptions about the nature of the scientific enterprise and what scientists really mean when they use such words as "laws" and "theories" and "truth," and the relationship of scientific knowledge to the external world.

The course readings of classic works by historians and philosophers of science (such as Pierre Duhem's *The Aim and Structure of Physical Theory* [1906], Karl Popper's *Conjectures and Refutations: The Growth of Scientific Knowledge* [1965], Thomas Kuhn's *The Structure of Scientific Revolutions* [1996], and Imre Lakatos's *The Methodology of Scientific Research Programmes* [1986]) made students recognize that the popular notion that science was inching ever closer to "the truth" and one day would squeeze religion out completely was not supported by the scholarly literature. Students began to realize that, while science evolved and progressed, producing more encompassing theories leading to spectacular successes in dealing with the world, there was no reason to think that this process was leading to "the truth," however one defined that philosophically slippery concept. The evolution of scientific theories seemed to have an almost perfect parallel with biological evolution in that while organisms evolve and become more sophisticated, there is no reason to think that the current species were *destined* to appear out of the primeval soup. There are no archetypal "true" forms of life that each species is evolving toward.

While this knowledge seemed to reassure religious students that scientific advances need not eventually squeeze out their particular religious beliefs, some had difficulty with the requirement that scientists practice *methodological naturalism*, postulating and testing one *natural* cause after another until a problem is solved. Appeals to a supernatural agent to explain phenomena are not allowed in science, since such hypotheses necessarily shut down further research. This explains why the community of scientists does not consider intelligent design to be a viable "scientific" theory.

It was not hard for students to see this as a reasonable requirement. After all, if our car developed a strange and disturbing noise and we took it to a mechanic to diagnose, and if, after trying out just one or two ideas and failing, the mechanic threw up her hands and said the cause must be something mysterious and inexplicable, we would very likely switch to another mechanic. We would do the same thing with a plumber trying to find the source of a leak or a doctor trying to find the cause of an acute pain. If any one of them told us the cause was some supernatural power, we would quickly dump that person and find someone new, even if we ourselves were religious and we preferred to have religious people as our mechanics and plumbers and doctors. We want each of these people to keep investigating, to try and find a *physical* reason for the problem and not give up until they have solved it. We expect them to practice methodological naturalism as part of their work, and the same logic applies to scientists.

However, *philosophical naturalism*, the belief that the natural world is all there is and there is nothing more, is not a necessary requirement to be a practicing scientist. Many scientists undoubtedly *choose* to be philosophical naturalists (and thus atheists) because they see no need to have a god as part of their philosophical framework while others reject that option and remain religious. But this is purely a *personal* choice made by individual scientists and it has no impact on how they do science, which only involves using methodological naturalism. There is no requirement in science that one *must* be a philosophical naturalist, and scientists don't really care if their colleagues are religious or not since this does not affect how the community evaluates their work.

In the end, the class seemed to have little difficulty understanding that adoption of a scientific paradigm, which represents an overwhelming consensus judgment by the scientific community, was often the result of a long and complex process. In arriving at that judgment, scientists had to weigh many factors, including evidence and reasoning (Lakatos, 1986).

The students similarly realized that there was no simple and unambiguous answer to the question of whether religious faith was compatible with a scientific outlook (Laudan, 1983). While that understanding may have come as a relief to those who feared that it was not, it also meant the onus was now on them to make a judgment about compatibility. Doing so required them to function at high levels of King and Kitchener's (1994) reflective judgment scale, and this, rather than their adopting any particular point of view, was the ultimate goal of my course.

The notion that the goal of the seminar is not to change people's minds may be unpalatable to some. After all, isn't the goal of any course to teach people something? And doesn't teaching something necessarily imply that the students have a different understanding of the subject at the end of the course from the one they had at the beginning?

My response to such concerns is that I believe strong belief structures (such as religious faith) are developed early in life, reinforced over many years, and rooted in powerful emotions. Such beliefs can and do change, but usually over a long period as a result of people mulling things over in their minds, hearing different points of view, raising questions about their own beliefs, attempting to reconcile contradictions, and trying to integrate their beliefs from a variety of areas into a coherent and comprehensive worldview. Factors causing eventual change could be things you read, deep discussions with friends, and personal experiences of some import. Over time these things lodge in your consciousness, and, as your mind tries to integrate them into a coherent framework, your views start to shift.

This kind of activity cannot be forced; to try and push change on someone who has a strong attachment to a belief is to encourage that person to build a shield around himself or herself and actually avoid the kind of contemplative action required for real growth and development. So while my goal of getting students to better understand why they believe what they believe may seem limited, the process of getting there opens up a way of thinking that I hope will last them all their lives. As a result some will change their particular views later in life, others will not. My goal is not to change their views but to change the way they think about the world and provide them with the tools for self-reflection.

When I look at how my own views have developed, I know some of them have changed so much that they are now diametrically opposed to the ones I had before. But the interesting thing is that, although I know my views have changed, I cannot tell you exactly *when* they changed or *why*. Dramatic epiphanies are rare; the process is more like being on an ocean liner that is turning around. The process is so gentle you are not aware that it is even happening, but at some point you realize you are facing in a different direction. That moment of recognition, however, is just an explicit acknowledgment of something that has already happened.

All of us, as part of our lives, accumulate a rich storehouse of experiences. My seminar is meant to provide students with knowledge and a framework to better understand and analyze those experiences so they are more open to move in new directions. That may be the most useful lesson I teach them.

References

Bartlett, T. (2005, April 22). Most freshmen say religion guides them. *Chronicle of Higher Education, 51*(33), A1.

Bransford, J. D., Brown, A. L., & Cocking, R. R. (Eds.). (1999). *How people learn.* Washington DC: National Academy Press.

Duhem, P. (1906). Physical theory and experiment. In P. Wiener (Transl.), *The aim and structure of physical theory* (chap. VI). Princeton, NJ: Princeton University Press (1954). In S. G. Harding (Ed.), 1976. *Can theories be refuted?* (pp. 1–40). Boston: Dordrecht-Holland Reidel.

Kahn, M. (1974). *The seminar.* Retrieved March 9, 2007, from http://www.ca se.edu/provost/UCITE/articles/seminar.htm

Kahn, M. (1981, Spring). The seminar: An experiment in humanistic education. *Journal of Humanistic Psychology, 21*(2), 119–127.

King, P., & Kitchener, K. S. (1994). *Developing reflective judgment.* San Francisco: Jossey-Bass.

Kuhn, T. S. (1996). *The structure of scientific revolutions.* Chicago, IL: University of Chicago Press.

Lakatos, I. (1986). Falsification and the methodology of scientific research programs. In J. Worrall and G. Currie (Eds.), *Methodology of scientific research programmes* (pp. 8–101). Cambridge, UK: Cambridge University Press.

Laudan, L. (1983). The demise of the demarcation problem. In R. S. Cohen & L. Laudan (Eds.), *Physics, philosophy, and psychoanalysis* (pp. 111–127). Boston: Dordrecht-Holland Reidel.

National Academy of Science (NAS) Committee on Science and Creationism. (1984). *Science and creationism: A view from the National Academy of Sciences.* Washington DC: National Academy Press.

Popper, K. R. (1965). Science: Conjectures and refutations. In K. R. Popper, *Conjectures and refutations: The growth of scientific knowledge* (pp. 33–65). New York: Harper Torchbooks.

Rushdie, S. (2005, July 2). Defend the right to be offended. *OpenDemocracy.* Retrieved March 9, 2007, from http://www.opendemocracy.net/faith-europe_islam/article_2331.jsp

Singham, M. (2000). *Quest for truth: Scientific progress and religious beliefs.* Bloomington, IN: Phi Delta Kappa Educational Foundation.

Singham, M. (2005). Moving away from an authoritarian classroom. *Change, 37*(3), 50–57.

11

TEACHING SECULAR BIBLE READING TO RELIGIOUSLY COMMITTED STUDENTS

Roger G. Baker

I generally don't sense that students in my Bible as Literature class are religiously challenged by the course until about five minutes after I take roll on the first day. The challenge comes as I start a cursory review of the syllabus and mention in passing that the course will consider the mythic narratives of the Bible. I say, "myth," and students hear "untrue." I say that our experience requires the support of mythic symbols, and they check to see what other courses fill the humanities general education requirement at both Snow College, a state college in Utah, and Brigham Young University, a church-sponsored university in Provo, Utah. I say that the Bible is part of our cultural DNA, and they double-check that they aren't in some philosophy of science course. And in the backs of some minds are fears that they may have discovered secular humanism in a course on the Bible.

I respect the students I've taught at a public college and at a Latter-day Saint university and their often literal Bible reading. I sometimes read literally with them, but although my evidence is anecdotal and involves only 35-plus years of experience, I think students seem to have moved to more conservative religious beliefs and to a more literal reading of the Bible. Students at both public and private schools seem to come to the class with a

Note: Some of the material in this chapter was first published in Baker, 2002; this text, written for public school English teachers, is now out of print.

reverence for the Bible that sits on the border of literal reading and bibliola-try. They worship the Bible and find answers in its words.

Since anecdotal evidence doesn't hold up well in the academy, perhaps I can state only what I know for sure. Most of my students are more religiously conservative than I was when I was sitting in their places. After all, my high school graduation date was in the early 1960s, and in my college days, we talked about relevance and Vietnam and weren't inclined to trust anyone over 30, or was that 40 or 50?

I do know that if my classes are typical, students come with strong reli-gious beliefs. If my students mirror the general population the Gallup Orga-nization (2006) surveyed in May 2006, 84% of them say that religion in their own life is important. Not only is religion important to those surveyed, 62% "believe that religion can answer all or most of today's problems." More specific to my classes in Bible as Literature is this finding from the Barna Group's latest annual survey: "In 2005 45% of all adults agreed strongly that the Bible is totally accurate in all of its teaching" (2006). The Barna survey notes that this represents a 10% increase since 1991. More people believe in the inerrancy of the Bible now than did a decade ago, and this has important implications for the way I teach.

Recent data on college students suggest they do mirror the general popu-lation. Although research method and data reporting make comparisons with the Gallup survey difficult, the recent work of the Higher Education Research Institute (HERI) at the University of California, Los Angeles (UCLA), indicate that 80% of the students who come to our classes "have an interest in spirituality" and 81% "attend religious services occasionally or frequently" (Astin & Astin, 2003, p. 5). And although the same study sur-veyed more than 40,000 faculty to discover that 81% of the faculty describe themselves as "a spiritual person," one often wonders if faculty and students are really on the same page with their definition of "spiritual" (Astin & Astin, 2004, p. 3).

Perhaps the most important bit of information for college teachers in the available data is that, for the most part, strongly religious students are tolerant of other religious beliefs and practices.

Despite strong religious commitment, students also demonstrate a high level of religious tolerance and acceptance. For example, most students agree that "non-religious people can lead lives that are just as moral as

those of religious believers" (83%) and that "most people can grow spiritually without being religious" (64%). Similarly, nearly two-thirds disagree
with the proposition that "people who don't believe in God will be pun-
ished" (Astin & Astin, 2003, p. 4).

Since most students at least express religious tolerance, an appeal to the best
instincts of these students can defuse many religious controversies and challenges in the classroom.

I have affection for the students who struggle and I don't want to be a
professorial iconoclast who breaks their often fragile images, images that still
want the refiner's fire of study and experience. Although good scholarship
requires that those who study willingly ask any question about any text,
being a teacher requires that the teacher only break an image that can be
replaced with something better, and I am often in no position to replace
what I could easily tear down.

A reading of *Matthew* 12:43–45 and *Luke* 11:24–26 may make my point.
In my personal reading of these Bible passages, I discover that when an evil
spirit is driven out of a person and there is nothing to replace it, seven other
spirits more wicked than the first enter in and dwell there. A bad idea driven
out of a student by professorial force and not replaced may spawn seven
more ideas worse than the first to take its place. Since I'm in no position
to replace religious beliefs, I must be cautious about casting out beliefs not
underpinned by rigorous scholarship. The best I can do is to provide knowledge that students may use to modify their very personal beliefs.

Perhaps a more modest goal than driving out bad ideas is to help students recognize new ways of looking for answers by reading the Bible text
closely. As they look, they may come to understand that mythic knowledge
is a matter of recognition. In a sense, we already know but do not realize it
without the help of myth. Then we say, "That's it. That explains it for me."

When I say "myth" on this first day of class, I am talking about something beyond verifiable truth. Myth is a way of reading that I use to explain
what I believe. Historicity is not as important. "Why is there sin in the
world?" For some the answer is in *Genesis*. It isn't in *Genesis* as a theological
discourse on sin, and it isn't there as an eyewitness account of events in 4004
BCE. The answers are there because *Genesis* is mythic literature.

It is at this point that I catch another glimpse behind the eyes. "Do I
really need this class?" Only a few are brave enough to confront me; that's a

shame. I enjoy the visits of those few students who want to look me in the eye across the desk and ask. Some will seek refuge in their religion, where good people will patiently answer questions and will sometimes call me to discover what I really said in class.

The most terrible consequence of my use of the "m" word is for the student who mentally capitulates and thinks, "Another class where I just have to put down what the teacher wants and hold my own belief and knowledge inside. Saying what I think will only penalize me in the class and open what I believe to ridicule and challenge by someone who could obviously clobber my true ideas with the weight of a grade and a PhD in secular humanism." The answer to this student is that course capitulation is the lie, not the myth.

I try to say "myth" with some reverence. It is the *summon bonum*, the highest good. How else could I explain the most personal and sacred of beliefs? Science and history, with reliance on the foundation of the verifiable, isn't enough. We need myth reading because it does what Elie Wiesel says it should do in the parable preface of *The Gates of the Forest* (1966).

> When the great Rabbi Israel Ball Shem-Tov saw misfortune threatening the Jews it was his custom to go into a certain part of the forest to meditate. There he would light a fire, say a special prayer, and the miracle would be accomplished and the misfortune averted.
>
> Later, when his disciple, the celebrated Magid of Mezritch, had occasion, for the same reason, to intercede with heaven, he would go to the same place in the forest and say: "Master of the Universe, listen! I do not know how to light the fire, but I am still able to say the prayer." And again the miracle would be accomplished.
>
> Still later, Rabbi Moshe-Leib of Sasov, in order to save his people once more, would go into the forest and say: "I do not know how to light the fire, I do not know the prayer, but I know the place and this must be sufficient." It was sufficient and the miracle was accomplished.
>
> Then it fell to Rabbi Israel of Rizhyn to overcome misfortune. Sitting in his armchair, his head in his hands, he spoke to God: "I am unable to light the fire and I do not know the prayer; I cannot even find the place in the forest. All I can do is to tell the story, and this must be sufficient." And it was sufficient. (pp. 1–3)

Maybe those of us who have forgotten how to call down the fire of Elijah to destroy false gods can read the stories together and that will be sufficient.

As I invite students to read with me, central points seem to defuse religious confrontations. Perhaps they can help a student navigate a sacred text in an academic context. The first point is that there are many kinds of writing in the Bible. The second is that there are many ways of reading these different kinds of writing.

Five Kinds of Writing in the Bible

This may seem pedestrian to the professor, but it helps if students understand that there are at least five kinds of writing in the Bible and that Bible as literature is mostly concerned with two of the kinds (Ryken, 1984). This shouldn't be too surprising to students since the Bible is not really a book, but a library of many books. In fact, the Bible is one of the few volumes in the world that really has no title. The word "Bible" is not a title. This word is a transliteration of *biblia*. The word means books.

Religious Writing

This writing is sometimes called doctrine, theology, or belief. It is this kind of writing people read when they want to know what the Bible teaches them to *believe* and it is usually read in a religious context. This is the kind of reading people do when they ask questions about grace, faith, redemption, or justice and mercy and other abstracts. It is not the emphasis of literature classes. This kind of reading is often prooftext reading. Proofs of doctrine or belief are found by verse mining and context is often ignored.

- Faith—Chapter 11 of *Hebrews* is an example of theological discourse. It defines faith and then supports the definition with reference to Biblical narrative. This passage is not a poem and tells no story.
- Grace—*Ephesians* 2:1–10 is a discourse on the relationship of grace and faith.
- Charity/Love—Even though *I Corinthians* 13 is poetic, it is not a poem but a lecture or speech on charity or love.

Legal Writing

The laws are read by those asking what they should *do*. Sometimes called commandments, the laws provide context for our study of literature but are not the focus of study in Bible as literature.

- The laws concerning uncleanness are in chapters 11–15 of *Leviticus*.
- Ten Commandments—*Exodus* 20 is a familiar example of law.

Historical Writing

This writing is concerned with such facts as genealogy, places, events, and data like census records. It includes long lists of begats. There is a lot of begatting in the good book. Sometimes history reads like a story but has a goal quite different from imaginative literature.

- Genealogy—*Genesis* 10 is the record of Noah's sons and their families.
- History—The books of *Kings* have a historical tone. Although some of the narratives read like short stories, chapters 15 and 16 of *II Kings* read more like history texts.

Poetic Literature

Poetic writing is characterized by parallel form and is most obvious in the *Psalms*. It is also characterized by the images it helps us see.

Psalm 23 is perhaps the most translated passage in the Hebrew Bible. It is easy to teach simile and metaphor with the images of the *Psalms*. The list of poetic symbols in Psalm 23 is rich; there is a shepherd, green pastures, still waters, and oil. This is Bible as literature; it speaks to the imagination.

Narrative Literature

This writing tells a story that speaks to the imagination. One of the characteristics of Biblical literature is understatement, which Robert Alter* calls the art of biblical reticence (1981, pp. 116, 163). This literature may be poetic and contain historical, legal, or religious writing, but it is also pleasurable for its own sake because it allows us to see images that we make in part for ourselves.

The story of Ehud in *Judges* 3:12–30 and the story of Susanna in the *Apocrypha* are places to start that can defuse some students' reluctance. There seems to be no contentious point of religious dogma in either narrative that can get in the way of a terrific short story. Susanna is clearly in the mainstream of Western culture and makes a good narrative for an introduction to

---

*Two books that qualify as classics are both by the same author: Alter, 1981, 1985; they are good resources for faculty and students.

Biblical literature. Somehow, the *Apocrypha* carries far less modern baggage than the canonized Bible.

Ways of Reading the Bible

The most important issue for students to consider in dealing with sensitive religious issues in the Bible is the notion that there are many ways to read the imaginative text. The ways of reading are even beyond the usual considered in most university English programs, since the Bible, for most, is literature in translation. First, an example of the translation issues and then an introduction to ways of reading this literature in translation may defuse religious confrontations in the classroom.

Translating the Ancient Text

What is proposed is not new. Bible scholars frequently compare Bible translations. The value of these comparisons is an argument for allowing/encouraging multiple Bible translations in the classroom. We all read through different templates anyway; why not allow translation to influence the template?

The variant translations of biblical texts offer a way to teach critical thinking and religious tolerance. This critical thinking is what many would call close reading, and Bible texts from various translations help teach this skill. The goal is modest. I want students to read carefully as they have a personal dialogue with the narrative.

A modest beginning in comparing variant Bible texts is to point out to students the use of italics in the King James, or Authorized, Version (KJV) of the Bible. Words are in italics to identify a translation issue. In fact, some italicized words can turn the meaning of some passages.

Perhaps an example of italics that do matter is in order for students to get the point and start to read critically. "And there was again a battle in Gob with the Philistines, where Elhanan the son of Jaare-oregim, a Bethlehemite, slew *the brother of* Goliath the Gittite, the staff of whose spear *was* like a weaver's beam" (2 *Samuel* 21:19). In at least five modern translations, "the brother of" is omitted. The italics in the KJV indicate that the translators had to add these words to give David the credit for killing Goliath. The translators may have been on safe ground here because their correction makes the passage agree with both tradition and *1 Chronicles* 20:5.

A note from the Bible Dictionary bound with many editions of the King James Version of the Bible explains the use of italics:

> In the King James Version italics identify words that are necessary in English to round out and complete the sense of a phrase, but were not present in the Hebrew or Greek text of the manuscript used. Such additions were necessary because in some instances, the manuscript was inadequate, and the translators felt obliged to clarify it in the translation. In other instances, italics were necessary in cases where the grammatical construction of English called for the use of words that were not needed to make the same thought in Hebrew or Greek. Italics thus represent the willingness of the translators to identify these areas. (Italics, 1979, p. 708)

There is something else interesting in the Bible Dictionary explanation of the use of italics; it refers to Hebrew and Greek manuscripts. A similar reference is made on the title page of the Christian New Testament. Teachers can at least point out the obvious to students that the title page says that the New Testament was translated from the "original Greek." Was Greek really the original? Was Greek the language of Jesus Christ and his disciples? Was Greek the language of the synagogue where the early apostles preached? The point is that what is claimed as the "original Greek" may be a translation of the original spoken words. Since the New Testament was an oral text long before it was a written text, the original language was probably not today's Greek.

The note from the dictionary makes another point. There are grammar challenges in translations. We are used to thinking in English, which means that we think in a three-dimensional time system of past, present, and future. This way of thinking is an artifact that can't be separated from our language. The challenge is what to do when we read or translate into a different way of thinking based on a different language. The Hebrew verb system allows for the *complete* and the *incomplete*. It is more two-dimensional.

Students know that the old idioms are long gone when I share a Biblical example: In *Judges* 3:24, the servants of Ehud are wondering why he is so long in his parlour:

> "Surely he covereth his feet in his summer chamber."

And what means "covereth his feet?"
I'll get right to the point. He was defecating.

"I'm sorry I asked."

There are other language points students ought to know before becoming close readers. In the second chapter of Genesis, the common word *da'at*, a cognate form of the verb *yada*, has three meanings: to know, to understand, and to have carnal relations with. Is it any wonder that translation is difficult? Instead of Eskimos who have a dozen words for snow (this isn't exactly true, but the example holds), we have Hebrew writers who have one cognate with three meanings. Gerald Hammond (1987) makes this point in his essay, "English Translations of the Bible." Hammond takes an uncommon word, *khiydah,* and finds eight different contexts for it (p. 653).

In these contexts, there are five different translations of the same word in the KJV. Reading these passages with the class offers an opportunity to ask about context. Is each translation good in its particular context?

> *Ezekiel* 17:2, *Judges* 14:12–17 = *riddle*
> *Proverbs* 1:6, *Psalms* 49:5, 78:2 = *dark saying*
> *Habakkuk* 2:6 = *taunting proverb*
> *Daniel* 8:23 = *dark sentence*
> *I Kings* 10:1 = *hard question*

Each translation does make a literary difference. A *riddle* may or may not be a *dark saying*. A *taunting proverb* is surely something different from a *hard question*. The different translations of *khiydah* may or may not make a theological difference to those who may read the Bible as prooftext, but the literary difference is profound. It is in fact the less dramatic and subtle difference that makes the literature interesting. It is the subtle difference between a *dark saying* and a *dark sentence* that speaks to our imagination more than the dramatic difference between a *taunting proverb* and a *hard question*.

It may make the point to look at a poetic difference. The following is the Hebrew text of a familiar passage from the *Biblia Hebraica Stuttgartensia*, commonly known as the Stuttgart Bible. The passage is *Genesis* 1:4:

וַיַּרְא אֱלֹהִים אֶת־הָאוֹר כִּי־טוֹב

that-good   the-light   ***   God   and-saw

I explain to students that the dots and dashes tell us the vowel sounds. The oldest Hebrew texts show no vowel sounds, so the reader had to know the sounds without visual cues. A commonly accepted way of indicating vowel sounds didn't come into use until about 900 CE. I ask students to write their names without vowels, then try to pronounce them, and they see the translation difficulty. The three asterisks represent the sign of the definite article.

I am certainly not the first to notice the differences in this passage. There is a very good analysis using this example in Hammond's "English Translations of the Bible" (1987, p. 647). His essay is in *The Literary Guide to the Bible* edited by Robert Alter and Frank Kermode. Turning the text in the familiar left to right direction and adding the literal translation, we find the following:

vayar	elohim	et-ha'or	ki-tov
and-saw	God	the light	that-good

And the translations follow:

KJV—And God saw the light, that *it was* good.
NRSV—And God saw that the light was good;
REB—And God saw the light was good,
NAB—God saw how good the light was.
NJB—God saw that light was good,
NEB—And God saw that the light was good.

When I ask students if there are differences, subtle or obvious, in the translations, they usually tell me that the KJV (King James Version) seems more poetic. They notice a certain familiar rhythm on each side of the comma since it is the only translation with this punctuation mark. They notice that the King James translation seems to make God the principal actor. Somehow, He sees to it that light is good. In other versions, He seems to notice that it is good. The NJB (New Jerusalem Bible) has the most passive God, who notices that "light was good." The NAB (New American Bible) translators seem to assume that there must be degrees of goodness by writing, "God saw how good the light was." Students wonder aloud if there is somewhat good light, good light, and awesome light.

Many versions are not translations from ancient or any other manuscripts; they are revisions. Some are revised to clarify particular sectarian doctrine. Others try to put the Bible in modern language. In the preface to the 1993 edition of *Black Bible Chronicles*, Andrew Young makes this argument:

The *Black Bible Chronicles* is an attempt to put the most important message of life into the language of the streets. This is in keeping with the very origins of the Bible. The New Testament was originally written in Koine Greek, the street language of the people. Subsequently, Martin Luther and others translated the Bible into the language of the people of their day. The *Black Bible Chronicles* stands in this tradition, bringing the Word to our younger generation in contemporary language. This book seeks to reach many of our young people for whom the traditional language of faith has lost the power to bring them in touch with their God. The *Black Bible Chronicles* attempts to express a faith which addresses the deepest longings of our younger generation for hope, love, and an encouraging vision of the future. (1993, pp. v–vi)

The notation on the title page of *Black Bible Chronicles* indicates that P. K. McCary is "interpreter." Significantly, it is not a translation. The results are interesting and students enjoy them. The passage from *Genesis* that was compared above reads: "And the Almighty liked what He saw and let the light hang out a while before it was dark again."

Translation does make a difference for the literary reader, but the difference isn't in doctrine, liturgy, or dogma. The difference the translation makes is in the images we see. Literature is writing that speaks to our imagination. The best analogy may be to the visual arts or to music. Because there are no words to express some ideas and emotions, artists paint and composers write music. However, some who have nearly inexpressible ideas can't paint or compose music: they write literature. They write stories and poems that speak to us in images, like music and pictures do.

When we read that God divided the light from the darkness, each of us sees an image that is ours alone. I can't explain my image of the awesome division of the light. It is in the literature that speaks to my imagination. Because it is somehow in the literature and in me, I see it as an image. The passage doesn't say how, or it would be a didactic textbook. It doesn't say why, or it would be theology. It just is. The light was divided from the darkness and God saw that it was good. I see it because it's literature.

Students may also have personal images of Biblical narratives, so I allow them to bring whatever translation they wish to class. If students don't have a favorite translation, I suggest the KJV for literary readers with a good vocabulary. Students who need a modern language translation will enjoy the *Oxford Study Bible*, which uses the Revised English Bible and has excellent footnotes. The New Revised Standard Version continues the lineage of the King James Version with more modern language and is a good choice; it is published as *The New Oxford Annotated Bible*. If recent is better, the NRSV is a good choice because it footnotes with the Dead Sea Scrolls.

Whatever choice is made, don't make the mistake of suggesting that students rent a cheap motel and steal the Gideon Bible (a King James Version). I did this at Snow College and received a present the following week from the Snow College Forensics Team. The team had a speech meet on the weekend and stayed at the Salt Lake Marriott. Team members returned with a gift of 23 Gideon Bibles and a serious question: "Is it a sin to steal a Bible?"

Over the years I have found that asking students to compare translations of particular Bible passages teaches close reading and builds bridges of understanding that defuse some religious issues. Students become critical readers when the meaning of a sentence can shift dramatically with the change of just one word.

Reading the Text

Instead of starting at the very beginning, whenever that was, the Middle Ages is a starting point for a brief introduction to the ways of reading. A verse that may have originated in the days of Augustine and was around in the 16th century has become a mantra in describing ways of reading the Bible:

> *Littera gesta docet, quid credas allegoria,*
> *Moralis quid agas, quo tendas anagogia.*

A translation that tries to honor the literary and theological intent of the poem is as follows:

> The letter shows us what Gad and our fathers did;
> The allegory shows us where our faith is hid;
> The moral meaning gives us rules of daily life;
> The anagogy shows us where we end our strife.

Now the class discussion can shift to ways of reading that include four perspectives. The classic example is *Galatians* 4:22. "Here 'Jerusalem' can be understood in four different ways. Historically it means the city of the Jews; allegorically it signifies the church of Christ; anagogically it points to that heavenly city which is the mother of us all; and tropologically (or morally) it indicates the human soul" (Grant & Tracy, 1985, p. 85).

The Venerable Bede elaborated on the uses the Jerusalem Temple to illustrate these four modes of interpretation: According to historical fact, the temple of the Lord is the house that Solomon built; allegorically, it is the body of the Lord, about which He said, "Destroy this temple and in three days I will raise it up" (*John* 2:19). It is His church, which was addressed as follows: "For the temple of God is holy, and such are you" (*1 Corinthians* 3: 17). Through the tropological interpretation, it signifies one of the loyal men, who are addressed as follows: "Do you not know that you are the temple of God and that the spirit of God dwells within you?" (*1 Corinthians* 3:16). Through the anagogical interpretation, it signifies the joys of the heavenly dwelling for which that man longed who said, "Blessed are they that dwell in your house; they will be still praising you" (*Psalms* 84:4; Grant & Tracy, 1985, p. 85).

Discussing the ways of reading the Bible could occupy an entire course when one considers the 13 "Modern Methods in Studying the Bible" proposed by Matthews and Moyer (2005). They include the following in their introduction: Textual Criticism, Historical Criticism, Source Criticism, Literary Criticism, Narrative Criticism, Form Criticism, Redaction Criticism, Canonical Criticism, Social-Scientific Criticism, Feminist Criticism, Reader Response Criticism, Rhetorical Criticism, and Tradition Criticism. Wow! And I suppose we could add Marxist reading, Psychoanalytic reading, and Deconstruction and. . . . Students soon get the point in spite of anachronistic historical reference. There are many ways of reading.

I often conclude the discussion of ways of reading the Bible with a citation from Robert Nash (1999). I use his words because the class and I can look at his text together instead of the class looking at my text or idea and my vested interest:

> Take the gospel of John in the New Testament. *This gospel is actually 5 different texts.* Text 1 is the gospel John thought he was writing. This is the *author's text.* Text 2 is the gospel each one of you thinks John wrote. This is the *individual reader's text.* Text 3 is the gospel that John actually wrote. This is the *objective text.* Text 4 is the gospel that each one of you is "writing" as you interpret this gospel from your own cultural and historical context. This is the *hermeneutical text-in-process.* And text 5 is the gospel you

and I might be able to agree on as the gospel that John intended to write. This is the *consensus text.*

None of us can ever know with any degree of certainty the truth of text 1, because we do not know what was in John's mind while he was writing. Neither can we ever fully capture text 3, because there is no such thing as an "immaculate reception" of a text, absolutely devoid of a reader's, or writer's, presuppositions. In fact, to speak of an "objective" text makes no sense at all, because without "subjects" to read and interpret the text, the text has no inherent meaning. The only texts worth studying, then, are text 2, text 4, and text 5; and while text 5 is certainly worth pursuing, universal consensus on *all* meanings in any text is virtually unachievable. Thus, we are left only with text 2 and text 4 as texts to analyze, and because these texts are always subject to very personal readings and commentaries, then, in a real sense, when we study the gospel of John, we are really studying ourselves. (p. 52)

Granted, this citation can raise as much dust as it settles for teachers and students trying to get past the emotion of belief in a Bible as literature course, but at the end of the day, students are at least inclined to admit that there are many ways to read the Bible, and the course can safely proceed on that assumption.

And there is some pleasure at the end of the course as some students seem to get it and use new phrases, such as "in the world of an author this could mean that . . ." or "I think we need to consider the context here." The new questions are wonderful: "Could that be allegorical? Is some modern meaning of the symbol hiding the author's possible intent? How have other translators rendered this text? Is it possible that this passage is part of a poem?" None of these questions requires that students alter some fundamental belief. In fact, the opposite is true. Students who understand there are many ways to read the Bible can find personal belief strengthened and broadened. At the least, there is strong evidence that students are willing to let the Bible narratives speak to their imaginations, and that is what good literature does.

References

Alter, Robert. (1981). *The art of Biblical narrative.* New York: Basic Books.
Alter, Robert. (1985). *The art of Biblical poetry.* New York: Basic Books.

Astin, John A., & Astin, Helen. (2003). *Spirituality in higher education: A national study of college students' search for meaning and purpose*. Higher Education Research Institute. Retrieved October 28, 2007, from http://www.spirituality .ucla.edu/spirituality/reports/FINAL_REPORT.pdf

Astin, John A., & Astin, Helen. (2004). *Spirituality and the professoriate*. Higher Education Research Institute. Retrieved March 10, 2007, from http://www.spiritu ality.ucla.edu/results/spirit_professoriate.pdf

Baker, Roger G. (2002). *Teaching the Bible as literature*. Norwood, MA: Christopher Gordon Publishers.

The Barna Group. (2006). *The Bible*. Retrieved March 10, 2007, from http://www .barna.org/FlexPage.aspx?Page = Topic&TopicID = 7

The Gallup Organization. (2006, June). *Religion*. Retrieved March 10, 2007, from http://poll.gallup.com/content/default.aspx?ci = 1690

Grant, Robert M., & Tracy, David. (1985). *A short history of the interpretation of the Bible*. Philadelphia, PA: Fortress.

Hammond, Gerald. (1987). English translations of the Bible. In Robert Alter and Frank Kermode (Eds.), *The literary guide to the Bible* (pp. 647–665). Cambridge, MA: Harvard University Press.

Italics. (1979). In *Bible Dictionary* (p. 708). Salt Lake City, Utah: Church of Jesus Christ of Latter-day Saints.

Matthews, Victor H., & Moyer, James C. (2005). *The old testament, text and context* (2nd ed.). Peabody, MA: Hendrickson.

McCary, P. K. (1993). *Black Bible chronicles: A survival manual for the streets*. New York: African American Family Press.

Nash, Robert J. (1999). *Faith, hype, and clarity: Teaching about religion in American schools and colleges*. New York: Teachers College Press.

Ryken, Leland. (1984). *How to read the Bible as literature*. Grand Rapids, MI: Zondervon.

Wiesel, Elie. (1966). *The gates of the forest* (Frances Frenaye, Trans.). New York: Holt, Rinehart and Winston.

Young, Andrew. (1993). Preface. In P. K. McCrary, *Black Bible chronicles: A survival manual for the streets*. New York: African American Family Press.

12

THE ROLE OF RELIGION AND SPIRITUALITY IN THE LAW SCHOOL CLASSROOM

David Hall

S ince I first began teaching law over 27 years ago I have seen a dramatic change in the ways that values morality and other interdisciplinary subjects are addressed in the classroom. Legal educators have come to grips with the sobering reality that systematically interjecting nonlegal perspectives enhances the study of law. Yet, when it comes to the sensitive topics of religion and spirituality, the change has not been as dramatic. Though various law professors have written extensively about the intersection of law and religion, this scholarship is generally a doctrinal analysis of the cases surrounding the separation of church and state. There has been no systematic attempt to make discussions of religion and spirituality, especially from a personal perspective, an integral part of the law school curriculum. Therefore law professors, who attempt this exploration, are going against the current and are swimming in some very dangerous and uncharted waters. The waters are filled with concerns that we may be using the classroom to proselytize our religious beliefs or to raise perspectives that don't pass the test of scientific rigor. Despite these fears, we swim just the same.

We swim because we believe a value is overlooked when we ignore this rich part of the human experience. We swim in these waters because, as lawyers face the unfolding of the 21st century, we face it with our vision encumbered by the blinders of the 20th century. The depersonalized and sometimes amoral approach to teaching law has produced too many lawyers who are estranged from their clients, themselves, and the deeper calling behind this sacred craft. So the need for a personal and intense exploration of religion and spirituality is not just a theoretical exploration, but a cry for help. There have been numerous calls for revitalizing or renewing the legal profession, and some of us believe religion and spirituality can contribute to this regenerative process.

The place where I have chosen to make this exploration more explicit is Professional Responsibility, which I teach at a private, nonsectarian university in Boston. Professional Responsibility is a required course in law school, offered to students in their second or third year. It is one of the few, if not the only, required courses in the upper level of the law school curriculum. This chapter explores the role religion and spirituality can play in a course on professional responsibility in the law school context. Though numerous law professors are attempting to interject religion and spirituality into the classroom, I am not aware of this perspective being applied to professional responsibility. Professional graduate education is a classic educational structure that strongly endorses the rules of the profession that provide the moral basis for the work. The American Bar Association's (ABA) Model Rules of Professional Conduct (Morgan & Rotunda, 2007) are a prime example of how the legal profession has defined its moral boundaries and constructed what it believes is a sufficient foundation for the ethical practice of law. However, these rules have proven insufficient in addressing some of the critical challenges of meaning, civility, and personal wholeness. Numerous studies have documented the high degree of depression, alcohol abuse (Cushman, 1989; Hennessey, 1984; Huie & Spilis, 1992), and professional dissatisfaction among lawyers (Fisk, 1990; Schlitz, 1999). Therefore various legal scholars are beginning to explore other nontraditional sources as aids for addressing this crisis within the profession.

For the last three years I have been teaching professional responsibility from a spiritual perspective. The catalyst for this endeavor was publishing my first book, *The Spiritual Revitalization of the Legal Profession: A Search for Sacred Rivers* (Hall, 2005). This book has created a framework for a more systematic exploration of the role religion and spirituality serve in student's lives and their vision of the legal profession. I have been able to apply some of my theories and insights to a concrete subject that I teach regularly. I have faced numerous theoretical and practical challenges in attempting to use spirituality as the framework for a required course in the law school curriculum. In addressing these challenges, I have gained a deeper understanding of the subject matter and of myself.

Definition, Framework, and Educational Goals

I explicitly chose to use the term *spirituality* instead of religion as the overarching conceptual framework to explore religion in the classroom setting. I chose not to use the label of religion as the backdrop for the course because I felt it would be too exclusive, and I could reach the same educational goal with a more inclusive construct. This created another challenge: developing a working definition of spirituality that was meaningful and inclusive. I define spirituality as consisting of two related concepts. The first is a sincere commitment on the part of individuals to live their lives in accordance with the highest values that are humanly attainable. The second component is a commitment to constantly "search for the sacred" (Hall, 2005, pp. 20–24). For many, this second component relates to one's search to have a meaningful relationship with God; for others, it is a search to find the deeper meaning in one's work or life. I have adopted this broader definition of spirituality in my scholarship and teaching because it accommodates religious and nonreligious perspectives. The other virtue of this approach is that tends to evoke less resistance from students. Even students without a religious orientation tend to embrace discussions of "values" and "meaning" as important aspects of their education and development. Thus all students feel included in the discussion and are not as fearful that the professor is attempting to impose religious beliefs on them. The downside of this broader definition is that it can easily transform a discussion of religion into a secular discourse on values. Since one of the major objectives of my work is to interject religion more explicitly into the discussion, this escape hatch has to be monitored carefully.

What is even more important than the definition of spirituality is the framework within which the course is presented. If there is no coherent framework that makes religion and spirituality relevant to the course, then these discussions appear to arrive from left field and can generate resentment and distrust. I devote the entire first class of my professional responsibility course to creating and unfolding this framework in an interactive manner. I begin by drawing an outline of a house on the board and label it, "Framework for Constructing the Temple of the Ethical Lawyer" (see Figure 12.1).

I tell the students that a primary goal of the course is to explore how a person becomes a moral lawyer. I purposely chose *constructing* to indicate that ethics is a process, not something one is born with or given. The ABA Model Rules of Professional Conduct, the primary focus of this type of course, are the floor in the diagram. I justify this positioning of the rules by indicating that mastering the rules does not ensure that an individual will always act in an ethical manner. Law students must pass this course and pass an examination on the rules before they can practice law; therefore, any lawyer who has been charged with violating the rules has already demonstrated an intellectual mastery of them or he or she would not have been admitted to the bar. If the rules were the entire temple, then there would be no violations since all lawyers would have become ethical actors. I argue that for lawyers to comply with the rules, or morally choose not to comply with them, there must be a secure *personal values foundation* on which the rules

FIGURE 12.1
Framework for Constructing the Temple of the Ethical Lawyer

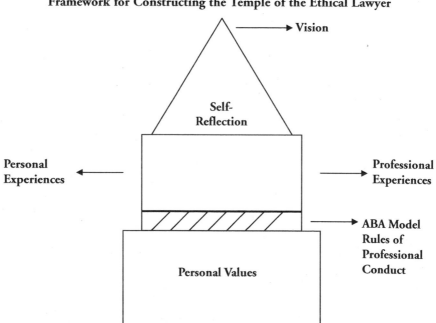

rest. These values are the forces that contribute to the development of a person's character and integrity.

At this point I invite the students to tell me the source of their values. Along with family, philosophy, education, and friends, religion inevitably makes the list. This permits me to explore with the students how religion (and the other sources) contributed to development of their values. It also permits a brief discussion of how one continues to stay in touch with those sources. What is important about this approach is that the students have interjected the concept of religion based on their own experiences. I have never conducted one of these opening sessions where religion was not one of the earliest sources suggested. This allows me to explore the connection between religion and the development of ethical lawyers, and, more important, it allows students to interject it into their comments and written assignments.

The remaining parts of the diagram also allow for spirituality and religion to become a part of how the students view their understanding of ethical practices. The walls of the temple are labeled *personal experiences* and *professional experiences*. The experiences we have and the manner in which we make sense out of those experiences allow us to become ethical lawyers. When students confront ethical choices at work or in their personal lives, the various sources of their values (religion, family, etc.) are put to the test and contribute to their development. The ceiling of the temple is labeled *self-reflection* to suggest that some process of introspection is necessary for the students to become ethical lawyers. Finally, the steeple of the temple is labeled *vision*. It is important for students to develop a vision of the type of lawyer they want to become. Though students tend not to think automatically in these terms, I am trying to suggest to them that one goal of the course is to help them develop some aspirational statements that will guide them as they enter into the practice of law. What is important about this framework is that each component involves fundamental religious practices. By creating this broad approach to educating students about the Model Rules of Professional Conduct, I am also giving them a structure they can revisit or in which they can discover those insights, values, and perspective that nurture their spiritual realities. The greatest role religion can play in educating our students in nonreligious educational institutions is conveying values, practices, and insights that contribute to the development of their spiritual intelligence (Zohar & Marshall, 2000). If our goal is solely to transmit religious doctrine and dogma, then we are least equipped for this enterprise. When we reaffirm the benefits of religion, challenge its limits, and reframe its contributions to our intellectual development, then, as educators, we have moved religion out of the dark ages of dogma and into the marvelous light of human transformation.

This framework is important to me because it is the primary justification for explicitly including spirituality and religion in the classroom setting. As educators we should not assume that mere insertion of the topic of religion leads to positive educational results. Since great risks are involved for the students and the teacher, it is very important that we understand why it is worth taking these risks. We risk being marginalized by those who see religion as a "soft" topic that does not challenge the mind. We risk making our students feel uncomfortable because they have shared a personal aspect of themselves that their peers or professor might misinterpret. Therefore, our efforts should always be rooted in a sincere belief that this approach is educationally sound and beneficial. I sincerely believe, though the empirical evidence is still lacking, that this more inclusive framework has greater potential in developing ethical lawyers than does the traditional approach, which focuses solely on the rules. My challenge is eventually to develop scientific instruments that verify my instincts and beliefs, but at least for now, this framework serves as my road map and justification for treading in these dangerous waters.

Reading Materials, Discussions, and Assignments

To provide students with a common perspective on how professional ethics and the legal profession can be viewed through a spiritual lens, it is important to provide reading materials that support this approach. Because I have written a book that explores the intersections between spirituality and the practice of law, this goal is not as challenging as it was in the past. Numerous legal writers have explored the practice of law from a religious perspective, but most do so from the perspective of a specific religious tradition. Joseph Allegretti's *The Lawyer's Calling* (1996), is a classic example of this type of approach. He eloquently demonstrates how Christian beliefs are fundamental to the manner in which lawyers can practice their faith through the practice of law. Though I am a Christian and was enormously inspired by

Professor Allegretti's work, it is somewhat inconsistent with the inclusive framework I attempt to bring to my course. More important, since I must devote a considerable amount of time in the course to the Model Rules, the supplemental readings on spirituality and religion are limited, so they need to embrace an inclusive perspective. Therefore, I provide the students with a selection of readings from my book that explores the relationship between spirituality and the practice of law.

Their first reading assignment is from the first chapter of my book, "On the Wings of Spirit" (Hall, 2005, p. 17). The material is intended to introduce students to my definition of spirituality and explore the fundamental connections between this definition and the key attributes of a lawyer. The reading suggests that there are some key spiritual values, such as love, loyalty, humility, forgiveness, service, faith, and integrity, that are essential to the enlightened lawyer. The reading material also demonstrates some of the "spiritual challenges" the legal profession presently confronts, such as lack of meaning, high indicators of lawyer dissatisfaction with the practice of law, and high levels of alcoholism and depression among lawyers.

This first reading assignment gives the students a backdrop to support the framework I introduce in the first class. It also documents for them the vices of the profession that aren't often discussed in the law school curriculum. We don't spend a great deal of time discussing the reading in the first class, but I do attempt to solicit their reactions to it. Students tend to be aware of the spiritual challenges, but don't appear to have concrete answers about whether a more spiritually oriented "calling" for the legal profession would solve the problem. This healthy skepticism is important for the course to create the real tension that exists within the profession and the world around the role of spirituality and religion.

Later on in the course students are expected to read and discuss in small groups a section of the book that deals with topics such as "Serving the Whole Client," "The Search for Truth," and "The Lawyer as Healer." This reading assignment goes directly to the heart of the matter because it challenges lawyers to see themselves and their clients through a spiritual lens. To serve the whole client, the lawyer not only must address the legal aspects of the conflict the client presents, but also must be willing to embrace the emotional, spiritual, economic, and other factors that are often at the heart of the conflict and the client's circumstances. The reading suggests that the client and the lawyer benefit more from this spiritual perspective to lawyering.

The search for truth attempts to reframe the goal of litigation or service to the client as more than the truth of outcomes, but as the truth of the relationship between the lawyer and the client. It is very easy for law students and lawyers to measure their success by whether they won a case or received a lucrative settlement for the client, instead of focusing on whether they "won" the client. Winning the client relates to the authenticity of the relationship the lawyer develops with the client and the lawyer's ability to stand with the client through difficult and challenging emotions without retreating behind the barriers of legal rules and procedures. It also requires the lawyer to enter into the relationship expecting to learn something from the client, just as the lawyer has something to give to, or to teach, the client. For students to see themselves as "healers" instead of technocrats with finely tuned legal skill is a major transformation. The spiritual concept of healer is strange to the legal profession, though influential members of the profession have invoked this label (Burger, 1982).

Discussion of these reading materials occurs on two different levels. First, I present the students with various emotionally and morally complex hypothetical cases. One involves a poor person facing numerous personal, emotional, and legal challenges. Another involves representing someone who is guilty of a crime but who has a procedural escape hatch that could get the person off. Still another concerns an entertainment lawyer representing a very lucrative and substantial client who appears to be addicted to drugs. Random students are asked to explain how they would proceed in representing each of these clients. Based on the reading and their own personal values, the students are asked to describe their strategy for engaging the client. There is no right answer to any of these scenarios, but the discussion elicits articulation of students' values and, more important, whether they feel comfortable bringing a more spiritually oriented perspective to the practice of law. Reactions and responses vary, but they consistently demonstrate that students do see the complexity of human relationships and appreciate that the lawyer has enormous discretion in how he or she chooses to frame the relationship. In the poor person hypothetical, I asked one student, "What would you do if the woman asked you to pray with her before the hearing started?" The goal of this question is to remind the students that religion is a part of the arena in which they will operate because it plays a central role in the lives of many of the people they will represent. Though it is often in the background of the relationship, it still is a valuable part of the lawyer/client dynamic and can be used in understanding the client's goals and needs.

The more profound ways in which religion is directly interjected into the work of the students in the course are in the two reflective papers they must write. In addition to a final examination based on the Model Rules of Professional Conduct, I require the students to write a paper during the first month of the class exploring their personal values, and one at the end of the semester describing their future strategy for becoming and remaining ethical lawyers. In addition to articulating their personal values, the first writing assignment asks them to describe the sources of their values and whether their personal values conflict with the fundamental values of the legal profession. Just as occurs in the first class, many of the students mention religion as the source of their values. Yet, now they are able to describe in greater detail how religion has shaped their understanding of self and how it will influence the type of law they want to practice or the manner in which they practice law. I am struck by the fact that more students seem to mention religion as a source of their values than did students in earlier courses when I used this same writing exercise but did not place the course within an explicit spiritual framework. In legal professional settings where religion is still viewed as a private matter that should be kept to oneself, the role of the professor becomes critical in whether students feel free to express their religious or spiritual views.

This writing exercise also demonstrates how some students often wrestle with their early religious belief as they mature and become more educated. Common statements I read in the papers that reflect this tension are, "Though I'm not a practicing Jew, those values are still with me" or "Though I don't attend church on a regular basis, or strictly adhere to the belief system, it played a critical role in the development of my values." These types of statements indicate to me that, even when religion is not primary in a person's orientation, it still lies in the background, shaping the person's self-image and waiting to be explored again. Some students describe a more direct conflict between the source of their values and their present worldview. A number of gay and lesbian students in the class have indicated through their writing assignment that, although religion played a role in the development of their values, they see it as being in direct conflict with what they presently believe and how they see themselves.

Regardless of the tone of the comments about the role of religion in the construction of values, it opens the door for a deeper exploration between the students and me. Since I do not grade the student paper, this becomes an excellent opportunity for me to raise questions and encourage them to explore the assumptions embedded in their positions. Even when students mention family as the source of the values, I write on their paper, "What was the source of your family's values?" This type of question sometimes triggers an e-mail response or private meeting, or the student tries to answer my question as part of the second writing assignment. Either avenue achieves an important goal of the exercise: to create ongoing exploration of values and deeper reflection about the function religion and spirituality serve in the development of ethical lawyers.

The final writing assignment asks the students to develop a mission statement to guide them as they enter the legal profession. It also asks them to identify the rituals or practices in which they will engage that will ensure they remain ethical lawyers. For many students, this is the first time they have been asked to write a mission statement for themselves. This confirms my belief that traditional legal education, like the rest of traditional education, does not create enough opportunities for students to reflect on their values and to create a vision of the type of person they hope to become. I am always extremely impressed by the thoughtfulness and sincerity students bring to this exercise. It is clear that many of them hope to keep what they crafted as a reminder of the things that are important in their lives. This part of the exercise opens the door for students to mention and embrace the religious practices of prayer, meditation, consultation, reading scriptures, and so on, that will assist them on their ethical journey.

By the end of the course, some students appear to be more comfortable describing their religious beliefs and the important role those beliefs play in their lives. These reflective assignments are the most extensive method through which students are willing to explore the role religion has played in creating their values and what they anticipate its role to be once they become lawyers. They reach a level of personal exploration the class discussions never reach. These writing assignments are often the first, and sometimes only, opportunity in law school students have to grapple directly with their faith and this new profession they have chosen to pursue. As a teacher, I learn more about them as students than I do about the students in other courses. The personal nature of the exchange replicates the type of relationship I hope they can develop with their clients.

Challenges and Obstacles

Though I am very pleased with the structure of the course and the way students are able to view the practice of law through a spiritual lens, some obstacles and challenges do occur with this approach. In the law school setting, the separation of church and state is a fundamental principle that most law students strongly embrace, and they have a visceral reaction to any attempt to contravene this norm. Therefore, the delicate balance between appropriate and inappropriate discussions and exercises remains challenging. I believe I have attempted to strike a good balance, but I'm not sure it is the right one. There is still some resistance to this approach at times. The size of the class (45–80 students) makes it difficult to engage students at a level that is necessary to overcome this resistance. There is also the challenge of teaching this type of course in a law school where many of the students have what we label "progressive politics." Religion in this country is often identified with more conservative political philosophies, so some law students and professors view religion as a repressive force. The reaction I described above by some gay and lesbian students is a classic example of this challenge. My broad definition of spirituality mitigates some of this tension since it is not restricted to any specific religious belief system, yet there is still an underlying tension that must be addressed more directly. The transformative power of religion and spirituality in the educational context can be drowned out by these political perspectives. When religion is seen more as a "hammer" we use to condemn those with whom we don't agree, instead of as a mirror that encourages us to engage in self-reflection, then we lose some of its inherent power.

Future Explorations

The greatest challenge for the future of this type of course is to demonstrate that this approach to teaching professional responsibility is more educationally sound than any other. The empirical evidence is not present to support this claim, so as educators and researchers in this area we must devote the next stage of this inquiry to these types of evaluative questions. In addition, there must be a more systematic intersection between the Rules of Professional Conduct and the religious and spiritual explorations I have introduced. The twin goals of mastery of self and mastery of the rules are daunting for a three-credit required course. Although I place the spiritual framework I use at the foundation of the course at the start, and at certain junctures during the semester, discussions about the rules dominate much of the course. Unless we develop casebooks that place the rules and the course within a spiritual framework, then the spiritual component of the course will still be viewed as secondary. The mere fact that it is now on the table is a major step forward, but it is not the place where legal educators must rest. Issues of conflicts, confidentiality, fees, communications with unrepresented parties, and honesty before a tribunal all have serious religious and spiritual overtones. Yet, we have not developed the tools and materials to make these connections seamless and more explicit.

Legal educators should be free to bring the virtues of religion and spirituality into the classroom, but we have to do so in a manner that meets the highest levels of excellence embraced by the academy. This project is very much in its infancy in the legal academy and doesn't always reach that level of excellence. This is not an inherent limitation of the subject matter but a testament to the limited number of individuals who are engaged in this project. The legitimacy of this exploration hinges on whether we have produced the indicia of acceptability the academy recognizes. I hope the work of Joseph Allegretti (1996), Jerold Auerbach (1993), Michael Hadley (2001), and James Pike (1963), as well as my own work, brings more credibility to this topic. However, until a casebook is written in professional responsibility that systematically explores the spiritual foundation on which the rules sit, the vast majority of law students will never be exposed to this approach.

Our search for an educational model that teaches to the whole student also hinges on our ability as legal educators to model the type of spiritual behavior and values this perspective offers to the world. The cry, "Physician, heal thyself," will be transformed to "Educator, teach thyself," unless we live the spirituality we offer to others. In our day-to-day interactions with students, we must, in the words of Mahatma Gandhi, "be the change we want in the world."

References

Allegretti, J. (1996). *The lawyer's calling.* New Jersey: Paulist Press.

Auerbach, J. (1993). *Rabbis and lawyers: The journey from Torah to constitution.* Bloomington, IN: Indiana University Press.

Burger, J. W. (1982). Annual report on the state of the US judiciary. *American Bar Association Journal, 68,* 274–277.

Cushman, J. B. (1989). Substance abuse in the legal profession: Facing facts. *Ohio Lawyer, 3*, 8–9.

Fisk, M. (1990). A measure of satisfaction: What America's lawyers think about the profession and their peers. *The National Law Journal, 68*, 2.

Florida State University Law School. (May 28, 1990). *Humanizing law school.* Retrieved March 27, 2007, from http://www.law.fsu.edu/academic_programs/hu manizing_lawschool/humanizing_lawschool.html

Hadley, M. L. (2001). *The spiritual roots of restorative justice.* Albany, NY: State University of New York Press.

Hall, D. (2005). *The spiritual revitalization of the legal profession: A search for sacred rivers.* Lewiston, NY: Edwin Mellen Press.

Hennessey, E. (1984). The state of the judiciary. *Massachusetts Law Review, 69*, 1–9.

Huie, W. S., & Spilis, D. (1992). Alcoholism and the legal profession. *Law and Psychology Review, 16*, 113, 118.

Morgan, T., & Rotunda, R. (2007). *Selected standards on professional responsibility.* Mineola, NY: Foundation Press.

Pike, J. A. (1963). *Beyond the law: The religious and ethical meaning of the lawyer's vocation.* Westport, CT: Greenwood Press.

Schlitz, P. J. (1999). On being a happy, healthy and ethical member of an unhappy, unhealthy and unethical profession. *Vanderbilt Law Review, 52*, 871–881.

Zohar, D., & Marshal, I. (2000). *SQ: Connecting with our spiritual intelligence.* New York: Bloomsbury Press.

13

TEACHING ABOUT RELIGIOUS AND SPIRITUAL PLURALISM IN A PROFESSIONAL EDUCATION COURSE

Robert J. Nash and Sue M. Baskette

T he two authors of this chapter are an educational philosopher/religious studies scholar and a university campus minister, respectively, who teach at a so-called public ivy state university. We write from the vantage point of co-teaching an interdisciplinary religious-pluralism course to graduate students (in master's and doctoral programs) enrolled in a professional college of education and social services. Among the several professions represented in our course are public school teaching and administration, higher education administration, health care, and a number of social service professions. We teach this course for a number of reasons:

- We are convinced that most Americans know very little about religion and spirituality, even though they might have many uninformed opinions they present as fact. This type of illiteracy is unacceptable in a 21st-century, multifaith, multireligious, global community.
- Whether teacher or administrator, counselor or lay person, believer, explorer/seeker, or nonbeliever, we believe it is crucial for social service professionals to think about the role the study of religion and spirituality plays in the education of students of all ages, at all levels, in public and private, secular and parochial, venues. Educators must

think seriously and systematically about the risks and benefits, the disadvantages and advantages, of dealing with such sensitive material in secular and private educational and clinical settings at all levels. To ignore religion and spirituality issues is to miss what is vitally important to educators, human service providers, and all of their diverse clienteles.

- Third, educators of all types in all settings need to reexamine their own latent biases for and against organized religion and private spirituality. This self-examination process, although difficult and time-consuming, is key to working with and understanding others. Its importance cannot be underestimated. Henceforth, we refer to the content in our course as *religio-spiritual*, because we do not know how it is intellectually feasible to separate religion from spirituality and vice versa. We believe this very popular dichotomy among our students represents an unstated bias against organized religion and in favor of private spirituality. We hear the following all the time: "I'm spiritual, not religious," as if the former is intrinsically superior to the latter.

- Fourth, it is important for professional educators to learn how to talk respectfully and compassionately with one another, and with their students, about a topic that, throughout history, has caused as much pain, suffering, and division as it has comfort, joy, and reconciliation.

- Fifth, if educators truly want to diversify their formal and informal curricula at all levels of schooling, and if they truly want to develop educational and clinical offerings that respect all kinds of difference, including religious and spiritual difference, then considering the nature and content of diversity education in a radically different way is necessary. Multiculturalism, diversity, and pluralism are empty catchwords unless they include religious and spiritual diversity, and nonbelief diversity as well, along with all of the other worthwhile types of cultural differences. In the 21st century, religio-spiritual identity is the core identity of billions of people on this planet.

One of the authors of this chapter, Robert Nash, has described his goals for this course in some detail in several books and articles/chapters he has written (e.g., 1999, 2001, 2002, 2008). An extensive bibliography of required readings for the course appears in his 2001 book. The other co-author, Sue Marie Baskette, has served the University of Vermont as a campus minister for several years, and she has fostered numerous pastoral and educational relationships with undergraduate and graduate students from all of the departments (and faiths) represented on our campus. She knows from first-hand experience what students of all ages are looking for in a religious pluralism course in a professional school.

The Quest for Meaning

Religio-spirituality represents, for us, the quest for meaning that lies at the heart of all cultures, people, and professions. As a philosopher and as a campus minister, we believe strongly that the quest for meaning in life is what a genuine, liberal education should be about. We think of professional education not as a social or practical science but as a series of interdisciplinary offerings that cuts across several of the humanities—including psychology, philosophy, religious studies, history, literature, art, music, theater, and others. For us, any professional training or preparation program needs to deal with the universal as well as with the particular, with the religio-spiritual as well as with the material needs of human beings. Most important, a professional training program that prepares teachers and administrators for a variety of positions must emphasize the quest for meaning in life as much as it does shaping particular pedagogical techniques and skill sets. "Know thyself," the great Socratic dictum, is as important to us in a professional classroom as the training imperative, "Know how to use the tools of thy trade."

Thus, we try to encourage our students to engage in what we think of as true liberal learning. We want them to explore their biases both for and against the religio-spiritual content of our course. We want them to understand as much as possible in a semester what the world's major religions hold to be true and why. We want them to engage in some deep, personal meaning-making. We want them to explore what they believe or disbelieve and why. We want our course to be intensely personal as well as information rich. Evidently, our students want exactly this type of course offering as well; every semester we offer this elective course, it is the first graduate course in the schedule to fill up, and waiting lists are always lengthy.

Our approach to teaching religious and spiritual meaning is a variation of the postmodern assertion that, at some level, all teaching and learning are autobiographical. Like religion, teaching for meaning comes out of highly personal narratives that educators create to elicit, and to answer, the most confounding existential questions, the ones that defy easy scientific, political, or technological answers.

For example, we teach that the most captivating religious narratives—Buddhism, Hinduism, Christianity, and Islam, among others—feature unforgettable characters, momentous events, and luminous ideals. And their languages are often sonorous and seductive. At its best, religion as a narrative, as a powerful storytelling device, reaches out and captures our imaginations, because the vitality of its message and the vividness of its language are potentially life transforming. We are moved to fresher understandings of the deeper, previously concealed meanings of our lives. The lesson here for educators is surely not an original one, but it is of the utmost importance, nevertheless.

An approach to teaching for meaning ought to recognize that good teaching, like the most powerful religio-spiritualities, is all about storytelling, and that the best pedagogy aims first at the heart and soul before it can ever find its way to the mind and hand. In Neil Postman's (1996) words, "do the stories provide [students] with a sense of personal identity, a sense of community life, a basis for moral conduct, explanations of that which cannot be known?" (p. 7). Postman captures for us the content and process of teaching about faith, spirituality, and religion in a secular classroom in a professional school.

As teachers of this course, we believe we are more likely to get students from a variety of religio-spiritual backgrounds to open up publicly about their guiding beliefs and leaps of faith whenever we deemphasize the revelational, doctrinal, and corporate elements of religion in the classroom in favor of the aesthetic and the poetic, the philosophical and the literary. While we do teach this very important, defining religio-spiritual scaffolding of the faith and wisdom traditions, we also work very hard to approach discussions of religion as a series of compelling and useful narratives that people have constructed for thousands of years to explain life's tragic anomalies as well as its unexpected gifts of grace. We know of no better way to mine the richness of an escalating religious and spiritual pluralism on secular college campuses throughout the United States (as well as in public school classrooms) than to get our students to exchange their religio-spiritual stories of faith with each other in a nondoctrinaire, mutually respectful manner.

As each week passes in this course, we have come to realize that, for each of us, our own co-teaching pedagogy is deeply spiritual. It is about helping students to name their doubts about themselves and their work with honesty and integrity. At the same time, it encourages them to create and nurture a faith (trust) in themselves, their students, and their work that is honest and integral. It also encourages us to do the same. Whether we are talking about religion or education, we struggle throughout the semester to help our students create individual professional narratives that combine the qualities of faith, doubt, honesty, and integrity in such a way as to deepen their understandings of themselves and their work. We try to create a sense of *vocation* in our classroom—getting students to see their professional work as a calling, as a commitment of faith without guarantee, as a risky response to the summons deep within them to minister to others wisely and compassionately.

The Types of Students Who Come to Our Course

Several religio-spiritual types of professional education students make their way to our elective course each year. The majority of our students have been raised in the mainline Christian and Jewish religions. We also get our share of Muslims, Buddhists, and Hindus. Occasionally, a few Pagans and Wiccans show up as well. Moreover, we notice that a growing number of self-acknowledged atheists and agnostics manage to find their way to our course on religious pluralism. Although the latter publicly eschew any overt interest in theology or theism, ironically, they are often the most excited of the students in our class. Within each of these formal denominational and religious identifications, however, certain types of believers and nonbelievers always seem to appear.

Some of these students are *orthodox* believers who come in all religious and philosophical stripes. Their confident, sometimes gentle sense of certainty attracts more than repels many of us throughout the semester. Many orthodox believers self-identify as fundamentalists, born again, nondenominational Christians, evangelicals, charismatics, and Pentecostalists. In class, however, a small coterie of outspoken antiorthodox skeptics always manages to remain unconvinced, and these students often have great difficulty concealing their disdain for any expression of uncompromising, orthodox belief.

As teachers, the pedagogical challenges with this particular group and its detractors are great. Each side manages to rankle the other with equal fervor. We believe, however, that, without knowing it, each group needs the other to define more clearly what they stand for and what they oppose. In a sense, this represents a complementarity between two oppositional groups that strengthens, rather than weakens, their respective belief systems. We see this type of oppositional complementarity being played out on the world scene in such locales as Iraq, West Bank and Gaza, Israel, India, Pakistan, and, yes, even here in the United States. We can better understand the dynamics of this belief/nonbelief complementarity on a macrocosmic scale, because we see it duplicated all too often in our microcosmic classroom. We make it a point to share this global insight with our students.

Some other students are *mainline believers* who are neither excessively conservative nor avant-garde. They dislike authoritarianism in religion as much as they dislike faddism. They prefer a life of traditional worship that balances traditions, standards, self-discipline, and moral conscience with a degree of personal freedom, Biblical latitude, and the *joie de vivre* of close community life. They often remain in the Catholic and Protestant churches and Jewish synagogues of their parents and grandparents. We have found, too often, that mainline believers are as uninformed about the details and complexities of their own religions as they are about the world's major and minor religions.

Our major challenge with these mainline believers is to help them understand that their need for religious stability and spiritual rootedness does not necessarily have to rule out important compromises and changes that any belief system requires to remain vital, responsive, and pastoral. The key, of course, is for our mainline believers to learn how to make reasoned compromises without falling prey to an array of compromises and dilutions of the original sacred messages in their own faith narratives.

Some of our students are *wounded believers* who define their religious experience mainly as a reaction to the physical and mental abuse (often perpetuated in the name of religion) they have suffered at the hands of hypocritical, overzealous clergy, lovers, parents, relatives, and friends. Their self-disclosing narratives of guilt, suffering, denial, reconciliation in some cases, and eventual healing always win our attention, believers and nonbelievers alike. We often hear stories of pain and bitterness from those wounded students who self-identify as "recovering" Catholics, Jews, or disgruntled members of any number of Protestant Christian denominations.

It is quite difficult, at times, for us to help our wounded students avoid overgeneralizing and projecting onto all religious institutions their own personal turmoil with religion. We try to listen compassionately to wounded believers, and we refer those who are in acute distress to the appropriate mental health professionals. We also remind them of Viktor E. Frankl's comment: "Suffering ceases to be suffering in some way the moment it finds meaning" (1978, p. 39). While religion has certainly wounded some people, it has also healed others. Reading dramatic, personal accounts of healing, reconciliation, and redemption in a variety of religio-spiritualities frequently helps these students put the problem of good and evil (what theologians call the problem of *theodicy*) into perspective (e.g., Lewis, 1962).

Some of our students are religio-spiritual *mystics* who continually remind us that more often than not genuine faith requires a discerning silence on the part of the believer, instead of a learned, theological disquisition. Some turn to the East, some to alternative American religions, some to folk religions and Native American spirituality, and some to private forms of spirituality. Most express a love of mystery, stillness, and balance that eludes those of us who too easily fit the stereotype of the fitful, ambitious, hard-driving Westerner. Mystics are a popular group of students in our class, and many are comfortable calling themselves *seekers* who are on a *journey* to find (some prefer the word *create*) larger meaning.

Most students in our classes (including even atheists and agnostics) have had at least one inexplicable, mystical experience that upsets their usual religio-spiritual routines or secular protocols. Whether it's a numinous awareness that comes through a transformative encounter with the magnificence of nature, or a loving relationship, or a vividly inspiring piece of writing, or a terrible accident, or an unbearable loss of some kind, most students see, if only dimly, what Peter Berger (1970) has called "fleeting signals of transcendence," or what we think of as quick glimpses of the extraordinary in the ordinary.

We remind our students that these mysterious moments can pull us all together at times, because, at the very least, they remind us that life is pretty much an unfathomable mystery, to nonbelievers and true believers alike. We just cannot explain all of life's enigmas, no matter how scientific or rational we might think we are. At some level of our existence, we are all stymied about how life works at those most difficult moments in time. Just when we think we have it all figured out, something breaks into our lives and upsets our comfortable philosophies of life.

Some students in our classes self-identify as *secular humanists*. Most secular humanists are convinced that, all too often, self-described believers turn to the supernatural to escape from the difficult responsibilities of individual freedom. For secular humanists, a humanistic, "self-centered" ethic can stand on its own as a defensible way of a person's being in the world and living an authentic human life. What is necessary is that all of us need to confront the inescapable fact of our human finitude and make a conscious choice to create ourselves through our daily projects—that is, through our courageous strivings to make meaning in an absurd universe. We have had some secular humanists in our classes who are believers and who even refer to themselves as *theistic secularists*, but these are rare.

Most of our secular humanists are skeptics, agnostics, and atheists who are deeply suspicious of any and all religious claims to absolute truth. Some are social justice activists on a mission to eradicate discrimination and oppression. Others are environmental advocates who proudly color themselves "green." And still others are civil libertarians for whom the First Amendment is a kind of "holy" scripture. As committed moral relativists, all of these types are dedicated to using science and reason to solve human problems. They also openly challenge all religious and moral certitudes, ethical universals, and what the postmodernists among them refer to as *grand spiritual narratives*.

They frequently encourage the rest of us to put our faith, not in church doctrines or dogmas, but in the awareness that we are all social constructors of our own religio-spiritual realities. Some of these nonbelievers are proselytizers; some are strictly scientific; some are inveterate questioners like Socrates; and others are militantly dogmatic and aggressive in their disdain for religio-spirituality. Some of the more temperate secular humanists in our classes agree wholeheartedly with Tennyson that "there lives more faith in honest doubt, believe me, than in half the creeds." (from "In Memoriam, A.I I.I I.," 1849).

We try to encourage theists and secular humanists in our class to avoid the trap of demonizing one another. We urge both groups to learn what we call the *art of mixed-belief capaciousness*. We ask, for example, if there is any way they might be able to embrace, or see the contiguousness of, even the smallest kernel of truth in the opposing narratives. Are their worldviews capacious enough to include even a fraction of a truth from a different religio-spiritual story? If not, then we urge each group at least to make a commitment to try to understand (not agree with) what is so precious and life-sustaining in the faith system of the other *for* the other. We believe that what Ninian Smart calls the practice of "structured empathy" is more than possible between believers and nonbelievers (2000). For Smart, "structured empathy" means getting at the "feel" of what is inside the belief system of another person by doing everything we can to get a genuine sense of (not necessarily agree with) the way the other person structures particular world-views of belief and meaning.

We let it be known very early in our course that each of us has a right to tell our stories of meaning with as much passion and conviction as we wish. However, we all must learn to honor, not critique, those beliefs that give people's lives special meaning, no matter how absurd or wrong they might sound. As teachers, we insist on the virtue of *respect* for one another when telling our religio-spiritual stories. The Latin root of the word *respect* (*respicere*) means to look back, again and again, to find value in what one might have initially opposed or dismissed.

To respect another's religio-spiritual story is to express a willingness to look carefully at what gives each of us meaning, what gets us up each morning and off to meet the day, over and over again. This is the pivotal communication rationale for our course: We need to show respect to one another by the way we listen, ask questions, and interpret information, no matter how discordant our differences may at first appear. Or, to say it another way, we are not *professors* in our seminar; we are *processors*—seminar participants whose main responsibility to ourselves and others is to collectively process a wide range of religio-spiritual phenomena to enrich and deepen our own faith understandings. What better way to discuss a controversial topic such as religio-spirituality than to be fully open to its possibilities and its liabilities?

One of the major advantages in identifying a number of religio-spiritual types like the ones above is becoming aware that there is as much diversity *within* particular religions and spiritualities as there is *between* them. The presence of each of these religio-spiritualities in every class we teach is proof that the search for meaning is multifaceted, never-ending, and complex—even though, at times, it might exist out of sight, just below the surface. Variety can, indeed, be the spice of life, as the old cliché goes. But it can also represent a grave threat to true believers of all kinds. Variety is an enemy of exclusivity. Thus, it is our double intention as co-instructors to try to maintain the wonderful distinctiveness of each of our student's religio-spiritual views, and, by extension, to encourage our teachers to recognize the uniqueness in the religious views of their students. At the same time, however, we

want to provide our students with accurate and helpful narrative classifications like the ones we have listed in this section. How better to understand
the rich variety of religious experiences among a number of middle- and
working-class Americans today.

Moral Conversation: The Most Important Goal of All

With such a rich religio-spiritual diversity of backgrounds and beliefs in our
seminars, we conduct classroom conversations in a particular way. We lay
out certain ground rules at the beginning of each semester, and we expect
full compliance with them. We talk about these rules and we revisit them
often during the course. We state, up front and early on, that we value the
conversational process as much as the *academic content* we will discuss
throughout the semester. Conversation and content are co-equal partners in
our religious pluralism seminar; one without the other is incomplete. Or to
paraphrase Immanuel Kant: "Ends without means are unachievable, while
means without ends are blind" (as cited in Fletcher and Childress, 1997, p.
121). In microcosm, this maxim is an excellent illustration of the process and
product called religio-spirituality. Our frank disclosure that classroom process is as important as religio-spiritual product is a truth-in-advertising statement we think is important for our students to know before our course even
begins.

What is moral conversation (Nash, 1996)? Here in a nutshell is what St.
Ignatius of Loyola said in his *Spiritual Exercises*: "Good Christians are dedicated to *saving* their neighbors' propositions rather than to *condemning*
them." Permit us to say this in a more secular manner: "Good teachers are
primarily interested in *saving* their students' propositions rather than finding
ways to *critique and ridicule* them." We do this by following what we call the
"Golden Rule" of seminar conversation: Respond to others in the class the
way you would like them to respond to you, unless you self-identify as a
sadomasochist. We stress that our chief responsibility to one another in our
seminar is to make the other person look good. In turn, we make ourselves
look good by making others look good. We make ourselves look bad when
we make others look bad. Critical, open-minded examination of intellectual
material can take hold only if it is undertaken in a mutually cooperative,
safe, educational environment. Angry, offended students are resistant students. What they usually end up learning is how to defend themselves

against attack. In this case, content often takes a back seat to zoning out, passive-aggression, or worse.

We include the following paragraph in our syllabus:

> We want to know what *you* think and feel about the readings and discussions; what meanings *you* are attributing to course content; what personal narrative *you* are writing for yourself in the areas of religion and spirituality. We do not want to spend a semester guiding you in the process of tearing apart texts, adroitly deconstructing an author's meanings, brilliantly ferreting out hidden assumptions, showing off background expertise and cleverness, or trying desperately to remain impartial and intellectually and emotionally unaffected. All of this, at least for us, is numbingly boring.

We also add this paragraph to our syllabus:

> If you are looking for a whirlwind, dispassionate tour through the world's major and minor religions, then please look elsewhere. This is not a comparative religions course, although our unit on comparative religions will be a large part of the course. If you are looking for an uncommon spiritual wisdom, eloquent homilies, inspiring metaphysical answers, and money-back guarantees of supernatural or secular truth from us, your instructors, then you will be sorely disappointed. We are as much at sea over these issues as most of you. We just thought you should know, so you can lower your expectations.

Truth to tell, many of our students come to us looking for experts and final words on the difficult religio-spiritual issues—even while, developmentally, they remain skeptics and naysayers. While in our more arrogant moments, we like to think that our ignorance on these matters is a "higher ignorance," in the words of Meister Eckhart, the great Christian mystic, in reality, our ignorance is no better or worse than our students'. Although each of us has spent our adult lifetimes studying and/or practicing religion and spirituality, what we are actually able to penetrate and to enjoin about our own, and our students', religio-spirituality will be nothing more than inadequate, to put it bluntly.

We tell our students that in a seminar such as this one, we think we have the ability to dispense some basic information; ask the provocative questions; explore the more controversial hot buttons; genuinely empathize with their discoveries, doubts, fears, bewilderments, and misgivings; and share some of our own compelling, personal concerns about religion and spirituality. But this is as far as we can go. In spite of our limitations, however, we genuinely have no hidden religious or spiritual agendas to push in teaching this course other than trying to make a case for respecting religio-spiritual pluralism.

We emphasize over and over again that all of this teaching and learning must be done in the spirit of moral conversation. No *conversation stoppers* allowed! We prefer, instead, *conversation starters* and *conversation sustainers*. Here, then, are our moral conversation *no-nos*, stated in their most concise form:

- No name-calling
- No predictable repetitions of the same old, same old, sharp (and dull) axes to grind
- No making others look bad so you, the speaker, can shine
- No bloviating, declaiming, denouncing, or arguing
- No proselytizing, advertising, or evangelizing
- No settling old (or new) scores
- No looking for reasons why the course, or the seminar participants, aren't working well (ask yourself why *you're* not working well)
- No positioning oneself on the highest moral ground
- No relegating others to the lowest moral ground

Here are the moral conversation *yes-yeses*, stated in their most concise form:

- Explain, clarify, question, rephrase, respect, and affirm
- Evoke, don't invoke, or provoke
- Support without retort
- Flow, glow, and let it go . . . don't fight or flee
- Respond . . . knowing that you (and I) made it all up . . . everything
- Be generous . . . at all times . . . without exception
- Attribute the best motive
- Look for the truth in what you oppose and the error in what you espouse
- Speak always for yourself and not for some group
- Come prepared, having done the background reading and writing

- Help others to shine, while concealing your own brilliant light under the proverbial bushel

We end this section on moral conversation with a quotation we share with our students that appears in the oldest and most sacred Hindu book in the world—the *Rig Veda*: *Ekam sat vipraha bahudha vadanti*: "Truth is one, but the wise call it by many names." If this Hindu aphorism is accurate, and we believe in its basic value, then each of us in our seminar is, at best, naming our truth with but one name. Who among us, we sometimes ask, has the right and the omniscience to impose one name on all the rest of us?

Some Educational Concerns That Continue to Challenge Us

There are times when we think we might be failing, when we wonder if it is possible to deal openly with religio-spirituality in public schools and colleges without offending a variety of people. Is offense inevitable given the low boiling point of the topic? This question comes up for us time and time again in our work with teachers and administrators, so we often introduce it as a conversation starter at the beginning of the course. We reveal our own hopes and fears for the course for students to examine publicly.

At first, most public school educators are skeptical about whether we can pull off such a course. As the semester unfolds, however, these professionals feel more empowered to raise religio-spiritual issues with their own students and colleagues, because now they have the basic conversational skills to do so. They have seen moral conversation work in their graduate seminars. One of our tasks each time we teach this course is to review the First Amendment to the U.S. Constitution, where the wall of separation between church and state is actually low, not high. Favoring or discriminating against religio-spirituality in public schools is impermissible, but studying about religio-spirituality is acceptable. No pandering or promoting is ever allowed, however, or else the First Amendment has been seriously violated.

Related to this issue of giving offense in discussing matters of religio-spirituality, is the question of whether it is ever possible to talk about any type of value-loaded subject matter in a relatively value-free way. Some of our professional students wonder why they should stir up the hornets' nests of religion and spirituality in their individual school systems when so much could be at stake for them, including possible job loss, public censure, and charges of stereotyping and pedagogical malpractice. Why not just leave well enough alone, they ask. Some educational administrators, in both public schools and higher education, believe that religio-spiritual beliefs are so deeply personal and private, it is simply beyond the jurisdiction of educators to discuss these in public forums of any kind.

We have found that, at times, it is necessary to separate out the *cognitive* from the *emotional* dimensions of religio-spiritual conversation in the classroom. At other times, we try to recognize and validate the powerful emotional content of our students' religio-spiritual convictions. To this end, we encourage our students to express the intensity of their beliefs freely, but always in a mutually respectful and sensitive manner. One way we try to maintain a balance between the cognitive and the emotional in our seminar is to rule out of order favoring one or another perspective. Rational and emotional approaches to subject matter have equal worth as learning styles in our seminar.

Also, we try to avoid raising questions about the validity of the truth claims of various religio-spiritual points of view. What criteria could we ever identify that would meet the unanimous approval of all the various believers and nonbelievers in our class? Even more fundamentally, what exactly does *validity* mean when religio-spiritual content is being taught? Our main agenda, therefore, is always to focus on the course purposes we identified at the beginning of this chapter. We are in the classroom to inform, clarify, and respond. We do not intend to reform or perform. We strive to establish a communication process that promotes no hidden agendas other than the goal of fostering a pluralistic philosophy of religio-spirituality in a stress-free, no-fire classroom zone.

Bibliography

Berger, P. L. (1970). *A rumor of angels: Modern society and the rediscovery of the supernatural.* New York: Doubleday Anchor.

Frankl, V. E. (1978). *The unheard cry for meaning: Psychotherapy & humanism.* New York: Touchstone.

Fletcher, J. F., & Childress, J. F. (1997) *Situation ethics: The new morality.* New York: Westminster John Knox Press.

Lewis, C. S. (1962). *The problem of pain: How human suffering raises almost intolerable intellectual problems.* New York: Macmillan.

Nash, R. J. (1996). Fostering moral conversations in the college classroom. *Journal on Excellence in College Teaching, 7*(1), 83–106.

Nash, R. J. (1999). *Faith, hype, and clarity: Teaching about religion in American schools and colleges.* New York: Teachers College Press, Columbia University.

Nash, R. J. (2001). *Religious pluralism in the academy: Opening the dialogue.* New York: Peter Lang.

Nash, R. J. (2002). *Spirituality, ethics, religion, and teaching: A professor's journey.* New York: Peter Lang.

Nash, R. J., Bradley, D. L., Chickering, A. W. (2008). *How to talk about hot topics on campus: From polarization to moral conversation.* San Francisco: Jossey-Bass/ Wiley.

Postman, N. (1996). *The end of education: Redefining the value of school.* New York: Vintage.

Smart, N. (2000). *Worldviews: Crosscultural explorations of human beliefs* (3rd ed.). Upper Saddle River, NJ: Prentice-Hall.

AFTERWORD

Miriam Rosalyn Diamond

When faculty unexpectedly encounter students' religious ideologies in the classroom, they may respond with apprehension, frustration, dread, or concern. Instructors may view this exchange as a confrontation that threatens the very heart of empirical study, and worry that this will lead to a dead end in the learning process.

The contributors of this book feel otherwise. While it is important to recognize the uneasiness that can result when students question the basic assumptions of a particular discipline, we see this meeting of worldviews as an opportunity for growth, reflection, and deep learning.

What can faculty learn from these scholars about how to respond to student disbelief and/or resistance to an idea on the basis of religion? According to Rosier, first, acknowledge that there is a (potential) conflict. Following the recommendations of Warren, Nash, and Baskette, faculty can find it useful to understand how the students arrived at their opinions, identify a "kernel of truth" (Nash & Baskette) in their stance, and appreciate the ways students benefit from believing as they do. Peggy Catron's piece provides meaningful insights that can serve this purpose.

A resounding position in these writings is the importance of creating a space in the learning for students to express their beliefs, dissonance, and emotions constructively (in writing or discussion) without fear of retribution. It is important to establish ground rules of respectful discussion for this process to be valuable and productive. If the professor wishes, he or she can share his or her own perspective—including how and why his or her views may have changed over time. Warren points out that it is helpful for the class to examine assumptions about ideologies that may not necessarily be true. One approach is to give students tools, such as the alternate translations of religious texts that Baker provides, to enable them to see different approaches to interpreting material. Nash and Baskette suggest engaging in "moral conversation," where students' ideas are maintained, rather than destroyed. The role of "professor" can then be viewed instead as "processor," where the class comes together to process, not necessarily change or dictate, opinions. After engaging in these activities, students can employ a metacognitive exercise to reflect on ways their stances have been challenged, altered, or solidified, as Rosier recommends.

On the other hand, it may be the faculty who choose to raise the topic of religion in their secular classes. Under the right circumstances, students are often keen to explore issues of faith and the meaning of life in their classes, according to the findings of Trautvetter, Rogers, and Love. Tending to issues related to religion in class can acknowledge cultural identities in ways that enhance personal validation and feelings of belonging for African American students at primarily white institutions, as Giles, Nance, and Witherspoon point out. This may also be the case for other groups of learners who are grounded in their faiths and feel marginalized on campuses where they are the minority.

A recurring theme in this book, as stated by Thomas and Bahr, is that providing students the opportunity to learn about faith can promote religious literacy, which in turn can lead to a better understanding of the world in which we live and of "the other." Discussing beliefs and listening to classmates who have differing perspectives can help students identify and articulate their own viewpoints. Koth, Hall, Nash, and Baskette indicate that the result can be increased self-awareness as well as clarification of personal values. These values may, in turn, affect what students do, as they explore how beliefs are manifested in the real world through the notion of "calling" or vocation, as well as ethical decision making and social action. These authors make the case that being aware of and grounded in beliefs and values can provide students with a sense of meaning that may support personal health and well-being, even in times of stress.

Lee recommends that faculty inform students at the beginning of the course that these controversial topics will be addressed and how they fit into the overall goals for the class. Singham offers a model that distributes power more evenly between learners and faculty and makes the class a group venture, thereby limiting student concerns over consequences of voicing a particular stance.

Nash and Baskette emphasize the value of encouraging students to become aware of their own attitudes toward the whole notion of faith and spirituality, and to appreciate perspectives of those who take a different approach to these matters. They state that it is important for people to have a language for constructively discussing these hot topics. Although their focus is on training educators, these objectives could apply to students preparing to work in a variety of fields including human services, international relations, and health care.

And what of online courses? Can lessons from classes conducted in a traditional format apply to distance education, as well? Most approaches listed here can be used wherever there is opportunity for students to explore and express their perspectives. Reflection is a key component of learning in any format, as is acknowledging and interacting with "the other." The ground rules for discussion become even more essential when communication is primarily written. Without nonverbal cues, such as vocal and facial expression, it is more difficult to accurately interpret intent and emotion. This challenge increases when the material has a tendency to elicit heated responses. It becomes even more important that ground rules and guidelines for written communication and clarification be clearly established from the outset (such as encouraging students to ask each other "Did I correctly understand your comments to mean that you believe . . . ?", or "Are you asserting that . . . ?").

In any class format, navigating discussions of religion in education can certainly be challenging and difficult. However, as the educators in this book assert, it can also be valuable, worthwhile and—often—vital.

Ann Marie B. Bahr is a professor in Philosophy and Religion at South Dakota State University. She is the author of *Christianity* (2004) and *Indigenous
Religions* (2005), and academic editor of the 11-volume *Religions of the World*
series published by Chelsea House (2004–2005). Her articles have appeared
in the *Chronicle of Higher Education*, McGraw-Hill's *Annual Editions: World
Religions*, and the *Journal of Ecumenical Studies*. Dr. Bahr is a regular colum-
nist for *The Brookings Register*. She is currently serving on the American
Academy of Religion's *Task Force on Religion in the Schools*. Dr. Bahr served
as president of the Upper Midwest Region of the American Academy of Religion from 1999 to 2001. She served on the South Dakota Humanities Council from 1994 to 2000.

Roger G. Baker, in 35 years of teaching, has taught at Snow College, a small
public liberal arts college in Central Utah, and Brigham Young University in
Provo, Utah, a large church-related university. In both schools, he taught
Bible as Literature in the English department, rather than in a religion or
Bible studies program. This experience gives him a unique perspective on
the challenges of teaching secular Bible reading to religiously committed students in both secular and religious schools. His most recent work is on the
first indexer of the King James Bible, the Scottish eccentric Alexander Cru-
den, who published his Exhaustive Concordance in 1737. Baker is also a col-
umnist for a small Central Utah newspaper, *The Sanpete Messenger*.

Sue M. Baskette was awarded an M.Div. degree from Princeton Theological
Seminary in May of 2003, and was ordained as a minister of the United
Church of Christ. Reverend Baskette is currently campus minister at the
University of Vermont and pastor of the United Church of Bakersfield and
Fairfield. Both communities of faith are venues where she invites all to dis-
cover their own vibrant spirituality.

Peggy Catron is currently a faculty member in the Communications Department and an adjunct instructor in the Department of Higher Education at

the University of Arkansas. Before coming to Arkansas in 2004, Dr. Catron founded the Center for Faculty Excellence at Drury University in Springfield, Missouri. After serving as a pastor and evangelist with the Assemblies of God, she began her teaching career in 1988 at Central Bible College in Springfield, where she developed the Church Communications program and taught courses in speech, church history, and theater. Dr. Catron has also served on the faculty at Missouri State University in Springfield, and on the staff of the Teaching and Faculty Support Center at the University of Arkansas. Degrees include a B.A. in Biblical literature, an M.A. in communications from Missouri State University, and an Ed.D. in higher education from the University of Arkansas.

Christina Copre teaches elementary school and serves as mathematics department coordinator and coach in Chicago. Previously, she was a graduate assistant with the Searle Center for Teaching Excellence and the School of Education and Social Policy at Northwestern University, where she graduated with a B.A. in mathematics and a minor in psychology. Christina holds an M.Ed. and teaching certificate in elementary education from the University of Illinois at Chicago. Christina's research interests include integrated curricula, peer learning, and alternative strategies for teaching mathematics.

Miriam Rosalyn Diamond has over 15 years' experience in faculty-curriculum development and is coordinator of Society for Values in Higher Education's Religion and Public Life Project. She has led programs for educators at many institutions, including Northwestern University, MIT, Northeastern University, London South Bank University, Claflin University, and the California State Colleges. Dr. Diamond has researched, published, and conducted workshops on ethical development, outcomes of creative interactive lesson plans, using technology to create learning communities, and holistic approaches to teaching and learning. She is on the editorial board of the international journal *Active Learning in Higher Education*, and she co-authored the book *Chalk Talk: E-Advice from Jonas Chalk, Legendary College Teacher* (2004, New Forums Press). Dr. Diamond holds a Ph.D. in educational processes from Northwestern, an M.A. in counseling psychology from Lesley University, and a B.S. in rehabilitation from Boston University. She teaches courses in adult and ethical development, education, and religious studies. Miriam may be contacted at mirdiamond@gmail.com.

Mark S. Giles is an assistant professor in the Department of Educational Leadership at Miami University in Oxford, Ohio, and teaches in the College Student Personnel program. Dr. Giles earned his Ph.D. in higher education administration from Indiana University and completed his dissertation on the life and influence of African American theologian Dr. Howard Thurman. He earned an M.S. in college student personnel from Miami University, and a B.A. in Afro-American studies from the University of Cincinnati. Dr. Giles brings a background in community affairs and social service to his teaching and research. His primary research interests focus on the social context and history of African American leadership in higher education (20th century), including dynamics of social change and spirituality. In addition, he is interested in using the lens of critical race theory to examine and understand the African American experience across educational settings (PK–20 model).

David Hall is a professor of law at Northeastern University School of Law. He served as dean of the Law School and provost and senior vice president for Academic Affairs at Northeastern University. He holds LL.M and S.J.D. degrees from Harvard Law School, Masters of human relations and Juris Doctor degrees from the University of Oklahoma, and a B.S. in political science from Kansas State University. He writes and lectures nationally on matters of social justice, racial equality, ethics, and spiritual values. He is the author of *The Spiritual Revitalization of the Legal Profession: A Search for Sacred Rivers*. President George W. Bush appointed Professor Hall to serve on the Board of Directors of the Legal Services Corporation. Mayor Thomas Menino appointed him to serve as a member of Boston's first Civilian Review Board for the Boston Police Department.

Kent Koth is Director of the Center for Service and Community Engagement at Seattle University, where he is also an adjunct faculty member in the Liberal Studies Program. He teaches an undergraduate service-learning course, *Leadership for Community Engagement.* He earned his B.A. degree in history from Grinnell College and his M.A. degree in religion from the Pacific School of Religion. He has worked in the areas of service-learning, student leadership development, and nonprofit management since 1990. Prior to joining Seattle University in 2004, he was Service-Learning Program Director at the Haas Center for Public Service at Stanford University and Executive Director of Youth Community Service in Palo Alto, California. A frequent consultant and workshop presenter, his scholarly interests have focused on the role of spirituality in service-learning and the theoretical conceptions of service and social change.

Barbara A. Lee is Professor of Human Resource Management at the School of Management and Labor Relations at Rutgers University, and its former dean. She is also counsel to the law firm of Edwards Angell Palmer & Dodge, LLP. Professor Lee has taught employment law and higher education law at Rutgers since 1982. She is the author of numerous books and articles on employment law, higher education law, employment discrimination, and academic employment practices. She is the coauthor, with William A. Kaplin, of *The Law of Higher Education,* 4th ed. (2006) and *Academics in Court* (1987) with George LaNoue. She is a former member of the board of directors of the National Association of College and University Attorneys and was named an NACUA Fellow. She also serves as an expert witness for litigation involving employment discrimination, sexual harassment, and academic personnel decisions. Professor Lee received her B.A. in English from the University of Vermont, her M.A. in English and Ph.D. in higher education administration from Ohio State University, and her J.D. from Georgetown University Law Center.

Patrick G. Love is Associate Provost for Student Success at Pace University. Before joining Pace, he taught at New York University, Kent State University, and Syracuse University. He earned his doctorate in higher education and student affairs from Indiana University and his master's degree in counseling psychology and student development from The State University of New York at Albany. Dr. Love has worked at nine different colleges and universities in such areas as residence life, new student orientation, judicial affairs, alcohol and drug programming, and summer conferences. He is author of four books, the latest being (with Sandra Estanek) *Rethinking Student Affairs Practice.*

Odelet Nance is the director of multicultural affairs at Goshen College. She also serves as an assistant professor of communication. She earned her B.A. from Indiana University and her M.A. from Purdue University. She received her Ph.D. in curriculum and instruction from the University of Illinois at Chicago. She has been in student affairs administration for over 10 years and has worked in various student services areas including pre-college programs, student support, admissions, and academic advising. In addition, her teaching experiences include teaching classes based on diversity in society, intercultural communication, and an introduction to research. Her research interests examine the first-year experience, church and university partnerships, and the role of religion in the lives of African American college students.

Robert J. Nash has been a professor in the College of Education and Social Services, University of Vermont, Burlington, since 1969 years. He specializes in teacher education, higher education, philosophy of education, ethics, religion, spirituality and education, and personal narrative scholarship. He holds graduate degrees in English/literary theory, religious studies, applied ethics and liberal studies, and educational philosophy. He holds faculty appointments in teacher education, higher education and student affairs administration, and interdisciplinary studies in education. He administers the Interdisciplinary Master's Program, and he teaches ethics and philosophy of education courses across three programs in the college, including the doctoral program in educational leadership and policy studies. He is the creator of an alternative research genre called Scholarly Personal Narrative writing (SPN), and in the last few years, he has supervised 25 dissertations and theses using this genre. His book on SPN, published by Teachers College Press, Columbia University, is the first of its kind in the field of education.

Judy L. Rogers is an associate professor in the College Student Personnel master's program at Miami University, Oxford, Ohio She teaches courses primarily in organizational theory, leadership and, most recently, she developed a seminar on spirituality and leadership. Her current publications explore the role of spirituality in leadership and in the preparation of student affairs professionals. She has given numerous presentations on the topic of spirituality in leadership and in student affairs work at national and regional conferences and on college campuses throughout the United States and Canada. She serves on the Editorial Board for the *College Student Affairs Journal* and was recently named a NASPA Faculty Fellow. Dr. Rogers received a B.A. in history from St. Mary College, Kansas, an M.A. in counseling, and a Ph.D. in higher education administration from The Ohio State University.

She worked in a variety of student affairs areas before becoming a faculty member in 1986, including career services, admissions, residence life, and learning assistance at both large public universities and small private colleges.

Tamara H. Rosier is assistant director for assessment in the Pew Faculty Teaching and Learning Center at Grand Valley State University. She received her Ph.D. in leadership for higher education. Her interests include application of learning theories, leadership development, authentic assessment of student learning, and differentiated instruction. She teaches courses in teacher education and statistics. She can be reached at rosiert@gvsu.edu.

Mano Singham is director of the University Center for Innovation in Teaching and Education (UCITE) and adjunct associate professor of physics at Case Western Reserve University. He is the author of the books *Quest for Truth: Scientific Progress and Religious Beliefs* (2000) and *The Achievement Gap in U.S. Education: Canaries in the Mine* (June 2005). A Fellow of the American Physical Society, he is also a winner of the university's Carl F. Wittke Award for Distinguished Undergraduate Teaching.

Nancy L. Thomas (democracyproject@aol.com) directs the *Democracy Project* for the Society for Values in Higher Education (www.svhe.org) and is a senior associate with Study Circles Resource Center and the Paul J. Aicher Foundation in Pomfret, Connecticut (www.studycircles.org). She assists campuses, education associations, communities, and public agencies that seek democratic ways to address pressing ethical and social issues and to effectuate change. Her experience includes conflict prevention and resolution, strategic planning, faculty development, curriculum reform, ethics training, diversity, and community building. Dr. Thomas graduated from St. Lawrence University (A.B., government, 1979) and Case Western Reserve University School of Law (J.D., 1984). She practiced as a university attorney before returning to graduate school to pursue a doctorate in educational leadership at the Harvard Graduate School of Education (Ed.D., 1996). Since then, her positions have included Special Assistant to the President for Legal and Policy Affairs at Western New England College and director of *Listening to Communities* for the American Council on Education.

Lois Calian Trautvetter is currently Assistant Professor in the School of Education and Social Policy and Associate Director for Higher Education Administration and Policy at Northwestern University. She received her Ph.D. in higher education administration from University of Michigan, an M.S. in chemical engineering from Carnegie Mellon University, and a B.A. in chemistry from The College of Wooster. She teaches college student development theory and research methodology courses. Her research interests include student development and faculty and professional development issues such as productivity, enhancing research and teaching, motivation, and new and junior faculty. She is also interested in the role of church colleges in American higher education. She recently coauthored a book, *Putting Students First: How Colleges Develop Students Purposefully.* She has written book chapters and articles on faculty teaching and other experiences, as well as how faculty and practitioners can foster college students' search for meaning and purpose.

Dona Warren received her B.S. in mathematics from Minnesota State University, Moorhead and her Ph.D. from the University of Minnesota, where she specialized in the philosophy of mind and the philosophy of language. In 1995, she began teaching at the University of Wisconsin, Stevens Point, working in an interdisciplinary department housing philosophy, religious studies, and anthropology. She has served as the coordinator for the philosophy program since 1999. At the University of Wisconsin, Stevens Point, Warren shifted her research program to focus on the philosophy of religion, critical thinking, and the philosophical issues that arise in the educational context. She's pursuing the Scholarship of Teaching and Learning and is particularly interested in studying how students analyze arguments and in determining how this ability can best be sharpened. Warren teaches Introduction to Philosophy, Critical Thinking, Symbolic Logic, and the Philosophy of Religion on a regular basis, instructing both lower-division and upper-division undergraduate students.

Noelle Witherspoon is currently a doctoral candidate in educational administration at the University of Alabama in the Department of Educational Leadership, Policy, and Technology Studies. In addition to graduate teaching responsibilities in social foundations and curriculum and supervision, she serves as a consultant for districts across the nation in the areas of literacy, math, instructional assessments, and culturally relevant teaching. Ms. Witherspoon has a strong interest in how social ideologies impact educational leadership; narrative methods; religion and education; ethics in education; women in leadership, particularly how women are socialized into leadership; leadership for social justice; and school-principal fit theory.